TALK OF THE TIDE

TALK of the TIDE

An oral history of Alabama football since 1920
as told to

JOHN FORNEY & STEVE TOWNSEND

CRANE HILL
PUBLISHERS
Birmingham, Alabama
1993

Library of Congress Cataloging-in-Publication Data

Forney, John
   Talk of the Tide / by John Forney and Steve Townsend.
     p. cm.
   "An oral history of Alabama football since 1920" — Cover.
   ISBN 1-881548-03-1 : $24.95
    1. Crimson Tide (Football team) — History. 2. University of Alabama — Football — History.
I. Townsend, Steve, 1951- .
II. Title.
GV958.A4F67 1993
796.332'62'0976184 — dc20   93 — 5275
                                                                    CIP

Cover design by Icon Graphics

Crane Hill Publishers
2923 Crescent Avenue
Birmingham, Alabama 35209

CRIMSON TIDE

An oral history of Alabama football since 1920
as told to

JOHN FORNEY & STEVE TOWNSEND

ACKNOWLEDGMENTS

The editors gratefully acknowledge the following, without whose generous assistance Talk of the Tide *would not have been possible.*

The University of Alabama

The University of Alabama Department of Athletics

The University of Alabama Sports Information Office

The Paul W. Bryant Museum Oral History Program, for the use of the oral histories of Byron Braggs, Sylvester Croom, and Marty Lyons as interviewed by Clem Gryska; and the oral history of Marlin "Scooter" Dyess as interviewed by Richard Reid

Kirk Wood

Collegiate Sports Partners, Ltd.

Centennial Marketing, for the use of the tape-recorded Team of the Century speeches from the 1992 "Golden Gala," and the interviews from the 1992 A-Day centennial celebration

The Collegiate Licensing Company

Dr. Finus P. Gaston

Kent Gidley, University of Alabama photographer

Britton Stutts, who interviewed Mike Dubose, Stacy Harrison, Martin Houston, Walter Lewis, John Mitchell, Gordon Pettus, Thomas Rayam, and Roger Shultz

Ronald Weathers, who interviewed Harry Gilmer and Tommy Lewis

Charles Thornton, who was kind enough to write a memoir of his broadcasting experiences with Coach Paul "Bear " Bryant

Virginia Fisher, who interviewed Linda Knowles

Bob Carlton and *The Birmingham News,* for the use of supplemental quotes from Bart Starr

And all the Alabama players and staff who gave so generously of their time to help make this book a success.

Finally, our deepest thanks
to one of Alabama's true fans — Logan Young of Memphis,
whose interest and support put us over the top.

TABLE OF CONTENTS

FOREWORD
by Gene Stallings

We all love to read the stories about Alabama football, all the great wins, the players and coaches. Now we have the unique opportunity to hear what some of Bama's outstanding players have to say about the tradition of football at Alabama.

You know, being at Alabama in my early coaching career was a special time. When Coach Bryant asked me to come to Alabama, it was an invitation Ruth Ann and I could not turn down. We knew that bright things were just around the corner, that hard work would pay off. And believe me, we know about hard work. All the coaches had their specific jobs, and none of us wanted to let Coach Bryant down. There was that spark that said we would do the very best we could do. We certainly didn't want to disappoint Coach Bryant. When I came here in 1958 for $4,800 a year, I thought I had the best job in the world.

Ruth Ann and I lived in a little house out University Boulevard past the Moon Wink motel. Our car wasn't running one morning, and Coach Bryant said he would be by at 6 a.m. to give me a ride into work. I was standing there on the corner with my briefcase in hand at 5:15. You can bet I didn't want to be late!

We had seven great years at Alabama — won some championships, went to some bowl games, and forged some wonderful memories and ties with coaches and players. Each player, each season, each coach is different. Each has his own story to tell, and John Forney has been on the Alabama scene long enough to pull those accounts together into a meaningful oral history of Alabama football.

Have fun listening to *Talk of the Tide* as John Forney and Steve Townsend bring to life the great tradition of Alabama football.

Gene Stallings
July 1993

9

PREGAME COMMENTS
by John Forney

This book had its genesis several years ago when I decided to come up with some sort of project in connection with the 100th anniversary of Alabama football in 1992. I wanted to use something that might involve a number of former and present Tide "voices" —Mel Allen, Charlie Zeanah, Maury Farrell, Dick Reid, Eli Gold, Doug Layton, and Paul Kennedy, in addition to myself.

Over the years I've had many people ask me if we had tape recordings of play-by-play football games going back far into the Bryant era. I'm sorry to report that there really were not that many. However, there were enough that I decided to put together a series of audiotapes entitled *Echoes of the Bryant Years,* which would cover the years of Paul Bryant's reign at the University. I was on the broadcast team during all those years.

In addition to using the actual play-by-play tapes, I did interviews with some of the players who were involved with Coach Bryant's Alabama teams. After getting into the audiotape project, I began to realize that there should be a book — an oral history, if you will — of the Crimson Tide that allowed the players to tell their stories in their own words. I decided it should go back to at least the early 1920s because the people who played on and worked with those teams are still living and deserve to be included in such a book.

I talked to Steve Townsend, University of Alabama Associate Athletic Director, who is an old and dear friend of mine going back to his days as Publicity Director for the Southeastern Conference. Steve is a very bright guy, has a good sense of history, and loves Alabama about as much as I do. We talked about the audiotape project and decided to take a shot at expanding it to come up with a history of Alabama football *told by the players themselves.*

There is a world of former players included within the covers of this book, and some of the tales they tell really have not been told publicly, or at least in this context. Let me give you a taste of what's to come.

At the Sugar Bowl this past January, my good buddy Jerry Duncan was down on the field getting ready to go on the air with the pregame show when the Miami team came out of their dressing room. Now those of you who were there know that they didn't come out as a group — they came out in intimidating ones and twos! Some of them who came out separately walked down one side of the field, making a point to stare up at some of the Miami cheerleaders or Alabama cheerleaders.

At one point a group of about eight Miami players came out to the 50-yard line, locked arms, and goose-stepped down to the goal line. One of their big guys, No. 99, whose name was Caesar, came out by himself, paraded down the sideline of the Superdome, made a right angle past the end zone, and came back up the other side. When he walked past Jerry Duncan, who was standing on the sideline with his Alabama sweater on, Caesar leaned over and said something to Jerry. I was up in the broadcast booth watching all this, and I was curious what had happened. So when Caesar proceeded on down the field, I got on the intercom mike and said, "Jerry, what did that fella say to you?"

Jerry replied, "John, he said that Miami was going to teach Alabama how to play football tonight."

I said, "What did you reply to that?"

Jerry said, "Did you see how big that SOB was?"

"I certainly did," I told him.

"I said, 'Yes, sir.' What do you think I said?"

Jerry is very much in these pages and so are many of the players from across the decades. Scooter Dyess tells the story of the first team meeting with Coach Bryant when he became head coach in 1958 — it's a story I'd never heard in its completeness. Roger Shultz, a very gregarious and well-spoken guy, tells how it was to play under Perkins and Curry and Stallings. The War Babies team is thoroughly recalled with some great stories from Norwood Hodges and others, and Norwood tells how Alabama almost won that 1945 Sugar Bowl game with a little bit of a different twist at the end.

In other words, there are a lot of stories that I, as an Alabama fan and nut, certainly have enjoyed hearing the players tell. Some of them I have heard before, and there are a lot of them that go back to the early 1920s. In fact, my father played on the Alabama team of 1920, and my recollection of his stories about his teammates and others at the University at the time will be where our oral history of the Crimson Tide begins.

However, in no way do Steve and I want to ignore the pre-1920 days of Alabama football. There are some wonderful stories as well as quotes from newspapers and *Corollas* from those early years that Steve researched for some of the Centennial projects. For instance, there is this story about W. G. "Bill" Little, who is acknowledged as the father of University of Alabama football.

Bill Little learned to play the game while he was a student at Phillips Exeter Academy in New Hampshire, and when he entered the University of Alabama, he introduced the game to his classmates. Little was a husky, broad-shouldered young man, fully up to the challenges and rigors of the game. He was also a good speaker, and below are words he spoke to some fellows and wrote to others as he went about assembling a team in the fall of 1892.

"Football is the game of the future in college life. Players will be forced to live a most ascetic life, on a diet of rare beef and pork, to say nothing of rice pudding for dessert, for additional courage and fortitude, to stand the bumps and injuries."
— Bill Little, Father of University of Alabama football

In those early days of Alabama football, the University had a number of coaches who claimed a knowledge of the game and were able to cloak their weaknesses, at least in the beginning. E. B. Beaumont, the first coach, apparently was not the most popular of pigskin mentors. Over the years coaches have been fired or gracefully released, but these words from the 1893 *Corolla* offer a very succinct explanation of why this particular coach had to go!

"We were unfortunate in securing a coach. After keeping him for a short time, we found that his knowledge of the game was very limited. We therefore got rid of him."
— 1893 *Corolla*

In the early years of college football, there was no NCAA or conference to observe and enforce rules and regulations, although some might have been welcomed — as this experience of the Alabama team of 1895 indicates. Alabama lineman Thomas Wert reports on that year's game with Tulane, and once you read about it, you won't find it surprising that Alabama did not return to New Orleans to play the Green Wave for over nine years.

"They had prizefighters, dockhands on their team. I don't know if they had any students, I doubt it. They kicked me, trampled me, and sometimes bit me — all at the same time. I remember returning to the hotel on the streetcar. I had two black eyes, and my nose was as large as my fist."
—Thomas Wert, Alabama lineman, 1895

Auxford Burks was one of Alabama's first big stars of the 20th century. His ferocious play in the 1906 Auburn game, which Alabama won 10-0, inspired these lines, by an unknown Alabama poet, in the *Corolla*. This poem might also have contributed to the ill feelings in the Alabama-Auburn game of 1907, which ended in a tie, and the subsequent brawl that resulted in the cessation of games between the two schools until 1948.

Long shall old Auburn, with groans and with madness,
Remember our halfback who played them so fast;
Long shall Sewanee, with wonder and sadness,
Remember our onslaught of November last.
Tho this season ends his fight,
Long shall the Auburnite
Think of Burk's tackling with fear and with woe,
Victory upon victory then,
Echoes his praise again,
B. Auxford Burks! Alabama! Ho! Ho!
— 1906 *Corolla*

13

President Abercrombie was known to be very lukewarm about athletics, especially football. So when Dr. George H. "Mike" Denny came to the Capstone from Washington & Lee in 1912, he delighted students and townspeople alike with his enthusiasm for the sport and for Alabama's participation in it. The Bama coach that year was D. V. Graves, and judging from this quote, he was a far cry from the unpopular Coach Beaumont of 20 years before.

"In September the squad looked light and of poor physical development. Everything was discouraging. I had not yet become familiar with the Alabama Spirit — that indescribable something which made the efforts of a light team bring seemingly impossible results."
— Coach D.V. Graves, 1912

The four sons of the VandeGraff family of Tuscaloosa distinguished themselves in many ways. Three of them lettered at Alabama, and the fourth, Robert, was involved early in the smashing of the atom at MIT. Hargrove became a lawyer, Adrian ran the family land holdings, and W. T. "Bully" VandeGraaf played tackle and fullback at Alabama and was designated an All-American, the Tide's first, by the Walter Camp organization. Bully later went to West Point.

Bully was a fairly large football player for that era, and he went all out on every play. My uncle, Dick Foster, told me he remembered one time when Bully scored a touchdown and cracked his head on the goalpost (which was then on the goal line) with a sound you could hear all over the stadium. Here is a tribute to Bully from a star Tennessee player who played against him.

"His ear had a real nasty cut, and it was dangling from his head, bleeding badly. He grabbed his own ear and tried to yank it from his head. His teammates stopped him, and the managers bandaged him. Man, was that guy a tough one. He wanted to tear off his own ear so he could keep playing."
— Bull Bayer, University of Tennessee

Jeff Coleman told me that three men had a lot to do with keeping the fledgling Alabama football and athletic program moving ahead. They were Dr. Eugene Smith, who was a professor of geology, Lonnie Noojin, and Charles Bernier. Dr. Smith helped with the details of each game, raised money when needed, and generally assisted the program any way he could. Lonnie Noojin was listed as an assistant coach in 1914 and 1915. Charles Bernier was a handsome, personable man who coached track but had an interest in all athletics. He counseled with Dr. Denny frequently and nursed the athletic department through World War I. (The University did not field a team in the war year of 1918.)

Bernier was interested in recruiting players, and he traveled the South extolling the virtues of the University of Alabama. He was a great salesman, and by the end of 1919, he had assembled a group of good athletes at the Capstone. Bernier had a deep interest in track, and he assisted in both track and football. Later he became head basketball coach and was the first one to raise any interest whatsoever in basketball at the University. The 1921 *Corolla* records this tribute to this energetic collegiate sports enthusiast.

"Charles Bernier came to Alabama in the fall of 1920 after three years service as head coach and graduate manager of athletics at Virginia Tech. Coach Bernier's role has been largely responsible for the exceedingly stimulated interest in every branch of athletics which the University has experienced this year. He assisted Coach Scott in developing the powerful 1920 football squad and accomplished wonders with the green squad of track men."
— 1921 *Corolla*

This is just a sampling of the many memorable stories told by and about the Crimson Tide that we're retelling in this book. I hope you will enjoy them as much as I have, and I hope this oral history will be meaningful to all of us who love the University of Alabama.

July 1993

The Crimson Tide, 1920. Top row (l-r): Coach Xen Scott, Charles Bernier, Hugo Friedman, unidentified. Middle row (l-r): B. Newton, Luke Sewell, Mack Forney, Tram Sessions, A. Hovater, Mullie Lenoir, Talty O'Connor, two unidentified players. Front row (l-r): unidentified, Riggs Stephenson, Al Simmons, "Bood" Montgomery, Captain Sid Johnston (with ball), remaining players unidentified.

THE TWENTIES
The Winning Tradition Begins

This oral history of Alabama football had to have a starting time, and the decade of the twenties was the logical one because my father was on the team in 1920. The picture to the left shows the Crimson Tide of that year, and they had a pretty good season, winning 10 and losing 1, with that one loss being to the Georgia Bulldogs.

Another reason for starting with the twenties is our intention of having actual conversations with the players tell the story of Alabama football over the years. And I have to say that some of my earliest recollections are my father talking about the team he played on and some of the men he played with. A number of those names will be familiar to those of you who really have paid some attention to the Tide — Riggs Stephenson, Luke Sewell, Tram Sessions, Talty O'Connor, and others who are identified in this picture.

My father was outspoken, but he always said that Riggs Stephenson was one of the greatest athletes he had ever been around, and certainly he was. Riggs was the father of Marla Stephenson Sayers, wife of the current president of the University of Alabama. He made his big mark in baseball, as did Luke Sewell, whose older brother Joe was a star for the Yankees and is in the Baseball Hall of Fame.

"Riggs Stephenson is the equal as an athlete to Jim Thorpe."
— Head Coach Xen Scott talking about his star back and future major league baseball star in 1920

When I was growing up, Dad used to tell me that it was hard to beat the camaraderie of having played together and fought together on the practice field and then enjoyed the excitement of the games on Saturday. Years later, Talty O'Connor, father of probably my best friend back in the thirties, Bill O'Connor, told me one day that he missed seeing my dad, who had moved to New York, because once you'd fought together in a common cause with someone, that relationship had great meaning to you.

Talty O'Connor was one of the world's great drop kickers, which certainly is a lost art. The ball back then was almost round like a volleyball. The kicker took the snap from center, dropped the ball, and kicked it as it bounced off the ground. As the ball was tapered over the years to make certain that the passing game was being facilitated, drop kicking became a lost art. But Talty O'Connor won some games for Alabama with his drop kicking ability.

The twenties was just a sensational decade for Alabama. It started off in 1920 when the head coach was a man named Xen Scott. He took the team to Philadelphia in 1922 to play the University of Pennsylvania, and the Crimson Tide won a big upset over Penn by a score of 9-7.

To put it mildly, this touched off a celebration and uproar in Tuscaloosa. Someone took a brush and painted the 9-7 score in whitewash on the red brick wall of Rex's Drug Store on University Avenue, just a few blocks from my boyhood home. The score could still be faintly seen more than two decades later when I left home to join the service.

I think it's significant that the Alabama-Penn game was played less than 60 years after Appomattox, and the idea of a Southern group going north was not all that commonplace. In fact, I guess maybe you could say that the Alabama squad, small as it was, was the biggest group to cross the Pennsylvania line to have a contest with Pennsylvanians since Lee's army crossed at Gettysburg in 1863!

At any rate, the 9-7 win was a big one, and that long-remembered game is described by Al Clemens, one of the men who played in it. I am saddened to report that Al, who was Alabama's oldest living letterman, passed away in late May 1993 at the age of 94.

AL CLEMENS:

The only way we traveled was by train. We went to Austin to play Texas, got back on the train, and passed through Tuscaloosa on our way to Philadelphia to play Penn.

We took off our dirty clothes, got some more, and went on. The reason we went up East was we felt we had reached a level where we could compete against the schools up there.

Coach Xen Scott contacted Penn to see about a game. They didn't think Alabama could challenge them, so they gave us a game for an easy win. We went up and arrived in time to see Penn State and Navy play in Washington.

We had to leave that game early to get to Philadelphia for our game with Penn. They had an All-American lineman named Thurman. We were going to pretend Thurman didn't exist.

Our game plan was to run right at him. During the game, between the plays, we'd say, "Where's Thurman? We thought he was supposed to be some All-American. When's he going to show up?"

We got him so upset, he slugged our fullback W. C. Baty.

The referee put him out of the game. He was a great player, and we dominated the game after that point. Their only score of the game came when one of their backs reversed field and went all the way for a touchdown. It was the only time they crossed midfield the entire game.

Our kicker, Bull Wesley, missed three field goals before he finally kicked one. That shows how many times we got into scoring area.

The night after the game we were one proud team. We paraded through the streets of Philadelphia with Coach Scott carrying the game ball under his arm. When people asked him what he had, he'd say, "It's gold, just as good as gold."

We played the game in Franklin Field, and what I remember most was that the field had grass. Most of the fields back then were really dusty and dry. You played on the same fields you practiced on, so there weren't any grass fields.

Franklin Field, in contrast, wasn't used much. It was also closed in. We had to have tickets to get in because fans would try to get in Franklin Field by putting on a football uniform and going through the gates. Back then, it was easy to duplicate uniforms — everything was made of canvas.

We had no pads to speak of, and we had leather-cleated shoes. We'd get a chunk of leather, punch holes, and drive nails into the soles of our shoes.

You hardly ever had shoes that fit. You'd just swap around with somebody. I remember getting a lot of bruises playing. In those days coaches couldn't substitute. If a man started a quarter, he couldn't come out of the game. I played three years without missing a quarter.

Coach Wallace Wade came to Alabama in 1923, replacing Coach Scott, who was dying of cancer. Wallace Wade was a legendary coach. He had been to Brown University, and he was as tough as a nickel steak. Even back in those days, he was called "Bear" by a lot of his players. After the team had upset Penn, Wallace Wade took the team to Syracuse in 1923, and the Orangemen shellacked Alabama 23-0. Wallace Wade claimed that he learned more about football that afternoon than he had in all the previous years he'd been around the game. I guess the Orangemen were ready for him.

Unquestionably Alabama was a leader in early recruiting. Dr. Mike Denny was a far-seeing man, and he quickly came to believe that having football at Alabama would play a big part in making it one of the South's leading institutions. Needless to say, Pooley Hubert was one of the great ones to come to Alabama in the early twenties. Through some fancy maneuvering, Dr. Denny was able to bring Bully VandeGraaf, who had just graduated from West Point, back to Alabama to head up the ROTC unit. From this perspective, one has to believe that Dr. Denny primarily had in mind getting Bully back to Alabama to help out with the football program — and he did. Bully was the head coach of the freshman team, while Coach Wade was building his powerhouses. There's some evidence that perhaps Bully and Wade did not exactly get along, and for that reason, Bully stayed at Alabama for only several years.

Bully was a very colorful man. He was a big, burly person who could quote poetry by the ream. He was a very intellectual guy as well as a helluva football player.

Another man who came to the Alabama athletic administration about that time and who was a very important part of everything was Coach Henry G. Crisp. He came from Virginia Tech and was as fine a line coach and general assistant coach as ever lived, in my estimation and in that of the people who played for him.

Coach Hank, as he was known, had been injured in a farming accident and had lost his right hand just above the wrist. Yet he was able to play football, handle the ball, coach, and do everything. In fact, my father told me that one of the tougher drills that he went through and a lot of Alabama players went through in later years was when Coach Crisp, whose amputated stump was covered in sort of a leather glove over the entire wrist, would have the offensive linemen get down in position and then give them a snap count. If they didn't anticipate the snap count and jump ahead and beat it by a nano-second, then the stump would come flying up and hit them in the groin. Dad told me this really kept the attention of the players!

The virtual Alabama Rose Bowl franchise began when the team of 1925 won all their games and beat Washington in the first Alabama Rose Bowl. Wu Winslett remembers that great season.

HOYT "WU" WINSLETT:

We gave up only 7 points during the regular season, and that was in a 50-7 win over Birmingham-Southern. During the season we had only two tough games, a 7-0 win over Georgia Tech and a 6-0 win over Mississippi State in Tuscaloosa. It was a wet day, and we struggled the whole game. Finally Pooley Hubert threw a little old pass to me, and I caught it and ran about 10 or 12 yards for the only score. We missed the extra point and won it 6-0.

Coach Hank (Crisp) gave one of the most inspirational speeches I ever heard that year. It was before we played Georgia. He made a helluva speech. He was in the middle of the starting lineup, and he started telling us one by one something to get us ready to play. He went up to our right end Ben Hudson and said, "Your home folks back in Montgomery think you're yellow as hell! We haven't made up our minds yet, but we will today."

Then he came to me and said, "Winslett, we're starting you at left end. We been keeping you around here for four or five years, and you haven't done a damn thing yet. We're giving you one last chance!"

He saved Pooley for last, and he dropped his voice real sad-like and said, "Pooley, your mama is sick in bed over there in Meridian, listening on the radio and hoping you'll do something to help Alabama beat Georgia." Pooley started crying, tears streaming down his face, and Coach Hank said, "Let's go beat the hell out of Georgia!" We did, too, winning 27-0.

That win got us the Rose Bowl bid to play Washington. On our first TD against Georgia, Pooley called a reverse pass. I was on left end, and he got the ball and gave it to me coming back. I threw a pass to Grant Gillis, and he ran it about 35 or 40 yards for a touchdown.

Old Grant had a lot of mischief in him. There was a promotion going on—a pair of shoes was going to be given to the player who scored the first TD. Well coming off the field, Gillis says to me, "You SOB! You knew you'd better throw that ball to me because the guy that makes the first touchdown gets that new pair of shoes!"

I didn't get a damn thing! But I threw the TD pass.

One of our best players was Herschel Caldwell. He was a great defensive player. He played on the left side backing me up. I got the reputation of not allowing a first down on my side of the field. Hell, it was Caldwell who made all the plays—he liked to knock the hell out of the opponents. I didn't mind getting the credit. That was all right by me, but believe me, Herschel was a player.

Look up the records—we scored 297 points that year and gave up only 7 in the regular season. We won a national title. It was quite a team.

Coach Wade was a tough disciplinarian. He expected you to carry out your assignment, but he was fair. He was a tough cookie. Bruce Jones and some of the other guys called him "Bear." I also played baseball for him. He was an entirely different person on the baseball field—he would let you have some fun! In fact, on a lot of trips, he would let me order the meals for the guys. They got pretty well fed when I ordered the meals.

I never saw Coach Wade spend any money, but he always drove a nice car. I took him deer hunting one time, and I swear he was the sorriest deer hunter I ever saw. He expected a damn big buck to run by every minute. He wouldn't be on a stand 30 minutes before he was calling me. He'd holler, "Hoyt, come take me home." He always called me Hoyt.

Let me tell you a little personal anecdote. I had been around Tuscaloosa a couple of years and hadn't done much on the football field. My sophomore year I had malaria fever and didn't play at all. My junior year, I was just so-so. I played in the games a little bit but not a whole lot.

One day I was walking across campus with Coach Wade, and he said, "Hoyt, I believe if you ever want to make a letter at Alabama, you'd better go out for track." It made me so damn mad, I never did get over it!

At the 1926 Georgia Tech game, I had the best day of my career. Played the entire 60 minutes. I threw the passes and made us the touchdowns. Beat them 21-0, the worst licking a Tech team had ever taken. Coming off the field, Coach Wade told me, "Hoyt, I don't know whether the media will give you the credit for it, but you played the best game any Alabama player ever played."

Champ Pickens, of Montgomery, was an avid, longtime fan of the University of Alabama and a pretty good PR man for those days. He created the special brochure of memorabilia for the people who were on the Rose Bowl trip in 1926. Parts of it are reproduced in the photo section beginning on page 27, and it should give you a little bit better feel for the stories on the Rose Bowls, which you will be hearing about from Wu Winslett, Jeff Coleman, and Johnny Mack Brown.

HOYT "WU" WINSLETT:

On the way out (to the Rose Bowl) we got off the train a time or two to limber up our legs and run around a little. We were all scared to death going out to California, a bunch of Alabama boys who'd never been far from home. We had heard how great Washington was and how they were going to romp on us. They were big, and they had the best player I ever played against, George Wilson.

It was the consensus that Wilson was the best player in the country, and he was the guy we had to stop. Washington made 12 points in the first half. We'd given up only 7 the entire season. Well, on a reverse play, Wilson and I collided. I was carrying the ball going around the right end. Coach Crisp used to say I knocked Wilson out. All I can say is Wilson was so tough, he must have knocked himself out because I wasn't capable of knocking him out.

We rallied to go ahead 20-12, but Washington came back and made it 20-19. There were no 2-point plays back in those days. Late in the game, Wilson got loose again, and the only man between him and a touchdown was Johnny Mack Brown. Johnny Mack was a great offensive player, but I never thought he was much of a tackler. Still, that good-looking thing made a sensational tackle on Wilson, and we won the game. In one modern Rose Bowl book they say that the 1926 Rose Bowl was the greatest ever played. That makes me proud.

I think Johnny Mack was the MVP of the game, and he caught a TD pass from Pooley and one from Grant Gillis. I think Pooley scored our final TD. Back in those days, we called all of our signals on the field, and I sometimes called the signals from my end spot! Can you imagine that in today's football? Whenever Red Barnes, our quarterback, was hurt, I'd call the signals.

I'll tell you one thing, it was quite a sight for a country boy from Horseshoe Bend to walk into the Rose Bowl Stadium and see 57,000 watching a football game!

> *It's hard to realize what a great streak of luck it was that Alabama was able to get the Rose Bowl invitation in 1926, and I guess you have to wonder what the difference would have been if Clark Shaugnessy had decided that he wanted to take his Tulane Green Wave team out there that New Year's Day. Clark was one of the major figures in football during that time. He invented the T formation in the late 1930s with the great Stanford teams and then took it with him when he went to the Chicago Bears. In the early 1940s, the Chicago Bears' T was invincible. Fortunately for Alabama in 1926, however, Clark didn't want to go to Pasadena and we did!*

JEFF COLEMAN:

There was a man who was a graduate manager for Oregon State, and he came South trying to get a team to go out to Pasadena and play. The first choice apparently was Tulane, and he went to New Orleans to meet with Clark Shaugnessy, the Green Wave coach. Coach Shaugnessy wasn't interested, and he recommended the Rose Bowl consider Alabama. So Alabama was invited to go West to meet Washington for the 1926 Rose Bowl.

After the first Rose Bowl, I would go to handle tickets for Alabama, but the first year I went on my own. I got a job serving as the representative of *The New York Times,* and I wrote for several other papers in the South. So I was a member of the official party, which was very small. There were only 22 players and 3 coaches on the trip.

We went on the northern route on our first Rose Bowl trip. Mr. Borden Burr was a big Alabama supporter, and he was a lawyer for the L&N Railroad. He talked Coach (Wallace) Wade into agreeing to go on the northern route, which was up through St. Louis. We were planning on coming back on the southern route on the Southern Pacific. It was not a good idea because we never went the northern route again. We were late getting into St. Louis. It was snowing and cold everywhere. From then on, we always went on the southern route.

It seems as if it took us three or four days to get out to Pasadena. We went through Williams, Arizona, and some of the players walked through some plays. Williams is on the northern edge of the Grand Canyon. Champ Pickens, who was on the trip, played marbles with the little Indian boys who were there.

We didn't have much connection with the movie people on our first trip, but Paramount Studio invited us to tour their facility. Since I was on the list as being a writer for *The New York Times,* they sent a chauffeur with a limousine to pick me up and watch them make a show called *Kiss in the Taxi* with Bebe Daniels. The next day they had the team out to see the same scene on the set, but that was about all they did for Alabama.

I had a little box camera with me. I was at the parade, and there was a flight of stairs going up to the second floor on the roof of one of the buildings on Colorado Avenue. I climbed up there and took pictures of the parade. It's a wonder I didn't get put in jail!

At the game, Johnny Mack Brown was chosen as the Alabama Man of the Game, an early version of the Most Valuable Player. Washington had a great back in George Wilson, and he was named their Man of the Game. Johnny Mack had speed, but his way of running made him different from any other back I've seen play. He could change direction quicker than any player I ever saw, and that's why they called him the Dothan Antelope.

We also had the great Pooley Hubert playing for us. He was just as great a player as Wilson was for Washington. Of course everybody played both ways back then, and on one play Pooley pointed to Wilson, and said, "We're coming right over you!" He did it, too, ran right over Wilson for a touchdown. We won the game 20-19, and it is still said it was the greatest Rose Bowl of all time.

On the trip back we came on the southern route. I know Bill Little, the father of Alabama football, got the train to stop in his hometown of Livingston, and he gave us turkeys and cakes for the team. There were thousands of folks at the depot to greet the team when we finally got home. It was quite a spectacle.

"Johnny Mack Brown will have enough experience posing for the cameramen to enter the movies after his stay at the Rose Bowl."
— Birmingham News' Zipp Newman's remarks, which proved prophetic about the Tide star

Johnny Mack, being a cowboy hero as well as a former Alabama All-American, was certainly a hero of mine. I will never forget meeting him and having a conversation with him at the Hotel Wellington in the early fifties. I asked Johnny Mack about the Rose Bowl game of 1926, a contest that really set Alabama on its way to being one of the top teams in football lore. This is what he told me.

JOHNNY MACK BROWN:

I'll never forget coming onto the field and looking up and seeing about 58,000 people at the Rose Bowl. All of the Alabama players were pretty well awestruck by this, and as the game started, we fell behind 12-0. Had it not been for Pooley Hubert, the score would have probably been worse than that early in the game.

Hubert made most of the tackles in the first few minutes. I can still see old Pooley (who was several years older than the rest of the guys on the team) as he made a tackle to save a touchdown and jumped up. His helmet was twisted around, he readjusted it and turned to the ref and said, "Time out, Mr. Ref!" The other ten of us were squatting there looking up at the big crowd and not knowing exactly what to do, and we saw Pooley walking toward us with a very businesslike look on his face. He walked up to us and put his hands on his hips and said, "Now just what the hell's going on around here!" That somehow resurrected the Alabama team, and we got together and managed to play pretty well.

Pooley was a great football player and a great leader. I haven't seen Pooley in about 16 years, but if he walked in that door over there, I'd get up and go hug him. I really love that man.

"He was the greatest player I ever helped coach in over 40 years. There never was a more fierce competitor. He was a born leader and at his very best when the going was tough. He was just as good on defense as offense."
— Coach Hank Crisp talking about Pooley Hubert

HOYT "WU" WINSLETT:

The season after the 1926 Rose Bowl, we'd lost people like Pooley and Johnny Mack and Grant Gillis, Pete Camp and Bruce Jones and Bill Buckler, so we weren't supposed to be that good in 1926. I had already graduated, but I came back to play, and by golly, we won all of our games! Just by a little bit. We beat Sewanee 2-0 when Fred Pickhard blocked a punt for a safety. I had to punt in that game, too, because our punter Red Barnes had gotten hurt. I was standing back there in the end zone. The goalposts were on the goal line, and I was looking right at the crossbar when I punted it. By the grace of God, I got it out of there far enough for us to hold them and win the game.

They had a man by the name of Mountain Helvey playing for them. He gave us the devil, but we held on to win it.

We were unbeaten again in 1926 and got our second straight invitation to the Rose Bowl. We went out there to play Stanford, Pop Warner's team. We held them to 7 points, which wasn't easy because of their speed. Herschel Caldwell must have stopped a dozen long runs by himself. They had a back, Tricky Dick Hyland, and he got loose one time and seemed on his way, but old Herschel caught him from behind. Really, the only time Stanford scored came when Archie Taylor, one of our fast backs, fell and some fellow got behind him and caught a pass. That was early in the game. We didn't score until late in the game, I believe in the final 3 minutes, to tie it 7-7.

Our score came when Jimmy Johnson, who was plum fresh because he hadn't played much the whole year, came in. I think I ran the ball and made 3 yards, and Johnson clicked off 7 yards to get us pretty close. I ran it twice more and thought I'd scored, but the referee didn't give it to me. On the next play, Johnson came over with the big one.

On the extra point, I was the holder and Caldwell was the kicker. In order to keep Stanford from trying to block it, Red Barnes yelled, "Signal's off." When he did that, Stanford's players stood straight up, and Sherlock Holmes, our center, snapped it to me. Caldwell kicked it right through. Prior to the kick, I looked at old Caldwell, and man, did he have ice water in his veins. I said, "Right through the middle, ole boy." And he put it right through the middle.

We kicked off and held them and forced them to punt back in the final seconds. Red Brown, Johnny Mack's brother, caught the ball and nearly ran it back all the way for a touchdown. I always thought that I failed to block one man or he would have scored. Quite a game nevertheless.

The Tide had a couple of down years in 1927 and 1928, going 5-4-1 and 6-3. I'm sure that Coach Wade was not happy about this, but Alabama was definitely getting ready for what was to be another national championship team in 1930.

Fred Sington, the Phi Beta Kappa and consensus All-American of the 1930 national champs, gave us an interesting contribution to the Tide lore of the 1920s. Back then, freshmen were not allowed to play with the varsity, and Alabama's big game during Fred's freshman year was against the Georgia Bulldogs in Athens on Thanksgiving Day 1927.

FRED SINGTON:

Our freshman team coach was Shorty Propst, and he was a good one. We were undefeated as freshmen, with some great players like John Henry Suther and Monk Campbell. Actually it was the nucleus of the championship team of 1930.

The freshmen had been working very hard against the varsity to get ready for the big Georgia game. We went over to Athens to play the Georgia freshmen the Saturday before

Thanksgiving, and during the first half we were pretty ragged. The game was tied 7-7 at the half. Coach Propst was really upset with us. Matter of fact, he wouldn't even take us to the dressing room. He took us over under some bleachers, and he was giving us down the country about how we were playing.

We just looked at each other during Propst's harangue. We knew we were better than that, and finally I stood up and asked to speak. I told Coach Propst that for the past two weeks all the freshman team had done was run Georgia's plays against the Alabama varsity. I said we hadn't run our own plays in so long we'd almost forgotten them. All of the guys were nodding in agreement, and I asked Coach Propst if we could just go out there and run Georgia's plays. After a pause Coach Propst said, "Let's try it."

We went out and scored three touchdowns and beat them relatively easy with their own plays!

"Dadeville was War Eagle country in 1922. They took it for granted I was going to Auburn and didn't do much. Later when I decided to go to Alabama, I got a nasty letter from Mike Donahue, the Auburn coach."
—Wu Winslett describing his recruitment to Alabama

"He has to make a living doing something."
—Coach Wallace Wade's remark about his star player Johnny Mack Brown becoming an actor

Fred Sington, Bama All-American 1929-30

Johnny Mack Brown (coming to ball) Alabama 27-Georgia 0, November 26, 1925.

"...when I decided to go to Alabama, I got a nasty letter from Mike Donahue, the Auburn coach." All-American Hoyt "Wu" Winslett about his recruitment in 1922.

Rose Bowl stars Johnny Mack Brown and Pooley Hubert return home to a heroes' welcome after Bama beat Washington 20-19.

Actress Bebe Daniels explains during a visit to Hollywood why she picked Alabama to win the 1926 Rose Bowl — Coach Wade and boys were greatly interested. This photo is from a rare copy of "The Will to Win," the commemorative post-game program produced by Champ Pickens.

Al Clemens, Alabama's oldest living letterman when he died in May, 1993, at the age of 94.

Cowboy star Johnny Mack Brown (right) shown here with John Wayne is featured in *Alabama's Family Tides.* This rare photo is one of many which appear in the book.

Pooley Hubert crashes through for a touchdown in the play that rocked the stands during the 1926 Rose Bowl game. (From "The Will to Win.")

THE THIRTIES
Alabama Thunders In

The decade of the 1930s would find Alabama going to the Rose Bowl three more times. It was a good time for the Tide.

Wallace Wade's fame was national, and certainly his coaching ability was widely envied. The tough-minded disciplinarian from Brown knew his 1930 team was a juggernaut, and he very much resented the small budget allotted to his team and his coaches. He was not a particularly happy camper in Tuscaloosa, and made his feelings known. Tuscaloosa people were not happy about this, but then as now, they love a winner and knew they had one in Wade.

Meanwhile, the Duke family, tobacco multimillionaires from North Carolina, had spent some of their megabucks to take over Trinity, a small Methodist college in Durham, and created Duke University. Part of their plan to give Duke major university status was to go into intercollegiate football in a big way, and they dispatched representatives to Tuscaloosa to make romantic overtones to Wade to be their head of athletics. Wade was interested, to say the least.

In one of the more unusual "changes of command" in college football, Wallace Wade announced in the spring of 1930 that the upcoming season would be his final one at Alabama. Dr. Denny and University executives began a search even while the season was being played out — a powerful Alabama aggregation scored 241 points while allowing only 13, winning 10 games, losing 0, and claiming the national championship.

Bully VandeGraaf, Alabama's first All-American and later the freshman coach, was considered as Wade's replacement. However, a group of Birmingham alumni was most influential in the decision. The group's choice was a Notre Dame grad and Knute Rockne disciple, Frank "Tommy" Thomas, who was assistant coach at Georgia and recommended by Coach Wade. Tommy got the Alabama job and made the trip to the 1931 Rose Bowl — not exactly with the team, however. Wade claimed the first two Pullman cars for his team, and the coaches and these cars were off limits to the rest of the train. Coach Thomas was not on one of the team cars but was relegated to the rear by Wade. Presumably Tommy watched the team work out, though, so he had some idea of the players who would be his the next autumn. Fred Sington remembers the 1931 Rose Bowl trip from a player's perspective.

"Football Freddie, rugged and tan; Football Freddie, collegiate man."
—words from Rudy Vallee's song *Football Freddie,* dedicated in 1930 to Alabama star tackle and Phi Beta Kappa Fred Sington

FRED SINGTON:

I have always felt it was a shame that they stopped the open team policy of the Rose Bowl. Going to the Rose Bowl was a tremendous experience for us boys from Alabama. There was a special train, composed of the front two cars with the football team and the rest of it with citizens from around Alabama.

It was a marvelous trip—four and a half days to be exact. I have often thought that today when they grab a plane and go out in 3 hours, the players miss that thrill of the whole trip. We got to see parts of the country that we would never have seen, and of course, we stopped along the way and practiced.

On our way out, we stopped in San Antonio for practice, and a well-meaning alumnus brought us a gift—a baby burro that stood about two feet tall. The burro was such a baby that Coach Crisp's wife gave it a bottle in the baggage car all the way out to the West Coast and back home.

Some of the players thought the burro was a good luck charm. I'd say, "He might be a burro in Texas or California, but back in Alabama, he's a jackass." We'd laugh. During the game, we tied him up under the stands. I don't know if he brought us luck, because we had a pretty fair team.

We stayed in a hotel in Pasadena, but we didn't get to see the Rose Bowl parade. Coach Wallace Wade was very strict, and he had his mind on beating Washington State. We practiced two times a day, and the day before the game, he said, "We're going to take a little outing." We thought, "Boy, Coach has relented!" We did go on a little trip—out to an orange grove. We picked two oranges each and came back. That was his big outing!

Coach Wade, much to the surprise of everyone, including everyone on the team, decided to start the second team versus Washington State. We had a good second string, but we didn't know if Coach Wade was trying to motivate us. I know he was very confident in the entire team, and when our second unit stopped Washington State, they had to be thinking, "I hate to see their first team."

One of my most vivid memories is the uniforms of Washington State. We had been used to putting on a pair of khaki pants and a jersey. It could have been white or red. Well, that day Washington State came bursting out of the dugout dressed entirely in red. They had red helmets, red jerseys, red stockings, red pants, and red shoes. Zipp Newman, the Birmingham sportswriter at that time, referred to them as looking like red devils.

Of course, the West Coast folks didn't think we could play. There had even been some articles questioning why Alabama had been picked for the game. Well, with our first team in, we worked them over in the second quarter. We used a single-wing formation. I played right guard, which was the whipping guard. I came out to lead the offense, and Foots Clement was next to me. Albert Elmore was next to him.

On the other side we had Frank Howard, who went on to be the great coach at Clemson, and our end was Jimmy Moore. We did a lot of spin plays out of the Warner Formation. Pop Warner invented it. The ball would go back to Monk Campbell, who was known as Spinner Campbell, and he would spin, and then he would hand the ball off to John Henry Suther or Jimmy Moore to pass it. Jimmy was our passer.

Well, we used the spinner, and Jimmy threw the ball to Suther, who made a remarkable catch. John Henry had a bad shoulder and had a brace where he couldn't raise his arm but so high. He caught the ball and went in for a touchdown.

The next time we got the ball we did the same thing. This time Moore threw to Ben Smith, our left end, for a touchdown. Ben made a sensational catch, jumping about 3 feet off the ground.

A few minutes later, we ran the same play, except Campbell faked it to Moore and kept the ball. I came around from my side and led him through interference for a 42-yard touchdown. We scored all three touchdowns in about a 6-minute span.

Washington State had a fellow named Turk Edwards, who was one of the first big men in football. He was 6-9 and weighed 290, and he played left tackle for them. He was a terrific ball player. I played right guard, and it was my duty to come out and block on cross-block plays.

The first time Johnny Cain called a number on an inside play and I came out and hit Edwards, I thought I had missed him and hit the wall. That's the impression I got.

Then a little later on, another funny thing happened. We went back into the huddle, and Johnny Cain, who was running our team from fullback, said, "We're going to get this guy Edwards. We'll go outside of him."

Elmore was our end, and Suther was the flank back. Cain said, "Elmore, you and Hogjowl (that's what we called Suther), you all knock that guy in — we're going to outside."

We ran the play, and Big Ed charged and hit Elmore, Suther, and the ball carrier for a 4-yard loss. It was an explosion. A minute later, we went back into the huddle, and John said, "I know we can run that play. Run it outside. Elmore, you and Hogjowl knock him in!"

We ran it again, same procedure, and he hit all three of us for a loss. Back in the huddle, Suther said, "Cain, you call that play this time, and I'm turning him loose on you!" It was a lighter moment, and we all got quite a laugh out of Hogjowl.

We haven't really mentioned this, but not surprisingly the Alabama teams that came to the West Coast were derided as being "hillbillies," "swamp students," and other not-so-flattering names. One of the leaders in trying to give Alabama football a bad name was a very prominent West Coast sportswriter by the name of Braven Dyer. He was one of the great colorful writers, and the fact that Alabama won him over was a major PR victory for the Tide.

I met Braven Dyer before Alabama played Southern Cal in 1971, and even then he was a very trim, natty, and interesting guy. I told him I remembered the lead sentence in his story after the 1935 Rose Bowl game. He had written, "Open up that golden book that has the names Friedman to Oosterbahn and

Dorias to Rockne, and add the names Howell to Hutson — and write those names in crimson flame." Braven smiled and really seemed to appreciate my remembering that.

After witnessing the 1931 Rose Bowl, Braven Dyer was so won over by the former "swamp students" that he was asked to do a special feature for the 1931 Corolla. We have reprinted it here.

1931 Corolla:

"Alabama — World Champions" by Braven Dyer, *The Los Angeles Times*; Dedicated to the 1931 *Corolla*

Alabama's mighty men of muscle, combining brains with brawn, hold the unique distinction of scoring the most decisive football triumph ever recorded by an invading team at Pasadena. The Crimson Tide's smashing 24 to 0 victory over Washington State on New Year's Day, 1931, brought that honor to the battling gridders from Tuscaloosa.

It was entirely fitting that this spectacular achievement should come on the first day of the year of the University of Alabama's Centennial celebration.

I saw Johnny Mack Brown, Pooley Hubert, Grant Gillis and others rally round the cause and defeat Washington, 20 to 19, in 1925. I saw Babe Pearce, Red Barnes and Jimmy Johnson come from nowhere and tie Sanford, 7 to 7, the following year. But I hadn't seen anything at all until Johnny Cain, Monk Campbell, Jimmy Moore, Flash Suther, Captain Foots Clement, Freddie Sington and other bone-crushing behemoths from the South broke out in a rash in the second period of the Washington State game and buried the Cougars under three startling touchdowns.

They had told us to watch out for 'Bama's power. They had told us to watch out for steamroller drives through the middle of the line. They had told us to watch out for Suther's end runs. But they didn't mention about passes. To some of us, however, who know Wallace Wade and had seen Gillis and Hubert bombard the Husky backs in 1925, it wasn't necessary to sound a pass warning. But the palpitating public did not expect the aerial barrage Moore unleashed, and therein lay the big kick of the game. Alabama did the unexpected, and the unexpected is always thrilling.

Speed and deception. Such were the keynotes of Alabama's success. I have never seen such big men exhibit such speed in a football game. It was criminal the way the 'Bama linemen committed assault and mayhem on the persons of Washington State's safety men. Deception — akin to that for which Notre Dame is famous. Cain's calling of signals from different positions on those two pass plays completely upset the Cougars. It was deception that approached perfection because of the efficiency of execution. To Wallace Wade then goes the major share of credit for that great victory, for he conceived the plays, trained the players and had his men in the right mental and physical condition to perform at their best.

Alabama will be welcome at the colorful Tournament of Roses classic any time the Crimson Tide can muster another great team. But it won't seem like old times with Wallace Wade gone. Wade belonged to Alabama, and 'Bama belonged to Wade. Those of us on the Pacific Coast who have followed with keen interest the success of Alabama on her invasions of Pasadena will miss something when the Crimson Tide comes west to uphold the honor of Eastern and Southern football.

Of the 11 starters on the 1931 Rose Bowl championship team, 10 were seniors, and fate played a cruel hand on Jimmy Moore who died July 9, 1931, of spinal meningitis at his Anniston home. After the season while Wade was on his way to Duke, another starter on that team, Frank Howard, accepted an assistant coaching job at Clemson under Jess Neely. Howard would become a Hall of Famer.

Sington, destined to be a football Hall of Famer and the focus of Rudy Vallee's hit song "Football Freddie," had to choose between pro football, pro baseball, or a coaching career under Wade. He would do all three and later become known as Mr. Birmingham for his altruistic life.

Whitworth would come back one day to coach at Alabama, and as fate sometimes has it, his old teammate Sington was on the committee that chose Paul Bryant to succeed him. Monk Campbell would go on to coach at Kentucky and Johnny Cain at Ole Miss. John Henry Suther would become Sheriff in Tuscaloosa County, but all of these men shared that one common thread of being champions in a lame-duck season.

"You never know what a football player is made of until he plays against Alabama."
—Tennessee's legendary coach Bob Neyland assessing one of his players back in the 1930s

"There's a young assistant coach (Frank Thomas) over at Georgia who played for Knute Rockne at Notre Dame. Rockne says he's one of the best young coaches in the business. I'd recommend you talk to him about replacing me."
—Wallace Wade to Dr. Mike Denny after Denny announced Wade was going to Duke in 1930

Frank Thomas did a fine job of picking up where Wade had left off. One of the features of Alabama's history in the early thirties was the emergence of Tennessee as the No. 1 foe. In fact, the Alabama-Tennessee rivalry, which featured General Robert Neyland from Tennessee and Frank Thomas at Alabama, was born then and lasted for a number of years. Coach Thomas's 1931 team won 9 games and lost but 1 — however, that loss was to Tennessee 25-0 in Knoxville.

In 1932 Alabama won 8 and lost only 2 — again, one of those to Tennessee in one of the most memorable games in that storied series. That game was played in a torrential downpour from start to finish at Legion Field in Birmingham. Tennessee's All-American tailback Beattie Feathers and Alabama's All-American fullback, left-footed Johnny "Hurry" Cain entered into a punting duel that will never be equalled. In that contest, Cain punted 19 times and averaged 48 yards a kick, about 1 yard better than Feathers's effort. However, the Tennessee jinx held, and the Vols beat Bama 7-3.

That year Alabama got an additional taste of intersectional games, taking on George Washington in Washington, D.C., and winding up with St. Mary's Galloping Gaels in San Francisco. Alabama won the latter by a score of 6-0, and I guess that sufficed for the bowl game.

In 1933 Alabama went to New York and played the vaunted Fordham Rams at the Polo Grounds. In a titanic defensive struggle, Fordham beat them with a safety, 2-0. But Coach Thomas was certainly gearing up for his great team of 1934, which was to be the fourth Rose Bowl team for Alabama.

YOUNG BOOZER:

Talking about the 1934 team, there was a good mix of players. Jim Whatley had played ball in Dothan a couple of summers — we had the whole Alabama team down there playing summer baseball. We had Dixie Howell from Hartford, who was a star in the ballgame, and Don Hutson, and it was a great team. I've said so many times that the only reason I was able to play at Alabama was because the team was so good. Anybody who couldn't run or couldn't do what they needed to do and had Riley Smith, Charlie Marr, Bob Ed Morrow, Bill Lee, and Jim Whatley blocking for them — well, there wasn't much to them.

Don Hutson came into the huddle in the Rose Bowl game, and back then there was a substitution rule that you had to play one play without speaking. I believe Joe Riley was the tailback, and when Hutson came in, Riley just figured Coach Thomas wanted to throw a pass. Riley wasn't supposed to, but he called a pass play, threw the ball to Hutson, and Alabama scored a touchdown.

At times, though, other teams accused Coach Hank Crisp of violating that "no speaking" rule. They claimed he put the play number in the bottom of the water bucket where the players could see it and not have to talk!

JIM WHATLEY:

Bear Bryant and I were freshmen together, and we started to school together. I played right end in the first game we played, and Paul played left end. And I did score a touchdown in that first game against Tulane — the only one I scored in my whole career. Even though I scored a 60-yard TD, the coaches moved me to tackle because we had an end named (Don) Hutson. I didn't have quite the speed Hutson had, but I could keep up with the Bear. One thing I am proud of is that in 1964 I became President of the American Baseball Coaches Association, and two years later Paul became President of the American Football Coaches Association.

The trip to the Rose Bowl was a wonderful trip. All of us gathered at the train depot around December 20, 1934. Some of us had our clothes in bags, some of us had them in paper bags. I do recall that I had one little suitcase. I had one suit, and I think Coach Hank had to help me buy it — it was his suit, and he sold it to me at a discount.

We were on the train about three days. We had about 35 or 36 players and maybe 20 or 25 extra people — now they carry that many defensive ends! I was suffering with appendicitis and practiced just a little bit. We stopped in Tucson, Arizona, to work out, and Coach Hank said, "Well, Whatley, just stay on the Pullman and enjoy yourself." I was glad to get out of practice.

Later on in Del Rio, Bill Young, one of our tackles, had an attack of appendicitis, and they had to operate on him. He was a sophomore that year, but he did come back and play in 1935 and 1936. (JOHN FORNEY'S NOTE: I was in the Navy in Tokyo Bay on board The Bountiful, a hospital ship, and met a young hospital corpsman 3rd class named Bobby Graham. He was from Del Rio, and it turned out that it was his father who had operated on Bill Young some 20 years before!)

Stanford was one of the best teams I ever played against. I'll tell you, they were terrific. They took the ball and got after us. When they got the ball the first time, they just ran us off the field and had a 7-0 lead early. One of the players told me that I was the only defensive tackle he'd ever seen who played defensive safety that day. They were terrific, but in the second quarter, we got started rolling and scored 22 points.

Dixie Howell led our second-quarter blitz. He was a great athlete. He could have been a star in basketball, but he didn't want to play it. With baseball, he was just great. He signed with the Detroit Tigers after he finished at Alabama, but he got beaned, and it ended what would have been one great career. He was cocky enough to do anything he wanted on the athletic fields.

Man, he could play. He could run, he could throw, he could kick, and he could return kicks. We were using the Notre Dame Box formation, and I remember one play when Stanford hit him on the goal line and knocked him in the air. He turned and came down on his feet and went ahead and scored a touchdown.

He got loose on a 67-yard TD run, and the story is he thumbed his nose at the Stanford defender. That didn't happen. He was in the clear, and he waved his left hand good-bye to the nearest Stanford player. Dixie knew he wouldn't catch him.

During the second quarter, I tackled one of their players just as he caught a pass, and he brought his knee right into my head. I missed about 10 minutes of the game, but I came back and played the rest. I was the acting captain, and at the end of the game, he gave me the football.

I went into the dressing room, and Coach Hank said, "Give me that ball, boy. You don't deserve it." Well, in 1985 we had a 50-year reunion of the game at Bob Ed Morrow's home. He had that ball. It was flat, and we all autographed it again. We had autographed it back in 1935.

"I'll never forget going to the Rose Bowl. I remember everything about it. We were on the train, and Coach Thomas was talking to three coaches and Red Heard, the athletic director at LSU. Coach Thomas

37

said, 'Red, this is my best football player. This is the best player on my
team.' Well, shoot, I could have gone right out the top. He was getting
me ready. And I was, too. I would have gone out there and killed myself
for Alabama that day. "

— Paul Bryant reminiscing about the 1935 Rose Bowl trip and Coach Thomas

*After the great 1934 national championship year (in all fairness it should be
reported that the national championship was shared with the Minnesota
Golden Gophers), Alabama was expected to be great again in 1935. The
opening game, played in Tuscaloosa, was with Howard College (now Samford
University). In one of the most monumental upsets that any Alabama team of
the thirties suffered, Howard tied Alabama 7-7. I particularly remember this
game because my father was supposed to take me to it, but he got an emergency
medical case that he had to take to Druid City Hospital. With tears running
down my face, I stood on the corner of Denny Stadium and Tenth Street as the
game began. I finally walked home, but I always felt that if I had been at the
game, we would have won!*

*I'll never forget Homecoming, 1935, either — that was when the University
announced that my uncle, Richard C. "Dick" Foster, a lawyer who had earned
his undergraduate degree at Alabama, had been selected to replace the retiring
Dr. George H. "Mike" Denny.*

JOHN FORNEY REMEMBERS DICK FOSTER:

Dick's appointment to the presidency meant that I could go to all the football
practices, that I always got a good seat at the games regardless of what sport it was, and that
I got to go on several trips with the special party of the Alabama team.

I'm sorry that did not include the next Rose Bowl trip, but I remember some
discussions of at least the possibility before it was given up. I'll leave discussion of the game
to players, but I will say that Dick took the trouble to come by and see me and tell me the
highlights of the trip. I was heartbroken that we had lost 13-0 to Cal, but Dick told me every
time we would get something going "that big No. 92 would break loose and keep us in
trouble." No. 92 was Vic Bottari, the Cal halfback who was the star of the game.

There is a picture on page 46 of Dick Foster talking to a young Warner Brothers
contract player by the name of Humphrey Bogart. I'm told that Bogart, who did not know
who the genial Southerner was, observed that here were the Alabama players and coaches
and that everybody seemed to know them. Then he wryly observed that probably no one
knew who the University president was. And Dick agreed!

*Alabama truly had a great team in 1936, and Coach Thomas figured that
we should have been invited to the Rose Bowl. We won 8, lost 0, and tied 1 —
naturally, the tie was to Tennessee, at a game played in Birmingham. That year
my parents took me to the Georgia Tech game in Atlanta, which at that time was*

the season's next-to-last game. It was a truly great football game, with Bubba Nesbitt and Tarzan White the big stars as Alabama won that exciting contest by a score of 20-16. Coach Thomas let it be known that he was unhappy the team had not been invited by a bowl.

"Can you imagine going unbeaten with only one tie and not get a bowl bid?"

— Coach Frank Thomas after his 8-0-1 Tide was ignored by the bowls in 1936

This changed in 1937, when Alabama's team was probably not as good as the 1936 team. Only two great field goal kicks by a young Arkansas boy named Sandy Sanford got Alabama to the Rose Bowl that year.

JEFF COLEMAN:

We had no idea to look to the future, and there were no closed circuit arrangements in those days for bowls. And the other bowls had not developed. It was not until 1937 that we really had a problem. We did not have too good a team, maybe, in the overall view. But we wanted to go to the Rose Bowl if we could because we had been out there three times by then. We had played in 1935, so the 1937 team was a prospect, in a way — at least we felt we were a prospect. But Fordham thought they were going to be invited. And the Eastern press was all pushing Fordham.

In the meantime, we played Vanderbilt, when Sandy Sanford kicked the field goal. Mr. Cousin from the Sugar Bowl attended that game—that was the first time the Sugar Bowl had attended any of our games. And to make a long story short, in a few days we were invited to play in the Sugar Bowl. So of course Coach Thomas and I discussed it, and we put them off....

About the third day after they invited us, Ken Priestly, who had the position of graduate manager, I believe, of the Student Association at Berkeley, University of California, called me and invited us to the Rose Bowl game. And so we called the Sugar Bowl people and told them we couldn't make it.

CHARLEY BOSWELL:

One of our top players of the 1937 season was Joe Kilgrow, one of the senior halfbacks. He was a good, tough running back, and he passed the ball pretty good, too. He didn't do any kicking, but he did a little bit of everything else. Herschel Mosley and I were sophomores on that team. In those days, sophomores didn't play a whole lot, but we both played some.

About the only negative thing that happened to us was losing to California 13-0 in the Rose Bowl. We have the dubious distinction of being the only Alabama team that ever lost out in Pasadena, but California had a great team that year and deserved to win it. We had a few chances to pull out, but we didn't make the plays they did.

We really went unbeaten in the regular season thanks to the kicking of Sandy Sanford, who was a fine player and particularly a clutch kicker. Back in those days, you didn't kick many field goals — you didn't try many. We were playing Tulane in 1937, and with 4 or 5 minutes to go, we drove down close. Coach Thomas said we were close enough to take a pop at the field goal. We had never tried one at that point. Well, Sandy went in there, and darn if he didn't kick it through, and instead of tying 6-6, we won 9-6.

The Tulane game was our seventh game that year — we only played nine. The next week we beat Georgia Tech 7-0, and we went up to Nashville to play Vanderbilt. They had really good teams back in those days, and their center Carl Hinkle was one of the finest players I ever saw; he was a big All-American. It was a rainy and drizzly day, and we were behind 7-6 with 3 or 4 minutes to play. Coach Thomas sent Sanford in there, and darn if he didn't kick another field goal. We won 9-7.

We finished 9-0, won the SEC, and the day after the Vandy game, it was announced we were going to Pasadena to play in the Rose Bowl. Boy, that was a thrill. All my life I had wanted to go to the University of Alabama, and one of the reasons was to play football and play in the Rose Bowl.

On the way to Pasadena we stopped and practiced in San Antonio, and we had an incident that upset Coach Thomas more than anything I'd ever seen. We were doing dummy drills, no tackling. In the Notre Dame system we used, both guards pulled. Well, the guards, Leroy Monsky on the left, and Lew Bostick on the right, ran smack into one another. Lew was going the wrong way, and his head hit Leroy right above his eyebrow and ripped it open. It took about 25 stitches to sew him up — he was bleeding like a stuck pig.

Coach Thomas was about to have a fit. When he got excited and nervous, his face would turn red and his little old black eyes would get to jumping and dancing. He was literally about to have a fit. They got Leroy to the hospital and sewed him up and put a big old pad on his face, and we were back on our way to the Rose Bowl.

On the day of the game we were down in the basement of the hotel having a little chalk-talk with Coach Thomas. We never saw the first rose!

We had a great defensive team, but we didn't score many points. We beat Tennessee 14-7, Georgia Tech 7-0, and of course, I already talked about the wins over Tulane and Vanderbilt. California had some great players, like their big old center Bob Herwig. He was about 6-4, which was huge back in the 1930s, and they had an All-American end named Perry Schwartz and two great backs in Vic Bottari and Sammy Chapman.

In the game, poor old Herschel Mosley fumbled — he was going across the goal line when he fumbled the ball. And I think my buddy, Charlie Holm, dropped one, too, and we had two or three other costly fumbles. Actually we got the ball on the opening kickoff and were moving pretty good. Joe Kilgrow threw a pass to Perron Shoemaker, and that big Herwig just stepped in there and plucked it right out of the air.

Frank Thomas had a reputation in the coaching profession of being a man who could plan and work for one single game as well as any coach in America. No doubt he was bitterly disappointed to lose the Rose Bowl game to California on January 1, 1938. It just so happened, though, that Alabama had scheduled Southern California at the Coliseum to kick off the 1938 season. This was an opportunity for Thomas to get vindication, and he made the most of it. He began planning in the spring and decided to have a coaching clinic at the University in early August, and there was more than just a generosity of spirit behind this gesture. It meant that the Alabama team would come back to school early and start practice 10 days or so before they were supposed to. Fred Davis picks it up here for us and tells the rest of the story.

FRED DAVIS:

Coach Thomas had most of the squad come back to the University of Alabama starting in the middle of August. They came to learn conditioning exercises to show the high school coaches how to get their players in shape. We actually had a couple of weeks extra practice for that game. Southern Cal was touted as the best team on the West Coast, and most of us had never played before a big crowd. We were afraid of them, really, but we were in real good shape, and we went out and played and fortunately were able to win. We had some good players. We had one boy who played that year and then left Alabama as a sophomore and never came back. His name was Red Gornto — he ran an end around play at least 60 yards to score.

Perron Shoemaker and Tut Warren were the ends on that team with me, and Bobby Wood, Walter Merrill, and I were the tackles. Lew Bostick was a good guard. Grover Harkins, Ed Hickerson, Charley Boswell, "Herky" Mosley, and George Zivich were the halfbacks. Vic Bradford was the blocking back, and Charlie Holm and Alvin (Pig) Davis were our fullbacks.

Coach Hank didn't give you many pats on the back! One time he was having us do wind-sprints, and I was about to die — or I thought I was. I said, "Coach I don't even have a last breath." And he said, "Always leave one breath in you!"

Coach Hank was our line coach, and he was a great believer in quickness. He did so many grass drills and stuff that you thought were going to kill you, but he believed in agility. He'd take quick guys like me and some others and just work the hell out of us. We appreciated him, I guess, but we really didn't appreciate him as much as we should have. Coach Hank was a great man, he was a nice man, and he thought a lot of us. When we needed a little help, we could go to him.

I came to Alabama from Louisville, got to play in the Coliseum on the West Coast, and the very next year I got to play Fordham at the Polo Grounds. I went to Alabama really because I wanted to play in the Rose Bowl, and they'd been going almost every other year — but the years I was there, Tennessee beat us every year. We were a "bunch of dogs" really. Tennessee beat us, and we didn't go to any bowl games.

People used to call me "the bulwark" in the Alabama line. I don't remember being much of a bulwark. But I remember being up in Knoxville when they had a little halfback named Johnny Butler. He ran by me, I swung at him, and he drop-ducked his head and started off running 50 yards to score. I missed him three times on the same run! He ran all over the field like a rabbit, and I was after him — but I never did catch him.

It so happened that the Alabama-Tennessee game, which had reached heavy national prominence, was being dominated at the time by the Volunteers. General Robert R. Neyland, one of the greatest coaches in football history, had a pretty good plan for how to maintain a solid, winning record. When he had a good football team, this West Point grad would stay in Knoxville and coach. But when he felt that the larder was a little bare and he was in the process of stocking it back up with good players, he delegated the coaching responsibilities to a man named Major Bill Britton, who would be the head coach for one year, until General Neyland came back.

Neyland had great teams from 1938 through 1940, as anyone who ever saw one of them would know. They had a lot of All-Americans, they were big and strong, and they beat Alabama three straight times. That's the way the thirties ended, and as the forties came on, a lot of Alabama folks hoped we could get even with the Volunteers.

"Stanford made a mistake scoring first. It just made those Alabama boys mad. That first score was just like holding up a picture of Sherman's March to the Sea."
— Humorist Will Rogers after the 29-13 Bama win in the 1935 Rose Bowl

"Dixie Howell was in great form and lived up to my belief that he is as great as the immortal Gipp (Notre Dame's George who was Frank Thomas's roommate)."
— Coach Thomas on Howell's play in the Rose Bowl win over Stanford

"Fordham had its 'Seven Blocks of Granite,' but it was cracked today by an incessant flood of the Alabama Crimson Tide."
— Coach Frank Thomas after his 1939 team upset the famed Fordham squad featuring its fabled line, which included Vince Lombardi, 7-6 at the Polo Grounds

"I would have gone out there and killed for Alabama that day." Paul Bryant talking about the 1935 Rose Bowl.

Alabama's legendary Don Hutson.

Arthur "Tarzan" White, 1935, All-American
Alabama guard.

Alabama 7, Fordham 6, October 5, 1939. Charley Boswell carries the ball.

The 1934 Rose Bowl team visits MGM studios. L-r: Bear Bryant, Happy Campbell, LeRoy Goldberg, actor Dick Powell, Joe Dildy, Charlie Marr, Don Hutson.

Alabama — 1935 Rose Bowl champs.

Don Hutson, USC Coach Howard Jones, Frank Thomas, Dixie Howell.

University President Dick Foster with Humphrey Bogart in 1937.

THE FORTIES
Playing for a Common Cause

The forties dawned with war clouds drifting toward American shores. Alabama football seemed on the upswing, though, and 1940 saw 7 victories and 2 losses. One loss was to perennial nemesis Tennessee, and the other was to Mississippi State, which had a very fine team that year and beat Alabama 13-0 in the closing game. A principal reason for the Tide successes in the 1940 season was a big, mobile line and a true triple-threat halfback from Live Oak, Florida, Jimmy Nelson, who led Alabama to a narrow comeback victory over Vanderbilt, scoring four touchdowns in the fourth quarter to win the game 25-21.

In 1941 Alabama had a good team with a lot of players who made names for themselves, and All-American Holt Rast will be telling us about them. We might just mention that Alabama beat Tennessee for the first time in several years, by a score of 9-2 in the game played in Knoxville. One of the biggest Bama wins that year was over Tulane, the preseason pick for national honors. Tulane had a gigantic team, and Coach Thomas's plan took advantage of Alabama's speed. The key play was a punt return reverse in which halfback Jimmy Nelson handed off to Dave Brown, who scooted past the slower Greenies as they tried to turn around from chasing Nelson.

But Mississippi State continued its brief mastery over the Tide, and Vanderbilt beat Alabama in the rain at Nashville. Paul Bryant had just gone up to be assistant head coach to Red Sanders, and he was gleeful about having laid it on Alabama. Needless to say, that did not sit too well with some of the powers that be at Alabama!

University President Dick Foster died the Wednesday of the week before the Vanderbilt game from a variation of Lou Gehrig paralysis disease. He was young, only 46. Denny Chimes played choruses of mournful songs, and Dick's body lay in state at the library while long lines of mourners wound around the building. I have a feeling that the drama and the general sadness of Dick's death had at least a little something to do with the loss to Vanderbilt. And the ever-growing threat of America becoming involved in the escalating World War surely had affected everyone, too.

Despite the two losses, Alabama received and accepted a bid to play a powerful and favored Texas A&M team in the Cotton Bowl on January 1, 1942. This was three weeks after Pearl Harbor was attacked by the Japanese, and the Rose Bowl game had been moved from the Rose Bowl at Pasadena to the campus of Duke University in Durham, North Carolina, because at that time there were fears that Japan might attack the West Coast of the United States. Nevertheless, Alabama headed to Dallas on New Year's Day. It was one of the most unusual bowl games in history, and Alabama's All-American end Holt Rast has a lot of wonderful memories of that trip.

HOLT RAST:

My senior year we were invited to play Texas A&M in the Cotton Bowl. It was the first Alabama had ever played in a bowl other than the Rose Bowl, so it was a thrill for me and the entire team to have an opportunity to play the Southwest Conference champions in Dallas.

As exciting as it was to have an opportunity to play in a bowl, though, the bitter part was the world problems at the time. Pearl Harbor occurred December 7, 1941, and here we were going to play football on January 1, 1942. I remember the day of the game was awfully dark and dreary and cold — it sort of reflected the entire mood of the country at that time. Really, the general feeling was to get busy and get our armed forces ready to attack overseas. I was a reserve officer in ROTC, and I knew I would be called up right away. So the emphasis on the ball game was rather secondary because we were all more concerned about the national welfare of our country.

My brother Tom was an undergraduate at Alabama that year, and he wanted to go to Dallas and see the game. Some of the players arranged for him to get into the baggage car when we got on the train. After we left the depot, we moved him up to where the players were seated and found a spot for him. When we got to Dallas, he wound up getting a ticket in the press box as a spotter for the famous broadcaster Don Dunphy. Tom being the spotter probably benefited me because whenever Don was in doubt about who made a tackle or good block, Tom would point to my name!

Jimmy Nelson was a great, great halfback on that team. He was about as fluid and smooth a runner as anybody I ever saw. He was truly an All-American player, and he was a triple threat. He threw the ball, he ran the ball, he received punts, he kicked the ball — he did it all!

I played end, and I played with some great ends — George Weeks, Sam Sharpe, Wheeler Leeth, and Babs Roberts. We also had some great linemen, like Mitchell Olenski and Noah Langdale, who later made himself famous as the president of Georgia State in Atlanta. We also had Jack McKewen, who became President of the Million Dollar Round Table as an insurance salesman, and old Don Whitmire, who went on and became an admiral in the Navy. And we had Joe Domnanovich, who would be an All-American the next year. He was only a sophomore, and since Alabama didn't have a team in 1943, he never played his senior year.

Donnie Salls was a back. He was from White Plains, New York, and in our last game of the regular season against Miami played down there, he scored two or three touchdowns and just ran wild. Russ Craft was a tough, tough player who played in the pros after the war. He was a great physical specimen and a great athlete.

I remember the day of the Cotton Bowl game was a cold one. In Dallas, they say that when the blue northerners come through, the temperature can drop 20 to 25 degrees in an hour's time. They said the crowd was 50,000, but after we got ahead 29-7, you could look up and there wasn't half that many left. The Aggie players came out wearing gloves, which was quite unusual back then.

A&M had a sophisticated passing attack for that era — they had developed a passing game. They ran 72 plays that day from scrimmage and threw about 35 or 38 passes — we intercepted 7 of those, and they had 5 fumbles. We recovered 5 fumbles, and Jimmy Nelson ran a punt back 72 yards for a touchdown. He also scored on a run of about 20 yards. Can you imagine a team running 72 plays and turning it over 12 times? Well, it happened! We only made 1 first down the entire game, and they made 13.

Before Coach Frank Thomas took me out of the game, they threw a desperation pass. I was playing defensive end, and back in those days, you played both ways — offense and defense. We had them backed up on their own goal line, and they threw sort of a flat pass. I just stepped up, picked it off, and walked into the end zone. Well, that put them out of business. We were up 29-7. At that time, Coach Thomas put in the second and third teams, and Texas A&M scored a couple of times to make it close.

Winning the Cotton Bowl was a great thrill. I was fortunate enough in 1960 to be selected to the All-Time Cotton Bowl team for its first 25 years.

The Alabama campus was a scene of frantic activity during the whole year of 1942, with students, including players, being called to the colors. Alabama had a good team but was beaten by the Georgia Bulldogs in Atlanta 21-10 as the 'Dogs went on to beat UCLA in the Rose Bowl. Several weeks later after the loss to Georgia, Alabama lost to Georgia Tech, also in Atlanta, when a halfback named Clint Castleberry had one of the great individual games against Alabama. Clint was later killed in the service.

Alabama scheduled a final game that year against the Georgia Preflight aggregation, which had a bunch of pros led by Frankie Filchock. They had beaten the Tide pretty good by a score of 35-19. Nevertheless, Alabama got an Orange Bowl bid to play Boston College. The team would disintegrate after that, and in fact, Jack McKewen has a great memory of how he got to play, as a senior, against the Boston College Golden Eagles.

At the end of the regular season, Jack McKewen, who was a tackle, and Sam Sharpe, who was an end, were called to Fort Benning for Officer's Candidate School. They left the Alabama campus in early December. Coach Hank Crisp told both of them to stay in shape because there was a plan to get them back for the Orange Bowl.

Jack said that was the most absurd thing he could ever imagine as he and Sam Sharpe were at Fort Benning in heavy, intensive training. However, they reckoned without one thing — the influence of an Alabama corporate lawyer named Borden Burr. Mr. Burr made contact with a general who had been recently assigned to the Birmingham area and began to lobby him.

Jack McKewen told me that one day in the midst of some extremely important drill, he and Sam were called to the office of the fort's general, who looked a little baffled. This man, who was a lieutenant general, said that his best friend at West Point was now a general stationed in Birmingham, Alabama, and had asked him as a favor to relinquish these two men and let them go join the Alabama football team in Miami. The lieutenant general appeared not to be able to believe the request and told them he wouldn't do it for anybody in the world except this man, who was his best friend. Lo and behold, they were released and went down to join the team.

So Jack McKewen and Sam Sharpe played in the game, which Alabama won 37-21. Now Jack and some of his friends host a meeting every other year in Birmingham for the players who played for Alabama from 1938 to 1942.

BOBBY TOM JENKINS:

Perhaps it's difficult to recreate the environment of the Orange Bowl game because most of the players left after the Orange Bowl to do their billets in the service. Most of the guys were set to be sailors, soldiers, and marines. It was Alabama's first appearance in the Orange Bowl, and we were lucky enough to rally from an early deficit to beat Boston College.

Boston College had a great back in Mike Holovak, and he went about 70 yards for an early touchdown. Later in the first quarter, he went about 35 for another score to give them a 14-0 lead. Finally, our great center Joe Domnanovich called a halt and said, "Let's talk this over. Let's start playing some football." After his talk, we started playing some defense. As Joe described it, I believe that we went outside on the defense's scheme, and the linebackers went outside, and the ends crashed, and they were able to stop that business with Holovak.

Donny Salls was our starting fullback, and I was his substitute. He played a wonderful game, and I just played some of the game, but I was fortunate enough to make a touchdown in the second quarter surge when we went ahead 22-21. I scored one touchdown, and Wheeler Leeth and Ted Cook caught touchdown passes. George Hecht kicked a field goal and an extra point.

We scored a couple more times in the second half to win it 37-21. We also scored a safety in that game when Joe Domnanovich, our captain, caught one of their players in the end zone.

Coach Thomas had given us a day off after practicing in Tuscaloosa, the day before we were going to Miami for the game. I came back to Birmingham from Talladega where I was with a young lady who I later married. I stayed a little longer than I anticipated. I came out of the dance and couldn't find a cab, so I ran all the way from Five Points South to Union Station!

"Don't give up. We haven't had a chance to go with the ball yet. We're going to receive, and we're going to run them into the ground."
— Alabama center Joe Domnanovich talking to his teammates at the 1942 Orange Bowl after the Tide fell behind Boston College 14-0 in the opening moments of the game

So that wound 1942 up in fine shape, and Alabama had no team in 1943. After the decision was made for Alabama to field a team in 1944, Coach Frank Thomas, with a limited staff, did a masterful job of pulling a team together from 17-year-olds, 4-Fs, and a few men in their mid-twenties who had already served and been released from the military.

This small team (small both in physical size and total number) would forever be immortalized as Bama's War Babies. They were my classmates at Alabama, and there were some great players — and great people — on that team led by Harry Gilmer and Vaughn Mancha.

They only played 8 games that season and ended with a record of 5 wins, 1 loss (to Georgia), and 2 ties (LSU and Tennessee). I'm sure only Alabama's great records in the Rose Bowl and Cotton Bowl earned them an invitation to the Sugar Bowl of 1945. The strong college teams all during the war were those that had large contingents from military service programs — Alabama had none of those. Schools with Navy V-8 and V-12 programs were particularly good. Duke University, who was to be Alabama's opponent in the Sugar Bowl, was a good example of this, and they had a very good, experienced team with a lot of talent and a lot of depth. To put it mildly, Duke was heavily favored over Alabama.

At that point in World War II, things began to appear favorable for an Allied victory, but the timetable was still long. Since I was just a few short months from entering the service, I really wanted to get to New Orleans for the game — at that time I didn't know when I would see another one. I was able to talk my mother into letting me go, so a couple of days before the game, I put on my ROTC uniform and set out to hitchhike to New Orleans.

Back in those days, people were used to picking up guys in uniform, so I made the trip down quickly and found myself in the St. Charles Hotel (long since demolished, but prior to that, a long-time headquarters for a number of Bama teams). I planned to keep a watchful eye for two friends of mine who were team managers that year — Jimmy Sewell (Joe's son) and Bobby Drew (Coach Red Drew's son; Red, too, was away in the service). Somehow I had faith that they could put me up somewhere in the equipment room and also figure out a way to get me into the game.

A few moments after I arrived, I spotted Dr. Mike Denny standing in the lobby. Dr. Denny had been called back to serve the University after the death of my uncle, Dick Foster, and had been given the title of Chancellor. Dr. Denny, with his coat over his arm, was a familiar person to the hundreds and hundreds of Alabama students. He smiled when he saw me and came over. "Hello, Johnny," he said. "I didn't know you were in the Army."

Although I was embarrassed, I told him it was my ROTC uniform and I had just hitchhiked in and was really trying to find Jimmy Sewell and Bobby Drew. He asked me if I was staying at the St. Charles, and I told him that frankly I didn't know where I was staying. "Well," he said, "I've got a suite here, and there's a big sofa in the living room. Would you like to stay here?"

The next thing I knew, I was heading up to the suite with Dr. Denny. He told me he had come down by himself for the game and some meetings and he was glad to have me stay with him. Then he asked if I had a ticket to the game, and I told him no, which I feel sure he suspected. He said, "Well, you'll be in the box with me then."

I was truly staggered by my good fortune, and when we got to his suite, we found that the Sugar Bowl people had sent him a fruit basket and several bottles of top-brand whiskey that I hadn't seen in several years. I told Dr. Denny that it was indeed a rare package and that the Sugar Bowl people were taking good care of him. Later on he telephoned one of his daughters, and as they were talking, he told her that he was in a very nice suite and that the bowl people had sent him several bottles of whiskey. To my huge embarrassment, he added, "Johnny Forney says they are some of the finest brands ever!"

I won't dwell on the game — the players can handle that, but I will say that Dr. Denny's box was right on the 50-yard line, low to the ground. Coach Thomas's wife, Frances, was with us, and I vividly remember her tear-stained face at the end of what Grantland Rice, the great sportswriter, called "the greatest college game ever."

War Babies Vaughn Mancha, Norwood Hodges, and Harry Gilmer talk about those years.

VAUGHN MANCHA:

When we went to play Duke in the 1945 Sugar Bowl, we were matched against a very mature team. Duke had a lot of V-12 kids on their team, while the majority of our players were youngsters right out of high school. We weren't even supposed to make a game of it, but we stayed with them pretty good, and we thought we should have won it.

In the last 15 years, I've been a professor teaching at Florida State, and I always get two or three ball players in my class. (I should mention that in my office I have an all-time Sugar Bowl book — I was fortunate enough to make the all-time Sugar Bowl team, and I am one of about 28 players to have played 60 minutes in the Sugar Bowl.) One of my students was Deion Sanders. I would tell him, "Deion, you go out there and hit two licks on defense, then come over to the sidelines, and get a rubdown and something to drink. Man, when I played, we used to have to play every play." I pulled out the Sugar Bowl book and showed him where I played every snap in the Sugar Bowl. He looked at me and said, "Coach, I knew you were bad, but I didn't know you were that bad."

Harry Gilmer was a real leader. He wasn't a tremendously big guy, but he took a beating on offense, and then he would punt and play defense or he would return a kick and play offense. Harry always had a smile on his face. I don't care if he was bleeding, he was just really a great leader and a guy that everyone admired. That was part of his leadership. Harry was truly one of the greatest football players I have ever seen, and he was more than just a triple threat because he not only ran, passed, and kicked, but he played defense and returned kicks. In 1947 he led us in passing, rushing, punting, punt returns, kickoff returns, scoring, and pass interceptions. They didn't keep records of tackles back then, or he might have led us in those, too.

I played with a lot of other players who weren't big like the players are today but who had huge hearts. Take Tom Whitley, a Birmingham boy. He was a 200-pound tackle — 200 pounds. Can you imagine a 200-pound lineman today?

I don't know who started calling us the War Babies, but we were a Cinderella story. We played together for four years and played in two Sugars and one Rose Bowl. There was no dissension on this team. We were like brothers; we had a common cause.

Back in those days we traveled on trains, and that added a lot of romance to our trips. In the old days, we would go down to the depot on Thursday night and load up. We had a bunk in the railroad car, and the train would pull out at 6 p.m. Golly, it was fun. When you'd get to a place like Knoxville to play Tennessee, the train would pull up in the train yards and all the press and friends would be out there on railroad tracks. We'd get in taxis and go downtown.

The most fun was going to California to play Southern Cal in the 1946 Rose Bowl. We had about 20 or 30 coaches, and we stopped about every 300 miles and the press would be there to take pictures of the team on its way to Pasadena to play the Trojans of USC. We got to Hollywood and went to all those big studios. There was a special glamour to Hollywood, the old Hollywood. We went to four studios, and one of our players sold a ticket to the famous actor George Raft.

Of course, we beat Southern Cal easily in the game, 34-14. Actually, we beat them a lot worse than the final score indicated. After the game their coach thanked Coach Thomas for not running up the score on them.

I signed to play with Alabama after the 1941 season, and then the war came. I had a problem because I only had one eye. I couldn't get in the reserve or anything. So I went to work for the Navy. I joined the Merchant Navy and took off for California. I stayed out there working on destroyers. I got inducted in June 1944. They gave me another test at Fort McArthur in San Pedro, California, and, they said they were going to ship me to Fort McPherson. I had about 2 weeks to report to McPherson. So I took off to Birmingham to say hello to everyone in town here.

I got to Birmingham, and they told me I could be leaving next week or next month. Coach Thomas called and said, "We are getting ready to start football again, why don't you come down and go to school and play until you have to leave for the service." I did because I never thought I'd play one second, much less an entire season. But I never was called to leave for the service.

Coach Thomas was a great motivator. I don't know who you'd compare him to because every coach has his own way of getting his team ready. I have had Tennessee players tell me General Neyland never said anything. Coach Tommy would start off really quiet, and pretty soon he'd explode. The guys still kid me about what happened in the Rose Bowl. I'm sitting there near the door, and Coach Thomas started beating on me and screaming at me and just pounding on my shoulders. He was screaming, "Mancha, are you ready to play for Alabama?" Well, dang the whole dressing room erupted and we went out there and just whipped Southern Cal.

Coach Thomas wasn't very inspiring-looking. He would start off with that little ole bitty mousy kind of thing, and then he got louder and louder and louder. He was a magnificent guy, though, and his record as a football coach speaks volumes.

NORWOOD HODGES:

The first year I was at Alabama I was 17 years old, and we piece-mealed together a team for the 1944 season, which of course was right in the middle of the war. Alabama didn't field a team in 1943 and we started practicing in June for the 1944 season. As you can imagine, back then there weren't many rules governing practice time. We even had a practice game against Mississippi State in Starkville during the summer.

I remember State having Shorty McWilliams who was a great player, and I remember how hot it was. Our team was comprised almost entirely of freshmen, and that's how we became known as the War Babies. We developed a pretty good bond on that team, a strong bond, I guess.

Well, I guess my claim to fame was scoring the first two touchdowns in the 1945 Sugar Bowl, which was a record for a number of years. Vaughn Mancha was our center, and we had Johnny Wozniak and Tom Whitley up front. In short yardage situations, we used a buck play where I would hit real hard right behind Vaughn's left leg. My objective on those plays was to make first downs, but in the Sugar Bowl, I scored a couple of touchdowns. Unfortunately for us, we came close but lost the game 29-26.

Going into the game I was scared to death, but it was a thrilling experience. I had been to New Orleans one other time in my life, and that was a short visit. Getting there and seeing all the festive atmosphere and the stadium full of servicemen — it was quite an experience for a 17-year-old. Each yard line in old Tulane Stadium had a big box of poinsettias, and it was a very picturesque day.

Harry Gilmer not only was a great passer but he also played with a great heart. He would make a first down if it were a short yardage situation. If he needed to run, he'd run; if he needed to pass, he'd pass. If you needed a big play on defense, he'd make it. If you needed a big play in the kicking game, he'd make it. Appearance-wise he'd didn't look that great. He weighed about 157 and was spindly-legged and had no shoulders, but he was a football player.

In the final play of the Sugar Bowl, Harry completed a pass to Ralph Jones deep in Duke territory. When he caught the pass, he was about five yards from the nearest Duke defender and Hugh Morrow was in a triangle about an equal distance from the defender. Ralph took a step and when he did, his foot went out from under him. If he had kept his footing, all he had to do was go over. He would have been in front of the guy, and Ralph would have been in for the touchdown.

We were No. 2 in the nation for the 1945 season, behind the Army team that had Doc Blanchard and Glenn Davis. We always wanted a shot at Army even though they were a lot older and a more mature team than we were. We went undefeated and got a shot at Southern Cal in the Rose Bowl. It was quite an experience traveling out there on the train. I remember seeing Harlen Hill, the famous bow-and-arrow shooter, and Edgar Bergen. I got a picture taken with him. Gordon Pettus and I were talking with him and his wife, who was pregnant at the time with Candace.

One of the lighter moments about the bowl came because all the West Coast writers had said we didn't deserve to be on the same field with USC. Well, there was this fan from Jasper who got all worked up about all the negative things being said about Alabama's team. He got his hound dog and his shotgun and hitchhiked to California to make sure Alabama started getting proper treatment from the press.

The game itself was so exciting. We ran out of the Notre Dame Box, and we had shift 51 right or shift 51 left play. That was an off tackle play with the halfback. So I remember one particular time we shifted right and ran 51 and Gilmer made about 15 yards. We shifted left, but the right halfback made 15 yards. We just ran it up and down the field on them. We really didn't have to throw at all. We won it 34-14, and it wasn't nearly that close.

HARRY GILMER:

Back in those years there weren't enough seniors in college to have the game, so they allowed underclassmen to play. I played in my freshman year, along with Mancha and some others.

When we played Duke, and lost to them 29-26, we only threw 8 passes. It wasn't unusual that we threw that number — back then we just didn't throw many times. It was unusual in that as we completed them all, we wound up not throwing more.

As I said, back in those days, we didn't throw the ball that many times, and I probably did it a little more than other people and maybe had a little better luck with it. The thing that the media failed to talk about or even mention was that you jump and throw when you're on the run, when you're throwing the ball moving. The reason for it is that as you go up, you turn your hips around so that you're throwing normally. Because of that, we were known as "jump passers."

I was not a good punter. I didn't have the natural snap in my leg that other punters had, but the reason I did the punting was that Coach Thomas knew it wasn't going to get blocked. My punts were consistent — consistently short! That was the only reason I did the punting — there were people there who could punt better than I could.

I wore the same shoulder pads from my sophomore year at Alabama through nine years of pro ball, and they weren't big enough to protect me any of those years! They were little bitty pads that I had found in the basement, and they had to repair them for me. They weren't cumbersome — they just sat down and laid flat on your shoulders. When I left there, I took them with me and played nine years of pro football with them.

Coach Thomas didn't mention Notre Dame much to us. He was so much like Rockne himself that he didn't talk about Rockne and he didn't use Notre Dame things. But he worked us the same way — he used little psychological ploys on us. He could sound just like Rockne when he talked, and he could inspire us, but he was himself.

One of my runs against Kentucky was a record — 94 yards. It was a record until little Chris Anderson broke it in 1991, when Alabama played Temple in Birmingham. I was there for that game, up in the press box. This sounds like an unbelievable story, but it's true. A man came up to me as I was watching the game—I kind of felt him standing over my shoulder. So I looked back, and he said, "Harry, do you mind if I ask you a question or two?" I said, "No." He said, "Last year a guy came within 1 yard of tying your record for the longest run. How are you going to feel when somebody breaks it?" I said, "I am going to be happy for the guy. They keep track of these records so that they'll know when they are broken." He said, "Well, I thought you'd had this record so long that you might not feel too good over somebody breaking it." I said, "Well, they're made to be broken. I'll just root for whoever does it."

His expression told me that I wasn't answering the question to his satisfaction, and he left. No sooner had I turned my eyes back to the field, than Anderson went across the line of scrimmage, turned out to his right, went to the sideline, and ran down the sideline 96 yards.

That happened immediately after that guy asked me that question! I knew he would be coming back after he saw that run — but he did not. I knew I would get a telephone call from him — but I have not. That's kind of an odd story, timing-wise.

Coach Frank Thomas suffered from the severest kind of hypertension, and more and more it became apparent that he would give up the reins as head coach at Alabama. This happened at the end of the season in 1946. Today people might wonder why Alabama didn't call Paul Bryant back at that point, and it is worthy to look at it in light of Alabama football history.

Bryant was certainly a favorite of Coach Thomas — he put him on his staff after graduation, and I'm sure he did not stand in his way when Coach Red Sanders wanted to hire him as assistant head coach at Vanderbilt in 1940. I'm equally sure that Coach Thomas, who was very loyal to his people, had to feel a definite loyalty to Harold "Red" Drew who had been on his staff for years before he entered the Navy. After being discharged, Red Drew was named head coach at Ole Miss in 1946.

Bryant had become head coach at Maryland (taking a number of Bryant trained players from North Carolina Preflight to form the nucleus of the team) in 1946. At the point when his doctors told Coach Thomas he must quit, Thomas was able to name Drew his successor and probably a number of athletic department people and coaches were able to keep their jobs. At the same time, Bryant was being romanced by the University of Kentucky and ended up taking the job there.

What I'm saying is that I really don't think an effort was made to hire Paul Bryant at Alabama at that time. Frankly, I think he would have had some high-ranked people against such a move.

It so happened that Alabama had a mid-season game with Kentucky at

Lexington in 1947, so Red Drew in his first year at Bama would be taking on his former pupil. (Drew was end coach at Alabama during Hutson's and Bryant's years.) Alabama won 13-0 with a young halfback named Billy Cadenhead starring. During the game Bryant threw his hat down a couple of times, and I remember pleasurable talk around Alabama about beating the "Bear," with many people feeling he was getting too big for his britches.

The renewal of Alabama-Auburn in December of 1948 was, to my knowledge, the first time Alabama performed in front of television cameras. My employers at the time, Ed Norton and Thad Holt, of WAPI Birmingham, made a deal with the embryonic CBS TV department to telecast the game on a closed-circuit basis. Originally the plan was to help the two schools with their ticket problems (yes, even then there was hellacious demand). The broadcast was to be relayed to the Municipal Auditorium in Birmingham (now Boutwell), where about 2,500 people could be accommodated.

Somehow this could not be worked out, so the second choice was the big armory right by Legion Field. Maury Farrell and I were to do the game, and we would split duties, each doing one quarter on radio and the next on TV. Several New York technicians were on hand, and we listened avidly to what these hotshots had to say. I remember they stressed that with TV, the announcer did not have to say too much. Funny that this was good advice in 1948 and some still ignore it!

Gordon Pettus played four years for Alabama and competed in the Rose and Sugar Bowls. Later as an SEC official, he officiated in the Cotton, Sugar, and Orange Bowls, giving him a unique honor of participating in the oldest and most prestigious bowls, still considered the Big Four. He also played for both Coach Thomas and Coach Drew during his Alabama career. We'll let the recollections of Gordon Pettus and Ed Salem wind up the decade of the forties at Alabama.

GORDON PETTUS:

The Tennessee game had always been the biggest of the year for Alabama, at least in my lifetime. There is a story about me that has been printed in the paper, and it is true. My freshman year I walked into the first meeting, and Coach (Frank) Thomas walked up to the blackboard. He picked up his chalk and wrote T - E - N - N - E - S - S - E - E across the board and walked out of the room. I leaned over and asked one of the other players what that was all about, and he said, "Don't be so stupid rookie, Tennessee is *the* game around here." I learned early on there were some big games at Alabama, but none matched Tennessee.

Georgia and LSU were also big conference rivals for us back in the 1940s, and they had players like Charlie Trippi at Georgia and Y.A. Tittle at LSU. Those were huge conference games for us, and generally the conference race was fought among Alabama, Tennessee, Georgia, and LSU. Ole Miss got into the mix when they hired Johnny Vaught, but we didn't play them back then.

Coach Thomas was adamant about playing Auburn — better yet about *not* playing Auburn. He was outspoken, feeling we shouldn't have to play them because we had nothing to gain and they had everything to gain. You must remember back then, we had already been to all the major bowls. Disregarding the 1943 season when the war kept us from having a team, Coach Thomas took Alabama teams to the Cotton, Orange, Sugar, and Rose Bowls in consecutive seasons. That's pretty strong in anybody's book. Auburn was really not much of a factor, and he felt it would only strengthen their program. I don't think he ever felt it would diminish what Alabama had accomplished, but as good a person as Coach Thomas was, he wasn't in for a lot of goodwill for opposing teams.

Coach Thomas retired after the 1946 season, and Coach Drew, who had been an assistant at Alabama and then head coach at Ole Miss during the 1946 season, came back to replace him. By that time the state legislature had gotten into the act of trying to force a game between Alabama and Auburn. As Coach Thomas said at the time, it was a good move for Auburn but not for us.

Well, the legislature did finally mandate the contest with Auburn and the first game took place in December 1948, my senior year. You know we were a bunch of 20- and 21-year-old kids, and we reacted to what our coaches said. To be real honest about it, we just didn't have a lot of respect for Auburn because Alabama had accomplished so much in football and Auburn really hadn't.

The game was set in Birmingham at Legion Field, and Governor Jim Folsom was there. I don't remember exactly how many people the stadium seated back then, but it must have been around 50,000. We drove down the field the first time we had the ball, and I carried it for what I thought was a first down deep in their territory, but the official gave me a bad mark. I say that in a humorous manner because I ended up officiating for years and being in charge of the SEC officials for about 10 more. Anyway, I did get a bad mark, and we didn't score that time.

The second time we got the ball, we moved it down there, and I threw a touchdown pass of 6 yards to Butch Avinger for the first touchdown. I don't guess I did a whole lot of historical things in my career, but I did help us get ahead 6-0 in the renewal of the Alabama-Auburn series. Of course, Ed Salem had an all-star game versus Auburn that afternoon. I don't remember how many touchdowns he accounted for, but it was several, and we went on to win 55-0.

Coach Drew was a fiery type on the sidelines, and I can still hear him yelling at us, "You have got to hit them, and block them, and tackle them." On that day, I guess we did a pretty good job. That was my last game at Alabama, but I honestly can't say it was the biggest. Like I said earlier, those games we had with Tennessee, LSU, and Georgia back then were much bigger contests; and of course, my freshman year we went out to the Rose Bowl to play Southern California and beat them 34-14. They don't come much better than that.

I will always consider Coach Thomas one of the greatest coaches of all time, a real tactician and motivator. He knew what strings to pull on each player to make him better or at least make him think he was better than he was.

There is an old war story out there about the 1934 Alabama team going to the Rose Bowl and LSU's athletic director Red Heard was on the train talking to Coach Thomas, and

Coach Bryant was sitting there. Coach Thomas tells Red, "You know who my best football player is? I'll tell you — it's No. 12." Coach Bryant says when he realized it was him, he just swelled up with pride and was ready to beat Stanford by himself. Of course, that Alabama team had Don Hutson and Dixie Howell and all those great players, but Coach Thomas obviously knew how to motivate his players, and I believe Coach Bryant learned this technique from Thomas and built on it during his career.

Coach Thomas was a student of the game. Remember he played for Knute Rockne at Notre Dame, and he probably was as good a pupil as Rockne ever had. I think Coach Thomas passed on what he learned from Rockne to Paul Bryant and on to Gene Stallings. You see total preparation with the Alabama team, and I think that was a trademark of when I played and what you see today. On Saturdays, Coach Thomas was totally into the game, and he was unflappable — like I said, a great tactician.

ED SALEM:

When I was just out of high school, I went down to Alabama when the freshman rule went into effect that you had to be in school by February in order to play your freshman year. We had a game with Georgia when it was raining and muddy. Since I was a freshman, all I could do was sit back and watch until the score got out of hand and they sent the freshmen in to play.

When we went in to the locker room at halftime, the score was tied. I was lying next to Charlie Compton who had just chipped a tooth, and he was in pain. He said to me, "Salem, go get a pair of pliers." Well, I thought he wanted the pliers to fix his cleats because it was so muddy, but he laid his head back and used the pliers to pull his tooth!

It seemed every time an incident came up, it was when we were playing Georgia. When we played Georgia at Legion Field, I was the starting tailback. As the game went along, I took a couple of passes, some were intercepted and I completed a couple of passes. Coach took me out and put in another tailback, Ed White. He went in and had one intercepted, so Coach pulled him out and put me back in. I had another one intercepted, so Coach pulled me out again and put in Bob Kospers. He had one pass intercepted, and Coach Campbell said, "Ed, you just keep getting all those passes intercepted." I said, "Coach, you played me longer than you played the rest of them! Anyway, I'm 12 for 12 — we caught 6 and they caught 6! So that's a pretty good average!"

The last Alabama game of the 1940s was against Auburn, and the heavily favored Crimson Tide team was shocked, stunned, and upset by a score of 14-13.

"That 1934 team was my greatest. It had what it took. But my favorite team of all was that green 1944 eleven. Oh, how I loved those War Babies! Those boys were just kids, but they worked with all their strength and heart to win."
— Coach Thomas on his memorable teams

"Vaughn, I never want a thing like that to happen again. No matter what the other fellow does, I don't want my boys to get in fights. We must uphold the dignity of the University of Alabama."
— Coach Frank Thomas reproving Vaughn Mancha after the Tide star had been lured into a fight in the 1945 LSU game

"I really didn't do anything special. I had great blocking from my teammates. They deserve the credit."
— Alabama star Harry Gilmer after rushing six times for 216 yards and completing 2 passes in two attempts for 50 more yards in a 60-19 win over Kentucky in 1945

"Alabama has won in the Rose Bowl before, but, Alabama, you have never met the likes of Southern Cal before. It will be a different story for you."
— A West Coast writer on the eve of the 1946 Rose Bowl

"There goes a great coach. I'll never forget what he did today. If he had wanted, he could have named the score."
— Southern Cal's coach Jeff Cravath talking about Frank Thomas after the 1946 Rose Bowl won by Alabama 34-14

Norwood Hodges, hard-running
fullback 1944-46.

Holt Rast, All-American Alabama end,
1941.

Gordon Pettus, 1946 Rose Bowl.

The Bama-Duke 1945 Sugar Bowl: Vaughn Mancha (41) about to hit Duke's Davis.

Vaughn Mancha (41) and Harry Gilmer (52).

ALL-AMERICAN
1945
Alabama Half
A passer second
to NONE

In 1944, every Bama fan knew Harry Gilmer was a great passer and punter. But in the opening game of the season vs. LSU, Gilmer took a kickoff and sped 95 yards through the entire LSU team. The game ended in a thrilling 27-27 tie.

Bobby Tom Jenkins

Herb Hannah

THE FIFTIES
The Best of Times, the Worst of Times

As far as the 1950s were concerned, Alabama football was best described by Charles Dickens's phrase: "It was the best of times; it was the worst of times." The decade started off well enough with the Tide rolling to a 9-2 regular season, but it was indeed a bittersweet experience because the bowls snubbed this team that was obviously qualified to participate in postseason activities.

Ed Salem, Al Lary, and Mike Mizerany were All-Americans that year, and only a pair of heartbreaking losses to old foes Vanderbilt (27-22) and Tennessee (14-9) prevented a run at the national title.

Pat O'Sullivan was probably the first defensive specialist of modern day Tide football. He burst onto the scene as an unknown freshman. (His first game at Legion Field, the PA announcer did not know who he was and simply said, "Tackled by No. 26," before the sports information people could get word to him!) Pat was a senior on the powerful Tide 11 of 1950.

PAT O'SULLIVAN:

We had a huge backfield in 1950 with Butch Avinger weighing 225, Ed Salem about 215 to 220, Tom Calvin a lightweight at about 205, and Bobby Marlow about 190 but packing a 250-pound hitting force. Marlow could run through the side of a wall. He could run around you, through you, or whatever just to get by you.

We didn't go to a bowl that year, even though we lost only two games. We went down to Florida and just blew them out (41-13). As I understand it, there were a lot of bowl people at that game, and they said, "Whoa, we're not going to touch Alabama. We've already made a selection, and we'll be embarrassed because Alabama will just absolutely blow them out of the stadium!" So we didn't get to go to a bowl that year.

I played for Coach Red Drew who was an excellent coach but not the greatest motivator. He would tell us some stories about his past football career and other teams he had coached, but he never fired us up like you think of a football coach firing up his team. I guess the thing that got us fired up back in those days was we wanted to keep our jobs. We wanted to keep our jobs so we could continue going to school so we could eat! Back then, if you didn't play football, you didn't eat.

We used to practice 11 months a year back then — there was no prohibition on practice time. I remember going down to Tuscaloosa in early June and practicing all of June,

July, and August. It would be 110 degrees, and we'd practice twice a day.

The new freshmen would come in, and I guess we must have turned over a couple hundred freshmen a year. They'd come in and practice two or three days and leave saying they couldn't handle that. So only the folks with the real ambition and the dying desire to play football and those of us like me – I wanted an education – stuck it out.

One of my most memorable practices came at center. It was one afternoon, real late. It was hot, and I was tired. The way we knew what time it was and how much practice we had left was by listening to Denny Chimes. So I was listening to Denny Chimes. Jack Brown was our quarterback, and we were running some plays out of the Notre Dame Box and some out of the split-T. Most of the afternoon we had been running from the T. I was playing center and snapping the ball. Jack Brown came up to the line of scrimmage and changed the play to a Notre Dame Box. Well I was listening to Denny Chimes, and upon the signal hike I snapped the ball to the quarterback who was supposed to be under me, but he wasn't under me! The ball went sailing about 50 yards in the air, and Coach Drew went berserk. After that I became a defensive starter – they didn't want me in there at center!

I can recall vividly, as if it happened yesterday, when I was initiated into the A-Club. *(EDITOR'S NOTE: In those days, athletes were initiated by being forced to parade in public, in costume.)* They dressed me up like a girl, with a wig, a slip, a brassiere, stockings, and high-heeled shoes that didn't fit – so I was walking on my ankles instead of the heels. They made me go into the restroom, dance in the Supe Store with the jukebox going full blast, and walk up and down. It was kind of fun but a little humiliating. I was a little shy back then.

Van Marcus played offensive tackle on the 1950 team.

VAN MARCUS:

The 1950 team always sticks in my mind when I remember my playing days at Alabama. You wonder what made that particular team so good, but if you look at the seniors who were on that team, you won't have any trouble figuring it out. We had Herb Hannah, Mike Mizerany, Ed Salem, and on and on. Just look at the scores of 1950 – I wasn't a starter, but I played a lot of football. We scored 328 points and gave up just over 100.

The story has been told and probably could be verified that the coaches turned down a Gator Bowl bid because they knew they had an Orange Bowl bid locked up. After we beat Florida 41-13 in Jacksonville in late November, it seemed a cinch. But it didn't work out, and we didn't get any bowl bid at all.

By the way, the coldest I've ever been in a football game was that win over Florida in Jacksonville. I was a sophomore, and I was playing on the specialty teams. I played a lot that day because we scored a lot, so we covered kickoffs a lot. It was about 28 degrees in Jacksonville, with about a 40-mile per hour wind that blew the entire ball game.

We were using what we called squaw fists on our hands to keep warm, and after the game we didn't even shower at the stadium because they didn't have any warm facilities. At the hotel where we stayed, our people had to go to an Army-Navy supply place and buy blankets to keep us warm. This happened the weekend after Thanksgiving when a cold front moved through the South.

Jeff Coleman and Hank Crisp, I reckon, were the people running the show at Alabama, even though Frank Thomas was athletic director in title. Coach (Red) Drew was the head football coach. He had a good staff but Hank Crisp stood out with all the players. He had left Alabama and gone to Tulane for a few years, but then he came back. As many Alabama fans know, he had only one hand. He chain-smoked, and he'd have two cigarettes going and be on the chalkboard writing away. Don't know how he did it, but he'd do it. And the cigarettes would have the longest ashes on the end of them you'd ever seen. He'd make Xs and Os on the board all at the same time, and he was doing this with one hand!

Coach Hank was just a real players' coach. He wasn't an elegant speaker, but you knew exactly where you stood with him. Coach Hank designed what we called the "chicken coop." It was about 3 feet high and 10 feet square, and it had four legs with a screen around the top that was held in place by boards to make a cage. One drill was to charge under it. Coach Hank wouldn't let us wear our helmets because the idea was to teach us to stay low and keep our heads up. Then we would do figure eights, and he would enjoy the hell out of it with everybody colliding in the middle. Of course we liked to collide in the middle because we got to lay around for a few minutes! He also kept a paddle out there, underneath the bushes. What he'd like to do was tell you to leave on the count of two, and if you were still there, you were going to get hit. Now he didn't have that much strength in one hand, but you knew to leave on the count of one!

I will say that to this day Bobby Marlow was as good a football player as I've ever seen in my life. He single-handedly tore up Georgia Tech when we beat them 54-19 in 1950. He scored three times in four minutes. On the first play, we were running some Oklahoma split-T offense, Bobby popped through Tech's 7-Diamond defense. He left their safety Billy Teas standing still and went 90 yards for a touchdown. That was one of the first offensive plays of the game, and with the game not four minutes old, he had already scored three TDs. Bobby Marlow was a hard player, and there wasn't an ounce of fat on him. He worked as hard as necessary, but he didn't overtrain. In fact, he might have been a little bit on the other side. He and a few others would smoke when they wanted to. Bobby could do it all.

After a 5-6 season in 1951, Alabama rebounded for the 10-2 Orange Bowl season in 1952, which ended on a resounding high note with the 61-6 rout of Syracuse. Among the stars of that season was a sophomore defensive back from Tuscaloosa, Cecil "Hootie" Ingram. During that year, he led the nation in interceptions with 10 and the SEC in punt returns with 329 yards.

HOOTIE INGRAM:

We lost early in the 1952 season to Tennessee, but our team got better, and by the end of the season we had a really good team. That was the last year of two-platoon football for awhile. We had a really young football team, particularly defensively. Our entire defense would have been back intact for the 1953 season, but they changed the rules, and it hurt Alabama.

Our key game was with Maryland down in Mobile. Maryland was the national champion the year before, and they had another great team in 1952. I think Coach Hank Crisp devised the defensive scheme we used that day, and I don't think those plays had ever been used before.

In our day and time, you had a basic defense and you did a little stunting off it, but we employed both an odd-man and an even-man front, pretty multiple. One of our players, Bill Oliver, was the key to our defense. He had to double as a defensive back in the 3-deep setup to a defensive end in the other setup. So it was an interesting thing, and we shifted our defense and gave Maryland a lot of trouble that day. I think it had a lot to do with our winning.

Our Georgia Tech game, earlier that year, was one of the first regular season Southeastern Conference television games. And we got the Orange Bowl bid to play Syracuse, who had won the Lambert Trophy, which declared them the champions of the East. That game was on television, which was quite a big deal back then.

Syracuse had an excellent quarterback in Pat Stark. He was a passing quarterback, and they did a lot of schemes in their passing attack that we hadn't seen all year. Syracuse scored first, and they shot off their cannon six times-once for each point. I think that made us more determined to stop them — to make sure we didn't have to hear the cannon again!

One of the most humorous things about going to the Orange Bowl was that we were going to Miami Beach with all the sunshine and to have a good time. Well we flew down, and the first day Coach Drew practiced us three times. We practiced early in the morning, before the press got out there, and had a big scrimmage. Then we put on our game uniforms for a picture-taking session. We thought we were going to go back to the hotel, but instead we had another practice. After we had some interviews, the coaches said they weren't satisfied with the practice, so we had a late-afternoon workout. It was quite a first day in Miami!

Coach (Happy) Campbell, who was also my baseball coach at Alabama, coached the defensive backs. I was kind of proud of making that 80-yard punt return for a touchdown, and when I came over to the sideline, Coach Campbell said, "As slow as you are, you ran out the clock. You did two things to help us, you scored and ran the clock down!"

We scored 40 points in the second half, mainly because we had a lot of big plays. We went into the game a little worried because Bobby Marlow, our best player, had a broken toe and was not supposed to play. Of course he wanted to play in the Orange Bowl, so late in the game, Coach Drew let Bobby go in for one play. Coach Drew told the quarterback, who was a youngster named Bart Starr, what play to run and not to involve Bobby because of his injury. Bart was a freshman, and Marlow grabbed him in the huddle and told him what play to call. Bobby, broken toe and all, ran off tackle for about 14 yards.

In 1953 Alabama claimed the SEC Championship with a rather remarkable conference record of 4-0-3, and thanks to a field goal by Bobby Luna, the Tide averted yet another tie in a 10-7 win over Auburn in the season finale. Overall, Bama was 6-2-3 entering a Cotton Bowl showdown with Southwest

Conference champions Rice.

There is little question one of the most famous plays in football history occurred that New Year's Day in Dallas when Tommy Lewis came off the sideline and tackled the Owls' Dicky Moegle, keeping him from possibly scoring a touchdown. After the officials conferred, however, they awarded Moegle a 95-yard TD run, and Rice rolled to a 28-6 victory. After the game, Lewis made his much-acclaimed remark in explaining his misdeed by saying, "I guess I'm just too full of Bama." Lest we forget, however — not only did Tommy make that infamous tackle, but he also made the only Alabama touchdown in that Cotton Bowl game!

BOBBY LUNA:

Dicky Moegle and I became pretty good friends later on. In fact, we were roommates in rookie camp. Dicky says he was looking at one of our defenders, Vince DeLaurentis, when Tommy Lewis came off the bench and tackled him. He thought Vince had him cut off, and he was looking his way when Tommy hit him. Dicky said it's the hardest lick he ever got in football.

Actually the game was 7-6 when that play happened, and we were on the verge of going ahead. We had the ball first and goal inside Rice's 10. Bart Starr ran an option play, and someone grabbed his arm and stripped him of the ball. Rice recovered on the 5-yard line.

The very next play Dicky broke loose. I was playing safety, and I saw the play developing. As I cut across the field, I got clipped, but it wasn't called. I told Dicky later that he was awfully lucky because they should have called a clip and it would have never been a touchdown.

BART STARR:

The game was very close at the time, 7-6. I really believe we had control of the game until that long run by Moegle. I was playing cornerback on his run, and I was blocked almost down. I had stumbled, and by the time I regained my footing, Moegle was beyond me. I could have chased him for a month and not caught him!

I had a great view from behind him, and I saw Tommy Lewis come off the bench and tackle him. When I saw that happening, the strangest thought crossed my mind. I thought, "What is this?" It was one of the most bizarre plays ever in the history of football.

Some years later, Tommy Lewis was doing some volunteer coaching and had a similar happening when his team of Huntsville high schoolers were playing Sidney Lanier in Montgomery. A guy came off the Huntsville bench and made a tackle like the one Tommy made had made in the Cotton Bowl. And guess what number he was wearing — Tommy's old number! Tommy told me about it when I was speaking in Huntsville years later, and he said, "Bart, for the first time in my life, I really knew how to counsel someone!"

Tommy Lewis actually came from the sideline, not the bench, to make his unorthodox tackle. During his career at Alabama, Tommy was one of the Tide's strongest players and as alternate captain, he was a leader of the team. Due to the public's unfortunate focus on the tackle made that afternoon almost 40 years ago in Dallas, Tommy found it a little painful to recall. At the end of our conversation, though, he thanked us for opening some doors to memories that he wouldn't have opened otherwise.

TOMMY LEWIS:

In the 1954 Cotton Bowl, Coach Drew took the first unit out of the ball game to give us a rest, so we were all standing on the sideline watching to see if our second team was going to keep Rice backed up there on that 10-yard line. The first play, Rice got penalized 5 yards for Moegle jumping or something. The second play, they knocked our end a flip and knocked down our halfback, and Moegle set sail right on course up the center. I was standing there on the sideline, but my head gear was under the bench somewhere — I didn't know where it was. Moegle was a pretty fast guy, and football is a pretty fast game, but I had time to turn my head to Corky Tharp standing on my right and say, "He's going all the way!" Corky said, "He sure is, Lew." When I turned my head back forward, Moegle was right in my face, and I unloaded on him.

I'd like to think it was reflex — I certainly didn't have time to plan it. There were at least 10 guys on that team who were more inclined to do something like that than I was. I guess I felt like Moegle had no business heading toward our end zone. But Moegle had a magnificent day, and I think on that play, I personally killed the desire and spirit for Alabama to win that football game.

What nobody remembers is that we got out in front in that game — we took the ball and rammed it right down their throats. Bart Starr found a fullback play for me that was going right off our guard — not tackle, but guard, and it was open on both sides. We kept running it back and forth, back and forth, and we ran it down to the goal line and into the end zone. Of course, when they think about that game, most people only remember my off-the-sideline tackle.

I really appreciate Red Drew putting me back in the contest. I went straight to Moegle and apologized to him. At the half, I caught Coach Jess Neely and apologized to him. He put his arm around me and said, "Son, you might as well get ready to live with it because it's going to be with you for the rest of your life." And that's been true — I've regretted it, and I wish to God it had never taken place.

After the football game, I had to stay in Dallas because Bud Willis, Billy Shipp, Ralph Carrigan, and I had been invited to play in the Senior Bowl in Mobile — we had to stay out in Dallas, but the rest of the team left. Somebody in Dallas found out that I was still out there, and the phone rang off the wall.

Bud Willis was answering the phone for me, and one time he said, "Lew, I think you'd better get this one — it sounds like something important." I said, "Well, it can't be too important. It's just somebody who's going to harass me." But I answered the phone, and a voice said, "Hello, Tom, this is Ed Sullivan from *Toast of the Town*." Well I thought it was somebody pulling my leg. I joked, "What do you say, *Ed*." He replied, "Listen, old Southern boy, I want you to come on up here and be my guest on my TV show." I said, "I'm not coming." Then the thought crossed my mind that maybe I can do this and let the people across the country know that I was not a total, absolute fool and apologize for this thing. That's the only reason I went, the only reason. I then went on to Mobile to play in the Senior Bowl.

1954 was a bizarre season that saw Alabama's fortunes plummet downward almost unbelievably. The Tide was upset by Mississippi Southern in the 1954 opener and then won four straight. But on a Saturday in Tuscaloosa, Mississippi State, under Darrell Royal, beat Alabama 12-7, and the Tide didn't win another game, finishing 4-5-2, with a 28-0 loss to Auburn at the end of the season.

A couple of things contributed to that devastating loss to Auburn. One was that the overall Bama staff was getting a bit long in the tooth. Another was Auburn's resurgence under Shug Jordan. No longer could Alabama pick and choose from high school stars. They had to actively solicit and recruit them. In 1953 Alabama had been fortunate to beat Auburn 10-7 on a Bobby Luna field goal, and they won the SEC.

Tommy Lewis, who played as a senior in the hard-fought game against Auburn in 1953, gives some insight into the Auburn win of 1954.

TOMMY LEWIS:

I personally had some indication that Auburn was going to come on like they did in 1954 because the 1951 and 1952 games were so easy. Don't get me wrong, they were clean, hard-fought contests, just like all the games with Georgia Tech and Tennessee. They were always hard, hard fought — I mean, it would take you a week to get over one of those games!

After the game my senior year, 1953, I thought to myself that Auburn had arrived. That game was a terrible struggle, and we were fortunate to win. I think we fairly dominated the game that day, but still, it was not the Auburn team from the two years prior to that year.

It was a 10-7 ball game, and it was fought right down to the wire. I remember the 1952 game in Birmingham at Legion Field where I had so many holes open because Auburn's defense was keying in on Bobby Marlow. If I were playing against Bobby Marlow, I would key in on him, too! Consequently that left some running room for me, and I had a good running day because of that — because they were keying in on Marlow and no other reason. In the 1953 Auburn game, though, Marlow was gone, and I didn't see a hole open all day! I'm telling you, I didn't see one hole open all day. It was a dog-eat-dog game, and it was a heated battle — a battle of the magnitude of the Georgia Tech and Tennessee games. Then I thought to myself, "They have arrived. Auburn has arrived."

After Auburn's resounding 28-0 win, it became obvious that Alabama would make a coaching change. Looking back over the decades, you have to wonder why Paul Bryant was not the immediate choice to replace Red Drew. There were several mitigating factors that kept this from happening.

First of all, Bryant had left Kentucky just a year earlier in a sudden and baffling move although his superiority as a coach was widely known. Bryant's Wildcats had beaten the Oklahoma Sooners 13-7 in a classic Sugar Bowl upset back in 1951. Probably unfairly Bryant had been labeled a job jumper, and I knew for a fact that Dean A.B. Moore, a powerful man in Alabama athletics and dean of the graduate school, was not a fan of Bryant's for whatever reason. Bryant had gone to Texas A&M, and in his first year there, he had the only losing season of his entire career, going 1-9. For all these reasons, Bryant was not high on the Alabama list.

Growing up in Tuscaloosa, my best friend was Joe Moore, son of Dean A.B. Moore. I remember very clearly calling Dr. Moore in 1954 and saying that although it was none of my business I hoped the University authorities would give consideration to the young, impressive coach at Mississippi State, Darrell Royal. He thanked me for my call, and I don't guess Darrell ever heard anything from Dr. Moore.

Subsequently, Darrell went to the University of Washington and of course, later to Texas. Alabama hired J.B. "Ears" Whitworth, who in his three years at Tuscaloosa had 4 wins, 24 losses, and a pair of ties. It was a disaster.

Coach Whitworth had played on the 1931 Rose Bowl team, and he was very popular with the powers that be at Alabama at the time. He was certainly a very affable fellow, and obviously, he was an excellent assistant coach. However, even though he had been the head coach at Oklahoma A&M (now Oklahoma State), I don't think anyone would deny he was ill equipped to handle the No. 1 job at a place like Alabama.

Bart Starr was certainly one of the more gifted Alabama athletes of any vintage, but ironically he played very sparingly for Coach Whitworth in his senior season of 1955, a year before he would travel northward to Green Bay, Wisconsin, where he would earn Hall of Fame recognition as one of the shining stars in the golden era of the NFL. Here are some of Starr's remembrances of his days at the Capstone and how he managed to be drafted by the Packers.

BART STARR:

Originally I wanted to go to school at Kentucky to play for Coach Bryant. I was locked in to going there until I discovered that a pretty brunette, who I had been dating in high school, would not go with me. I think I was smart enough at 18 to recognize that if I went to Lexington, Kentucky, and she went to Auburn where she wanted to go to study interior design, I'd lose her. So, I called the greatest audible of my life and went to the

University of Alabama.

My high school ran a version of Coach Bryant's offense. Our coach Bill Mosley had played for Coach Bryant. I had been to Kentucky the summer prior to my senior year, which was the year before Babe Parilli's final year at Kentucky. He tutored me for three weeks.

I'm delighted I went to the University of Alabama. I made tons of friends and received a great education. I've always been pleased about that decision, but I regretted not being able to play for Coach Bryant. I was blessed later, because I played for Vince Lombardi, who was very similar to Coach Bryant.

Most of my memories of my first two years at Alabama center around the records we compiled that led us to the Orange and Cotton Bowls. I look back on that experience and realize I played with talented players like Bobby Marlow and Hootie Ingram. I learned a lot as a freshman sitting there watching them play, and once we got far enough ahead, I'd get a chance to get into the games. Watching Bobby Wilson, I used to sit there and gawk at how well he could punt. I wanted to be able to punt like him.

I was pleased to have a wonderful teammate like Nick Germanos, and I developed a great relationship with Curtis Lynch, a name that won't quickly come to the mind of some people. But Curtis was a free agent or a low-round draft pick like I was, and he went to Green Bay with me.

There was a lot of talent at Alabama in every area when I was a freshman. When we went to one-platoon football, I think it hurt us. I enjoyed playing defense, I really did. It was a change, and it required a great deal of concentration and a different mindset. It was a wonderful challenge, and I enjoyed it.

One of the persons responsible for me having an opportunity to play with Green Bay was Johnny Dee, who was the basketball coach at Alabama at the time. He had gone to school at Notre Dame with a gentleman named Jack Benissee, who was the personnel director for the Packers. I had two good first years at Alabama, but the last two years really were nonproductive.

It was a tough experience because I was injured my last two years. I guess that was the toughest part of it. When you're injured you feel inadequate. You're concerned that you're not contributing as you would like to. So it was very frustrating. Our last years, when we were seniors, one or two of us played a considerable amount. But most of the seniors didn't play very much. That was really tough, just having to sit there.

I guess that was probably the most disappointing period of time I've ever had in anything that I've been in — college or professional, as a player and as a coach. You have no control. You just had to sit and endure, and it was extremely difficult. I played almost none as a senior, so I had nothing to show for my final years. Jack talked the Packers into literally taking a chance on me. Here was a guy who had an injured back and not much productivity in his final two years of college, and they took a chance.

Coach Dee not only did that, but I had a difficult time getting some footballs from the athletic department to practice with after my senior year. Johnny Dee got me three new balls, and I threw those balls so much and worked so hard in an effort to make the Green Bay Packers as a rookie, that I swear, they looked like some of those balls back in the early 1900s. They were closer to being round than oblong!

Coach Whitworth went 0 and 10 in 1955, and his second and third years, the Tide was 2-7-1. To put it mildly, most Alabama alumni were furious and demanded a change. This feeling was nowhere more evident than it was among the Birmingham alumni after the first of those 2-7-1 seasons. The University prided itself on not firing a coach, and I think they were determined to keep Whitworth. Nevertheless, a large group of people in the alumni association in Birmingham wanted to go on record as having lost complete confidence in Whitworth and asking that a new coach be sought.

Bob McDavid, a great guy, was the president of the Birmingham alumni association at the time. It was the strongest chapter around, and it had participated in giving watches to the seniors all the way back to 1923.

Bob was simply trying to be a good president and respond to the wishes of his members, and so it was determined in January 1957 to have an open meeting at the auditorium in the Liberty National Building on South 20th Street. People were jammed in there to the rafters, with close to 300 on hand. Bob told the reason for the meeting, and there were a number of loud and vocal contributions made. One of the most interesting speeches was a long one made by Tram Sessions, who was a wonderful, gentle-souled guy and a former Alabama football player.

In addition to the football team having lost its luster, for some inexplicable reason — the University said it was because of the laundry bills — the Million Dollar Band had gone from its usual crimson-coated and white-trousered uniforms to black uniforms with just a little red around the shoulders and on the hats. Tram — who I'm sure was trying to defuse a hot situation — made an impassioned speech that the first problem to address was an objection to the band uniforms! Because he was such a popular man, people were inclined to humor him, but when he got through, the bitterness over the football situation took over.

Finally they voted on whether or not to issue a formal statement from the alumni. In a very dramatic scene, alumni president McDavid said for all those in favor of issuing a formal vote of no confidence in Coach Whitworth to line up along one wall and those willing to let him take the final year of his three-year contract line up on the other. To put it mildly, there was a lot of stir and a lot of last-minute hollering and buttonholing, but when the final vote was made there was only a one vote difference.

So it was determined the Birmingham Alumni Association would not issue a vote of no confidence. That vote is known in the annals of a lot of alumni as "The Battle of Liberty National Auditorium." The meeting came to a close, and no one was happy!

However a number of things were going to change in the months ahead, and one of the best of all was that Dr. Frank Rose was going to take over as the president of the University of Alabama. In the meantime, Coach Hank was like a rock amid the turbulent waters. Alf Van Hoose, well-known sportswriter, recalls those difficult years.

Alf Van Hoose:

During the Whitworth years' rebellion, there was never, never any movement at all to include Coach Hank. He was the athletic director at the time.

In the spring of 1957 they had an absolute rebellion of the football players at Alabama. That's the only time that's ever happened. Coach Hank got that stopped. Things had deteriorated so bad that the players knew they would have the backing of the Alabama fans. They just had a rebellion, and it was a big story for about a couple of weeks. The reason I remember it is that I wrote a column — sort of a column, I wasn't a columnist then — and the headline was, "Alabama, Who's to Blame?" The coaching staff or the players, somebody's to blame for 60 to 65 young men rebelling against the authorities. That was the spring before Whitworth's last team.

I just remember from 1940 to the summer of 1942, when I was there, that Coach Hank was such a revered person, such a cornerstone of Alabama football. I worked in the bullpen with him, where they fed the athletes. Like Coach Bryant later, when Coach Hank walked into a room, he was the presence in the room. He had great rapport with the players. Coach Thomas never did have that. Coach Thomas was respected, but he wasn't loved by his players. But Coach Hank had that air about him, and when there were any problems at all with the players, Coach Hank would be the one to settle it. They would go to him.

When I came in 1947, I don't think he was there — or maybe he was there in 1947 but not 1948. Then they brought him back in 1949. Here's a story about him that happened late in a practice on a hot September day in 1951 or 1952. Alabama had a tackle named Al Wilhite from Tuscumbia who weighed about 200 pounds and was a real fine player. They also had a tackle from Mobile who weighed about 300 pounds, which meant that after he finished his eligibility at Alabama he was a cinch to play in the pros because he weighed 300 pounds — not because he could play. He wasn't a good player at all. Anyhow, Wilhite was blocking him, and all at once they got into a fight, and Wilhite decked him, I mean cold knocked him out, in a fair fight. Coach Hank walked up and said, "Get him out of here. Drag him out of here, and let's go on with practice." So they dragged the big guy out — it took about six guys to do it. When they got him to, he began to talk about Wilhite: "He hit me when I didn't see him. Wait 'til tonight, I'll get him. I wish I had another chance at him." Coach Hank, as he always did, was standing behind the safety man on defense with his hands on his hips, when finally he had had enough of that trash-talk. I remember him coming over and telling him, "Hey, fellow, there he is, right out yonder!" It was a great lesson in life: There's your problem right out there — no need to talk about it, go get it! That was typical Coach Hank. That sure stopped all that mouthing.

By some point in early October 1957, probably after the 28-0 loss to TCU, the decision was rendered to extricate Whitworth from the coaching office, and three days after a 40-0 blowout defeat at the hands of Auburn, Paul Bryant was announced as the new head coach at Bama. He inked the dotted line for a 10-year contract at the Shamrock Hotel in Houston, Texas.

Approximately one month earlier in the same hotel, Bryant had met with Dr. Rose, national alumni president, former Bama megastar Fred Sington, and Tuscaloosa banker and University board member Ernest Williams about the job. One major issue Bryant wanted to resolve before he accepted the job was the status of his old coach at Alabama, athletic director Hank Crisp. It was not until after Crisp assured Bryant that he wanted him to return to Tuscaloosa and the ADs job would be relinquished and turned over to the Bear, that the deal was sealed.

In those waning days of 1957, while Bryant was preparing his Texas A&M team for a Gator Bowl game with Tennessee, assistant coach Jerry Claiborne moved to Tuscaloosa to oversee the transition and the recruitment of the class that would be seniors in 1961. One of the first true stars, signed the year Paul Bryant assumed his duties at Alabama, was Northport lineman Billy Neighbors. He reveals his feelings about Coach Bryant and the impact he would have on his life.

BILLY NEIGHBORS:

I was a freshman at Alabama in 1958, the year Coach Bryant took the job. I had already signed with Alabama before he actually committed to take the job. Pat James (an assistant under Bryant) is the guy who brought the scholarship to me to sign, but I had already actually signed with Alabama with Coach (Red) Drew, who had been the head coach and was the track coach in 1957.

I had never heard of Coach Bryant before he took the job at Alabama, but I soon heard the stories about him — how tough and how mean he was. One of the stories that went around was that while he was at Texas A&M, they'd dig a pit and throw one or two players into it, and the ones who came out got to play!

So when I went out there to play, I was scared to death. It wasn't quite that bad, but there were 117 freshmen who came with us and only 7 of us were seniors in my last year. One of the things I'll never forget is the first meeting we had with him. He told us that if we did certain things and stayed in school, we'd win the national championship.

The seven of us who stayed there and did what he told us to do did win the national championship, the first time Alabama had won a championship in years. Matter of fact, Alabama had won only four games in the three years leading up the time I enrolled.

We were lucky enough to play for someone who really knew football. But more than that, Coach Bryant knew people. And he worked us probably harder than he did anybody. He prepared us to win.

I guarantee you we were in better shape than any team we played. He'd walk up to you after a game and ask you if you were tired. Well somebody made the mistake of telling him they were. You know you *are* tired after a game, but you don't tell the coach that because, boy, the next week he would run the devil out of you. So we had a little rule at Alabama: Keep your mouth shut when anyone asked if you were tired after a game — unless you told Coach Bryant you were *not* tired.

When I played professional football, the coaches would always come to me and talk about Coach Bryant. And I'd get on an airplane flying some place and a guy would look at me — you know I'm bigger than most folks — and ask me if I played football, and I'd say yes. Then he would ask where, and I'd say, "Alabama." And he'd know all about Coach Bryant, about Alabama, and about Alabama football. It's all over the country and has been ever since he came there and started winning championships there.

There's another thing I will always respect about him. When you leave professional football, they send you your pictures in the mail, and that's the last time you ever hear from those people. But Coach Bryant always welcomed us back, and matter of fact, he called me one time when I was playing professional football and asked me how come I hadn't written him a letter!

Then when I came back to Alabama after I retired from the NFL in 1970, he and I became real good friends. I did a lot of business with him and talked to him about once a week on the phone from 1970 until he died in 1983. I had a great relationship with him. What a wonderful guy he was. He always tried to help his ex-players.

One thing that used to impress me about Coach Bryant was that he always returned his calls. It was unbelievable. I was in his office one day, and some woman had called him and wanted to borrow some money from him. He didn't know who she was, but he returned her call. And I've been doing it ever since — that taught me to do it.

Another thing he did was when you went to a restaurant or some place with him and people mobbed him. You know most people would get uncomfortable with that or get bothered by that. He never did. He'd get little children and set them in his lap and talk to them, and he'd sign autographs and pictures. He'd sit there and sit there for an hour and do that.

In our team meetings, if they lasted 30 minutes, he'd talk about life 20 of those. He'd talk about having ups and downs. I keep that in the back of my mind all the time. He'd say you're going to have ups and downs in your life, but what you need to try to do is not have the peaks too high or the valleys too low. Try to keep on an even plane. You know that makes a lot of sense because a lot of the time we get to doing things really well and we get a little too sure of ourselves and make some mistakes and knock ourselves down in a hole and we have to crawl back out again.

I think if you keep yourself on an even keel, you'll be a lot better off. That was a lesson I always remember even today. When things get going good, I try not to get too excited about them, and when they get going bad, I try not to get too depressed about them.

You know you hear a lot of talk now about education and players getting a degree. Buddy, let me tell you something: It was big to Coach Bryant back in 1958. I wasn't doing too well in school my freshman year, and my second semester, matter of fact, I wasn't doing anything. I was cutting classes. So Coach Bryant asked me to eat lunch with him, and man, I was scared to death because I knew I had a problem, but I didn't know why he was mad. To tell you the truth I didn't think he knew what kind of grades I was making!

He had the dean of the school with him, and I went and sat down with them. He introduced me to the dean, and we started talking. He pulled out my IQ and pulled out how many classes I'd cut, and boy, I didn't look up — I just kept my head down.

Coach Bryant said, "Look up at me, boy, I'm talking to you!" So I looked up, and he said to the dean, "Now this boy right here can help us win, but if he doesn't start getting better grades, he isn't going to be here!" The dean started talking about the classes I'd taken, what I should take, and all this stuff, and Coach Bryant said, "Well, I'm going to give him one more semester. I'm going to move him into my house with me, and I'm going to do him like I do Paul, Jr., when he comes home with a C, I'll beat him with a damn dictionary." So I got straightened out real fast!

One holdover from the Whitworth days, Scooter Dyess, was seated ringside for the arrival of Paul Bryant. He remembers with clarity the effects the Bear immediately clawed into the mindsets of the Alabama players.

SCOOTER DYESS:

I'll start with the very first time that we saw and met Coach Bryant. Naturally, when you go through a coaching change, the players all huddle in dorm trying to figure him out. We did too. We would congregate at night. We would vote, which meant nothing, among ourselves or discuss who we thought would and wouldn't come and who we didn't want to come. The one we didn't want to come was Coach Bryant. We had heard of his exploits at Texas A&M, and we just didn't think he was the guy for the job. To make a long story short, he did come.

I was a sophomore when Coach Bryant came to Alabama. Those were the years before freshmen were eligible to play on the varsity, and I had played my freshman year under Coach (Ears) Whitworth.

When I came to Alabama I was the first one in my family to attend college. I grew up in Elba and I had been an avid Alabama fan all my life. One of my heroes was Bobby Marlow, who came from a children's home in Troy. He played against Elba, and as a kid, I used to go watch him play. He was the player I always wanted to be like. Of course, Bobby was about 6-2, 195 pounds, and I was about 5-6 and 150 pounds. So our size never matched up, but he was always my hero. From the beginning, Alabama was always my team, even though, during recruiting, I went to other schools. I almost went to Georgia Tech because during those years Bobby Dodd always had small backs playing for him.

Butch Avinger, one of the ex-Alabama greats, recruited me to play at Alabama when Coach Whit (Whitworth) was the head coach. Their selling point at the time, for kids like myself, was that we could be part of building the program back. We knew the tradition at Alabama. We knew how bad the program was when we signed. I loved Alabama and wanted to be part of the rebuilding.

Coach Whitworth was one of the finest gentlemen I have ever known. He was good to his players. During Coach Whit's era, he just never seemed to have control of the players. I don't think he ever had the full respect of his staff like Coach Bryant did. He did not instill the confidence in the players that Coach Bryant did. As we all know, Coach Bryant made you a lot better player than you thought you were.

Our first meeting with Coach Bryant came at one o'clock. Jerry Claiborne had been sent ahead as his lead man. One of my favorite people and one of the finest coaches I've ever known was Jerry Claiborne. He came in and led the change over.

Coach Claiborne told us to congregate in our football meeting room there in the dormitory after lunch. When Coach Bryant came in, everybody knew who he was, where he came from, and what he planned to do. He came into the meeting, and everybody was seated. It was quiet as a mouse. One of his pet peeves was, "Don't be late for a meeting!"

When he walked into the room he checked his watch. He did not talk to anyone, and he did not walk around the room. He didn't try to cut the ice, which was thick. Nobody said anything. He kept looking at his watch and precisely at one o'clock, he closed the door and started his spiel. He said the past problems that Alabama had was not because of the ex-coaches. He said the problem started right here in this room. I'll never forget him saying, "We don't plan to discuss the past coaching staff. We don't plan to discuss anything in the past. I'll advise you to be ready when spring practice starts. I'm telling you now to get into shape. You haven't been through anything like you're going to go through." I'll never forget those words.

With that he left the room. He never told a joke or spoke to anyone one on one. We got ready for the hardest spring we'd ever had. He didn't leave any stones unturned. He did exactly what he said we were going to do.

We lost about 22 people that spring. When they were quitting, you kept wondering, "This guy is a maniac. How is he going to build a team with what we have left?" When we came in, in the evenings, and three of the first teamers would be gone, he'd move the second ones to the first team. He didn't care. He was going to play with what he had left.

He told us he wanted to have an individual meeting with each player before spring practice in his office. Everybody was scared to go. One day I went between classes, and I was hoping to meet him in the hall and not his office, and I did. He almost walked by me, and I was afraid to speak to him. Finally, I said, "Coach." He stopped, and I told him who I was.

I said, "Coach, you indicated you wanted to have a meeting with each of the players. He said, "Yes, I did." Back then everyone wore crew cuts. I'll never forget him rubbing my head and saying, "What the hell are you, the water boy?" That was my first introduction, and you can imagine how I felt. I went on down to his office, and then he came in.

One of the first questions he asked me was, "Do you think you're good enough to make this team?" I'll never forget, I told him I was going to try. He came right back to me and said, "Let's get something straight right off the bat. We either are or we are not. We're not going to have any triers."

Naturally I told him I was going to make the team. That's the kind of attitude he instilled in us from the beginning. If you didn't think you were good enough, you might as well leave. He didn't want anybody just trying.

Alabama opened the Bryant era in Mobile against LSU, a powerful team sparked by backs Billy Cannon and Johnny Robinson. The Tigers were so good, in fact, that by season's end they would wear the crown of national champions, but that September eve on the bay Alabama fans would be treated to the revival of their own downtrodden program. Scooter Dyess and Duff Morrison, a pair of the survivors of the Bryant boot camp, remember the commencement of Alabama's new age of football.

SCOOTER DYESS:

We had lost another 15 or 16 players in the fall drills, and we traveled to Mobile with 30-something players. We went down there with a ragtag group. We weren't very good, but we had them 3-0 at the half. That's the year LSU won the national title, and they came back to beat us 13-3.

You could tell from that game that things were going to be better. Coach Bryant just made you a better football player than you thought you were. One of his philosophies was he could coach the average athlete and make him better and get 100 percent out of him. I think that is the true trademark of Paul Bryant.

Alabama's lone score that night was set up by a fumble recovery and return by Morrison in the second quarter.

DUFF MORRISON:

I have fond memories of that particular incident. They gave the ball to Billy Cannon on a reverse, and he made it around our end and was heading up field. I was playing safety that game, and just as I came up to hit him, one of our other players — I think it was Bobby Smith — hit him from the right side. The ball flew up in the air, and it was one of those deals where you say, "Thank you, Lord!" I grabbed the ball and headed down the sidelines.

I picked up a blocker, Wayne Sims, who was my roommate, and he started running with me from somewhere around midfield down toward the goal line. All of a sudden, LSU's Max Fugler comes from across the field, jumps clear over Wayne, hits me, and knocks me out of bounds on the 4-yard line. I'll never forget it — the stands in the end zone had collapsed, and there were fans all in the area.

We ran three sweeps on the goal line and didn't gain an inch. Then Fred Sington, Jr., came in and kicked the ball right through the uprights for a field goal that put us ahead 3-0. We were tickled to death at that point. At halftime, Coach Bryant told us not to let down because we had another whole half to play. We were playing against a team that was ultimately the national champion, and Cannon later won the Heisman. We did a respectable job.

I still get chill bumps thinking back to that night. It had been a dreary three or four years in Tuscaloosa but Paul Bryant brought back hope. When the team left the field to go into the locker room at halftime, the Alabama fans stood as one and cheered the team's effort. It's something I'll always remember, I'm sure.

Highlighting that 1958 season, which ended with the Tide posting a 5-4-1 record, was the 17-8 upset win over Georgia Tech in Atlanta. Scooter Dyess recalls how he respected Coach Bryant's intricate mind.

SCOOTER DYESS:

Coach Bryant was a psychologist from the word go. We played Tulane the week before we played Georgia Tech. The only game we favored in all year. Well Tulane had won 13-7 — we had a touchdown called back, and we just didn't play very well.

We came back from New Orleans knowing we were in for one of the toughest practice weeks of the year. We had been through a spring and most of the 1958 season with Coach Bryant, so we didn't expect anything else. On the plane coming back, we talked about how much we dreaded Sunday and Monday.

Sunday afternoon, we had our meeting after lunch, and we expected to go out in pads. Well there was no practice schedule posted. We got over there, and not only are we not in pads, we're in sweat clothes, and Coach Bryant said, "We're going to work out in the gym."

We were all sitting on those benches over in Foster Auditorium, where this all took place. It was his planned activity. We were all sitting in there, quiet as a mouse. We knew Tech was coming. Then we heard Coach Bryant's feet walking down the hall, and he came in right on time. He never mentioned the Tulane game or whether we played poorly, which we did. He told us he wanted us to go out and loosen up on Sunday afternoon. We didn't go out in pads on Monday either. He let everybody get their legs back under them.

I've never seen a team get higher than we were for Georgia Tech. We were on Tech like June bugs. Everybody was fresh, and we won 17-8. Coach Bryant knew that he couldn't take our poor performance against Tulane out on the practice field. He knew what it would take for us to get ready. That was how Coach Bryant was. You never knew what to expect from him, and like he preached: Expect the unexpected.

After that 5-4-1 season, including the narrowest of losses to unbeaten Auburn, optimism continued to spiral upward in Tuscaloosa. When the Tide rolled into the 1959 Tiger contest with a 6-1-2 record, Bama was ready to erase five years of forgettable losses to the Tigers.

SCOOTER DYESS:

We were going into the Auburn game as underdogs, but two weeks before we had beaten Georgia Tech in Birmingham, and I think our team had a lot more confidence than it had in 1958 or the previous years. Alabama had not beaten Auburn since 1954.

After our first meeting in preparations, Coach Bryant said he wanted to have me, Billy Richardson, and Jerry Spruiell come to his office. He wanted to talk to us along with Coach Jerry Claiborne before our next practice. The first thing we three did was get together and see what we had or hadn't done. We didn't know what he wanted to meet with us about.

I got to his office first, and while we were waiting on the others, Coach asked,

"Scooter, how would you like to play end against Auburn?" I jokingly said, "Coach, I don't think I would like it." I had seen Auburn's Jerry Wilson tear heads off. He told me he was serious, and I said I'd try.

He said, "I'm going to wait until Jerry and the others get here, and then we're going to discuss what our plans are. In watching their films, we think that this play, if it ever comes about, may work." He drew his strategy on the board. Later on when we played the game, that very situation did occur.

When the others arrived, Coach Bryant said, "If Scooter is in the game, he's going to be in this position. If he's out for any reason, Richardson will be in this position; and if he's out, then Spruiell will be." The idea was to put one of us in a one-on-one situation with their defensive back. If we could ever get their linebackers all trying to blitz the quarterback, we felt this play would work for a big play.

Well they didn't do anything early. We threw two or three jump passes. I caught three across the middle. Then the situation finally arose. We were either in the latter part of the third quarter or early part of the fourth quarter. Bobby Skelton was in at quarterback, and just like Coach had drawn it up on the board, it happened. Bobby checked off and color-coded to me. We were leading 3-0 at this time. Bobby rose up and hit me with the ball. The defensive back was about 10 yards from me, and he missed me, which is what we were hoping for. I scored, and we won 10-0. Coach Bryant always gave Coach Claiborne credit for the play, but it was Coach Bryant who came up with it.

I have read numerous times that Coach Bryant said that game was the one that really turned the program around. I'd like to think it did. Coach had told us going into the game that it would be low scoring, and if it were a high-scoring game, Auburn would win. That's exactly what happened.

At the conclusion of the season, despite having a 7-1-2 season record, there was only a spattering of talk of Alabama appearing in a bowl game. Yet Paul Bryant manuevered the Tide into a trip to the first ever Liberty Bowl. Billy Richardson, a halfback on those 1959-61 teams, recalls how the Tide got that invitation.

BILLY RICHARDSON:

The key win for us was the 10-0 victory over Auburn. Coach Bryant put in a special play for Scooter Dyess where we'd try to get him the ball in the flat and let him do his thing in a one-on-one situation. The play worked like a charm, and we won the game. Frankly, we felt the Auburn game was our bowl game. It had been a difficult year but a successful year. It was Coach Bryant's second at Alabama, and we felt we had accomplished all we could when we beat Auburn.

Thinking back on it, I believe our seniors had pretty well decided that they didn't particularly care to go to a postseason game. Coach Bryant had told them that a new bowl in Philadelphia, the Liberty, was interested in Alabama. It was very interesting hearing Coach Bryant talk about a bowl, and how much fun it would be, what a great trip it would be, all the publicity the University would get, and he even threw in a trip to New York after the game. So he sold the seniors because it was their decision, and it was a very interesting trip.

There were a number of firsts for a lot of us. Some of our players had never ridden on a train, and Coach Bryant was afraid the weather would be too bad to fly into Philadelphia.

We'd never seen, much less played in, a stadium that seated 106,000, and the weather was so cold, they had us in long underwear during the game. The wind was blowing, and I believe you could have seated all the fans in the stadium between the 40-yard lines.

Penn State had an All-American quarterback in Richie Lucas, but their only score came on a fake field goal. Pat Trammell was one of our defensive backs, and he lined up on the side to try to come in and block the field goal. Galen Hall, the holder, just flipped the ball out in the flat, and they scored a touchdown, the only one of the game.

Coach Bryant was so upset with our first half play that he fired all the starters and started the second half with a bunch of players who probably thought they'd never get in a game. We were in this old dungeon of a dressing room, and it was cold, and Coach was mad. By the second series of the second half, he had the starters back in, but we never scored, and the final was 7-0.

Coach Bryant, who had been to all the big bowls, had told us when we got to Penn Station, there would be press and official parties with pretty girls there waiting to greet us. We rolled into Penn Station, and of course, none of us had ever been in a place that big in our lives, and we get off the train and start gawking and looking for the people meeting us, but there was no press to be seen anywhere.

So the next day at practice, Coach Bryant put together the chair drill in the stadium. We had 11 chairs lined up in the offensive position and 11 in the defensive position, just plain old folding chairs. We sat down in the chairs, and Trammell would call a play and the snap, then we would point at whatever direction or chair you were going to. It was a mental drill. Well the next day we got the headlines in the Philadelphia papers. None of those guys had ever seen anything like Coach Bryant's chair drills.

The 1959 Liberty Bowl was also the first time Alabama had ever played against a black player. Penn State had a great lineman named Chuck Jenarette. I know Billy Neighbors will tell you that to this day Jenarette was one of the best players he ever played against. He was a helluva player.

On that wintry day in Philadelphia, Alabama wrapped up a decade replete with seesaw ups and downs, with a 7-0 loss to perennial Eastern heavyweight Penn State. Despite being on the negative side of the ledger that day, the vigor was back in the steps of those whose blood runs crimson, and the 1960s certainly offered a challenge that promised new horizons would be explored.

"The game demonstrated the superiority of the Southern teams over any aggregation that the damn Yankees could send across the Mason-Dixon line."

— Sportswriter Charles Israel of the *Philadelphia Bulletin* after the Tide's 61-6 win over Syracuse in the 1953 Orange Bowl

"I guess I'm just too full of Bama."
— Tommy Lewis explaining why he came off the bench to tackle Rice's Dicky Moegle in the 1954 Cotton Bowl

"He was more than a coach to me. He was more like a father. I never made a move without seeking and receiving his advice. It was always the right advice, too."
— Alabama star Harry Gilmer in mourning Frank Thomas's death in May 1954

"We're going after the best boys, boys who want to come to work here and uphold the great tradition that is Alabama football. I'm going to work to keep that tradition, the coaches are going to work, and the players are going to work."
— Coach J.B. "Ears" Whitworth upon being announced as head coach at Alabama in 1954

"If I would have coached as hard as you played for me, we would have won more games. The football season is over, and my jurisdiction over you is ended. Keep your feet on the ground, study hard, work hard, and give the new coach as much effort as you have given me, and a year from now I'll be mighty proud of you."
— Coach J.B. "Ears" Whitworth after his final game in 1957

"If you believe in yourself and have dedication and pride — and never quit, you'll be a winner. The price of victory is high but so are the rewards."
— A favorite quote of Coach Bryant's

"He can take his'n' and beat you'rn', and he can take you'rn' and beat his'n'.
— Famous Florida A&M Coach Jake Gaither's evaluation of Paul Bryant as a head coach

"I thought this must be what God looks like."
— Former Kentucky and NFL megastar George Blanda in talking about Paul Bryant

Hootie Ingram returns a punt 80 yards for a touchdown in 61-6 win over Syracuse in the 1953 Orange Bowl.

Bobby Marlow (32) and Tommy Lewis (42) enjoy Bama's 61-6 Orange Bowl win over Syracuse. Marlow played with a broken big toe.

In his four years as Alabama's varsity quarterback, 1952-55, Bart Starr completed 155 passes for 1903 yards. Under coach Vince Lombardi at Green Bay, Starr went on to become one of pro football's greatest stars.

L-r: Bart Starr, Ralph Corrigan, and Bobby Marlow.

A-Day game 1951, l-r: Ralph Corrigan, Don Colegrove, Hyrle Ivy, Tommy Lewis, Sid Youngleman.

L-r back row: Jim Cain, Clem Welsh, Tom Calvin, Herb Hannah, Rebel Steiner, Ed Salem, Ed Lary. Front row: Mike Mizerany.

Bill Oliver, Al Elmore, Rocky Stone, Hootie Ingram, 1953.

Curtis Lynch, Al Elmore, Bart Starr, Nick Germanos, 1953.

THE SIXTIES
Bama Surges Forward

The decade of the sixties was an exciting one for Bama fans. It was filled mostly with highs, but there were also a few lows.

The decade began with a 21-6 victory over Georgia in Birmingham, a televised opener that featured the Tide defense containing Fran Tarkenton, the fabled Bulldog quarterback. This was Bryant's third season at Alabama, and he had a record of 12 wins, 6 losses, and 3 ties going in. Before the sixties were over, he would have added some 90 wins to that list, won 3 national championships, and become recognized as the nation's premier college coach. At the end of the sixties, the Tide would enter a down period, as we will see a bit later, but for the time being, Bama was on a roll, led by junior quarterback Pat Trammell and sophomore linebacker Lee Roy Jordan.

By the time Alabama went to Atlanta for the Georgia Tech game in 1960, they had only 1 loss and 1 tie on their record for the season, and hopes were high they could continue at a high level. However, at the end of the first half the Yellow Jackets led 15-0 and were handling the Tide fairly easily. The second half was to be different though, and the man who accomplished that was Bobby Skelton.

BOBBY SKELTON:

Although it has been a lot of years ago, it still seems like yesterday to some of us who played in that game. It was a gloomy day in Atlanta, really overcast. We played poorly in the first half. Matter of fact, when we went in at half, we felt we would get a pretty good shaking from Coach Bryant.

When we got to the dressing room, no one took their helmets off—those things stayed snapped on, and everybody was quiet. Coach came in, and we felt like it was doomsday for us. All of a sudden he started clapping his hands and saying it couldn't be better, that he had planned it this way, and it was like he wanted it. We didn't play very well in the first half, and we were behind 15-0. He told us we weren't going to change much, we were just going to go out there and play Alabama football.

It was back and forth in the second half. We got down to the fourth quarter, and I think Leon Fuller scored a touchdown. We went for 2 and missed it, so it was 15-6. Then we had another drive going, and I threw a touchdown pass to Norbie Ronsonet. Later we held them, and they punted into our end zone. We had 80 yards to go with a little more than two and a half minutes to play.

Someone jumped offsides and hit Pat Trammell on his bad leg — he had a bad knee. I was on the sideline, and there's a funny story behind it. Coach Bryant had fired me for a play that was called, but it wasn't my fault. Back in those days, you just couldn't arbitrarily substitute like you can today. So we had halfbacks who came in with a mimeographed paper with a red pencil mark circling the play the coaches wanted us to run. We had a sophisticated system for calling formations and since the halfbacks weren't used to doing it, they would give the folded paper to the quarterback, who opened it up and read the play. Well, the halfback came in and gave us the piece of paper, and I read the play. We fumbled the ball, and Coach Bryant took me out and told me to sit my little can on the bench over there and I'd never take another snap at Alabama! He fired me right there.

Well, I got rehired when Pat got hurt — hopefully, it was good for Alabama and good for Bobby Skelton, and it was in the nick of time. We found out more about that particular piece of paper later on in the dressing room after the game. Coach Phil Cutchin asked me about the play, and I pulled that paper out of my pants. I used to stick the papers down my pants instead of throwing them on the ground. He said he had written another play on the back of that paper, but the halfback didn't see fit to notice it or know how to tell me that, so I called the wrong play!

Anyway, Trammell got hurt and Coach Bryant put me back in the game. We stopped the clock no less than 10 or 12 times during that drive with passes out of bounds, and we probably had no less than four measurements for first downs, and most of those were in good fourth-down situations. We got it down there in pretty good range.

We had a play with Butch Wilson, who was our halfback. The play called for him to go out in the flat, then I was going to hit him, and he was going to run out of bounds toward the sidelines. But at Grant Field, there were so many people on the sideline, you couldn't tell where the sideline was. I rolled and sprinted out to the right. Mike Fracchia was the fullback, and there was nobody rushing. Butch was covered, and I looked back inside, but there was nobody open in there. Then I looked back at Butch, and he's running 180 degrees from where he's supposed to. He'd already run out of bounds and come back in. He's wide open, so I threw it to him. Or supposedly, he had gone out of bounds. I really don't know.

Anyway, the officials didn't see him. Butch gets it down inside the 10 to about the 7. We didn't have any timeouts left, and the time was running down under 30 seconds. We didn't know if we could get a field goal kicker in there or not.

Richard O'Dell was our second team kicker — Tommy Brooker was hurt. Heck, I had kicked in high school, and Leon Fuller was going to hold it. That was what we had planned to do. Then Richard O'Dell came in and brought the tee with him, and we lined up. The last thing I remember was looking up at Richard — that was the procedure. We'd just been trained in those things, and we had to go through the same routine.

So I looked up, and Richard looked down at me, and I said, "You ready?" He said, "Yeah, Rob, give me a good hold, and lean her back a tad."

I looked at the clock, and it was three seconds left and ticking. John O'Linger was flitching his tail around trying to get his hip path straightened out so he could snap the ball. He did, and that was a beautiful sight seeing the ball go through the uprights. Then all heck broke loose. Everybody ran onto the field, and I thought I was going to suffocate! I was right at the bottom of the pile.

Everybody at home thought Brooker had kicked the field goal because that's how it was announced on the radio, and when we got back home to Tuscaloosa everybody mobbed him. And Richard O'Dell – bless his soul – nobody hardly spoke to him! *(EDITOR'S NOTE: That was the only field goal O'Dell ever attempted in his Alabama career!)*

That come-from-behind win over Georgia Tech was a major one in the Tide's resurgence. Bama's next game was with Tampa University at Tuscaloosa. I remember before the game talking with B.W. Whittington and Finus Gaston who told me that this was an important money game for Tampa and in the interest of adding to their coffers, Tampa had taken buses overnight from Florida to Alabama. B.W. observed in his dry fashion that the players looked a little weary.

"To tell you the truth," he said, "I'm not sure they can go the distance."

The Auburn game was a great defensive struggle, and Tommy Brooker remembers his field goal that ensured the Tide a spot in the Bluebonnet Bowl. Tommy Brooker also told me a story about the 1960 Tech game that I had never heard before. It pays tribute to Paul Bryant's penchant for being a stickler for detail and preparedness.

With Brooker injured and unable to play for place kicking, Richard O'Dell from Lincoln, Alabama, worked hard all week. In pregame practice, though, both men warmed up, Brooker kicking without shoulder pads on. His injury apparently did not impede his kicking.

Just before the game Coach Bryant called Tommy aside and said, "Tommy, you're my kicker. The only thing is if we have a real time problem, you'll have trouble getting out there. So if that's the case, I'm going to send Richard in. But don't you dare tell him. Not a word. I mean it!

Bobby Skelton has already described the battle with the clock for us, and in the end, Richard was called on to make the kick. It's another example of Bryant's near clairvoyance!

TOMMY BROOKER:

Before we went to the Bluebonnet Bowl in 1960, we played Auburn in Birmingham. I was fortunate enough to kick the winning field goal in a 3-0 game. Auburn had a great field goal kicker in Ed Dyas, and Coach Bryant said that if we let him cross the 40, we were in trouble. I think they did it one time, but we held them off as far as them being a threat kicking a field goal. The next day the headlines in the Birmingham newspaper read: *Brooker Boots Bama to Bluebonnet Bowl.* At our senior banquet later on, they gave me that picture, and I always will recall those Bs being mentioned.

"Regardless of who was coaching them, they still would have been a great team. I said early in the season that they were the nicest, even sissiest, bunch I ever had. I think they read it, because later on they got unfriendly."
— Coach Bryant on his 1961 team

Every Alabama fan expected the 1961 season to be super with the likes of Lee Roy Jordan, Mike Fracchia, Bill Battle, Charley Pell, and Pat Trammell. Bob Ford was a young coach who had been on the Bryant staff and moved to another staff after the 1960 season. I went to the Masters Golf Tournament in April 1961 and ran into Bob. I asked him how he was doing and how he liked his new spot.

He said, "Very much. But, John, I really miss Tuscaloosa." Then he looked me straight in the eye and said, "John, they are going to have a great team this year. I mean great."

He was right. Bama rolled through the regular season games reaching a peak against Georgia Tech in Birmingham. Texas led both polls that year, and Alabama moved into second place. The Tech game was hard and close, but early in the second half, the PA announcer reported that TCU had beaten Texas that afternoon, and the roar at Legion Field was unbelievable. A win could put Alabama in the No. 1 spot. A bit later Trammell pitched out to Mike Fracchia who got a great block from Butch Wilson, turned on the after burners, and scored to give Bama a 10-0 win.

Another story seldom told on the 1961 team was an almost-bid to play UCLA in the Rose Bowl. The contract between the Pac-8 (now Pac-10) and Big-10 was in abeyance, and it appeared the committee was set to select Alabama to come West to play the Bruins in the Rose Bowl.

Behind closed doors in Tuscaloosa, it seemed a certainty, because Coach Bryant had assigned ace assistant Dude Hennessey to travel to Los Angeles to scout UCLA. Hennessey, with airline ticket in hand, was set to embark on his trip to California when a race riot broke out in Montgomery. The University's football team became a victim of the side effects of that riot when the Rose Bowl Committee decided not to invite Alabama and stick with the Big-10. Minnesota was asked to play the Bruins and the Crimson Tide settled for a roll to New Orleans and the Sugar Bowl.

TOMMY BROOKER:

Already crowned the national champions, we went to the Sugar Bowl to play Arkansas. One play really sticks out in my mind. Pat Trammell threw a pass to me in the end zone, and I went up for it, but so did Billy Richardson and several Arkansas players. We came down on the ground, and the ball never hit the ground. The ball landed on my chest, and little Billy Richardson was trying to pull it away from me because I think he thought I was from Arkansas. Anyway, they ruled the pass incomplete, and we didn't get the TD, but we hung on to win it 10-3.

Another key play for me, and it ended up being humorous later on, happened on a cutoff play. Coach Bryant taught us that if you can't get the player, you go for the cutoff position. Arkansas had a great scatback by the name of Lance Alworth, an NFL Hall of Famer later on and known as Bambi because of his speed and grace on the field. Alworth started around the opposite end that I was playing, and I ran for the cutoff position. I always said I caught Alworth from behind, but I did prevent him from scoring a touchdown.

I remember Mike Fracchia having a great game and being named the MVP. He was the original Italian Stallion — he had a high knee step and strut. We were a great defensive team, and including the Sugar Bowl, we didn't give up but 25 points for the entire season.

JIMMY WILSON:

Lance Alworth was one of a great number of players from Arkansas who had a lot of speed. Arkansas was a lot like us — they were small, quick, and very, very aggressive. I remember a lot about the Sugar Bowl that year. Coach Bryant was concerned that if we went to New Orleans and stayed in New Orleans, we would have so many distractions that we might lose sight of the toughness of the team that we were playing.

We had had an encounter with the University of Texas before and knew that we had a plate full when we got into the Sugar Bowl game with Arkansas. So we decided, or rather, they decided that we would have our pregame practices in Biloxi, Mississippi. We were to report to Biloxi the day after Christmas.

The weather was just atrocious! It was cold and rainy every day, and we couldn't get outside. Coach Bryant was pacing the floor. We would go over to one of the ballrooms and walk through plays, and he was very frustrated about the fact that we couldn't get any outside work in. We went out in the parking lot of the motel at one time, if I remember, and put on our tennis shoes and worked out in the parking lot just to get some outside work in. We went over to New Orleans the night before the game. We got very little sleep that night.

I think the significance of being No. 1 in the country at that time hadn't really soaked into me or probably a lot of the other players. We were just glad to be through the season undefeated, but we were concerned about the University of Arkansas and their quickness. And we had lost a lot of valuable outside work prior to that game.

Coach Bryant could see that once we got to be the No. 1 team, with the defeat of Georgia Tech and the real big defeat of Auburn that year, we had lost a little bit of an edge because we had a lot of distractions once the season was over back in Tuscaloosa. And in Birmingham, we were having dinners and tributes. We had a lot of things going on.

I think his decision for us to go to Biloxi was the right one. He couldn't do anything about the weather. If we had been in New Orleans, it would have been the same thing. We couldn't have worked out there either.

But I remember very vividly the day of the game. We hadn't gotten much sleep because people were up all night. New Year's Eve in New Orleans, you can imagine, was very noisy.

We went out to the stadium. Generally, the practice would be to walk around on the field before we ever went into the dressing room to get dressed. I was amazed at the pageantry. They had Dixieland bands out there. It was in the old Tulane Stadium, you know. The biggest crowd we had ever played before. The stadium was almost full at the time we got out there for the walk-around. They had all the floats, the cars, and I just distinctly remember that cold, cold air blowing in there. There were all the girls and majorettes out there in uniforms, and they were freezing to death.

Our minds were somewhat on the game, but I don't think we realized until the game started what a fight we were in for that day. They had two quarterbacks, McKinney and Moore, who were threats to go deep on us the whole time. We had a very conservative game plan, as we did all year. But the coaches were very concerned that they would get deep on us, and one play could beat us.

One of the things that I remember in the drive that we did manage to score on epitomized what Pat Trammell was. I will never forget it. We were starting the drive, and we had moved down to 30- or 40-yard line, maybe even closer than that, and Trammell came into the huddle and said, "If anybody misses an assignment on this drive, if we don't score, I'm going to call time-out and kick your ass right here on national television." And knowing him, he probably would have!

Alabama entered the 1962 season No. 1 in both AP and UPI polls despite the fact the Tide was going with an untested sophomore quarterback in place of the great and graduated Pat Trammell. That sophomore's name was Joe Namath.

Alabama opened against Georgia in Birmingham, and early in the game Namath hit Richard Williamson on a long down-and-out for the first of his many Alabama touchdown passes. The floodgates were open. Alabama gave Georgia a 35-0 thumping. The only people who took a worse beating than Georgia that night would feel the sting later — the owners of The Saturday Evening Post.

Namath, perhaps 19 years old at the time, was determined to show his cool after that first touchdown pass. He loped off the field in what was to become that familiar Namath shuffle. However, when he reached the bench and his teammates, he leaped into the air with great exuberance and was mobbed by a group of Southerners, who welcomed the Beaver Falls bomber with open arms.

The Bryant-Wally Butts versus The Saturday Evening Post *affair has been so well-chronicled I'll touch on it only briefly. In the winter of 1963, rumors kept cropping up of a major expose regarding scandal in college football.* Sports Illustrated *alluded to it in veiled terms. Finally* The Saturday Evening Post *came out with a story that former Georgia Coach Wally Butts had talked with Bryant long distance (true, since Bryant was also athletic director and since the two were friends) and that Butts had given Bryant all of Georgia's "secrets." This was patently absurd and judged so in federal court. The only "secret," as anyone who watched the game could attest, was that Alabama had a very fine football team and Georgia a very poor one. Namath and company probably could have doubled that 35-0 score. Bryant and Alabama needed inside information to beat Georgia that year about as much as Dolly Parton needs foam rubber.*

A man purported to have overheard the conversation through a crossed telephone line and was able to generate interest in his claims from a lot of smart people who should have known better. When the story broke, Bryant decided to go on television with a rebuttal. I was out of town on business, but I talked by phone with Bryant about his statement. I was unable to be on the show, but in retrospect I think that was best. The closeups of his coldly angry face and the slow-paced, measured tone of his voice were unforgettable as he denounced the story as a lie.

Benny Marshall of The Birmingham News *covered the trial in Atlanta. He told me later that Bryant on the witness stand was the embodiment of barely controlled fury, as if it were a real effort for him not to get off the witness stand and tear his accusers apart by hand. He said the malevolence in every aspect of him, his absolute conviction he had been wronged beyond repair, hypnotized the entire courtroom. After that, Benny said, it was all over except for how much he would collect.*

Although the episode probably had its genesis in Atlanta media circles, it was The Saturday Evening Post *that absorbed the loss. The magazine begun by Ben Franklin was ended by Paul Bryant.*

Linda Knowles joined the staff at Alabama in 1961 as a receptionist in the athletic department. By the time The Saturday Evening Post *story broke, she had moved up to the position of Coach Bryant's secretary.*

LINDA KNOWLES:

I was working directly for Coach Bryant when *The Saturday Evening Post* story broke. According to the story, a man claimed that he was on his telephone and was patched into a conversation between Coach Butts and Coach Bryant and the two men were "fixing" our game with the University of Georgia. The score of that game was 35-0, and it seems to me that if you're going to "fix" something, you would make it a little more competitive.

I remember we had FBI agents come into the office and confiscate financial and phone records. We didn't have a coffeepot in our office, and all of the coaches would take a break in the middle of the morning and go to Druid Drug (which has been torn down now) for a cup of coffee. Coach Wally Butts's trial was going on in Atlanta, and when Coach Bryant left the office he told me, "Linda, you'll get a phone call, and they will tell you that a decision has been reached and what the settlement is. I want you to call me at Druid Drug and tell me that the verdict is in — but DO NOT tell me what the settlement is."

I did exactly as he instructed, and he came back to the office. I don't remember the exact numbers of the settlement, but Coach Bryant said that if Wally had gotten that much, he would get a million or two million or something like that. He felt that he would be vindicated. What hurt him so much was that his integrity and honesty were questioned.

Earlier, when he was at A&M, he had been put on probation. Following that, he had told every coach that ever worked for him that if he were ever discovered breaking the rules, he would be fired on the spot. He would be allowed no explanation whatsoever – he would be fired. Coach Bryant was very strong about following the rules and doing it the right way.

Day-to-day, Coach Bryant was a very demanding boss, and from my personal viewpoint, he inspired different feelings in me. One day I would want to "mother" him – you know, "Did you take your medicine? Did you eat your lunch?" and that type of thing. Then there were days when I would go in and ask what I thought was an intelligent question, and he would just make me feel like a three-year-old. Now that I look back, I think he did that to keep you off balance and not ever feel that you truly knew him–his thoughts or his way of doing things. That's just my opinion. But I think he handled the team much the same way. At that time in his career, there were very, very few players who were close to him. Pat Trammell was one of his favorite players. There were not many who called Coach Bryant "friend." And yet he inspired so much loyalty and that feeling of, "Well, Coach, if you want me to bang my head against the brick wall today, you just tell me how many times and how many bricks." You wanted things to go well for him, and it was because you cared about him. I did not realize how much I truly cared for him as a person until he died, and only losing my father compared to his death.

Coach Bryant inspired such awe and respect. I remember one time we had a reporter in from one of the major newspapers–it seems like it was *The New York Times* – who I'm sure had interviewed kings and presidents and whatever. That man went into Coach Bryant's office and never sat down throughout the whole interview. He was that awed by Coach Bryant's presence, and he made a comment about it when he came out of the office. He said, "I've handled a lot of things, but this is pretty awesome."

I'll tell you another funny story. We had a coffeepot in our new office, and you had to take the coffeepot to the restroom to get the water, and then go back to pour the water in. Well Coach Bryant didn't mind going to get the water, but he would go back and pour it into the part of the coffeepot where it went and stand there and watch while just plain water came through. He'd say, "What's wrong with this coffeepot?" I'd say, "I don't know, Coach. We've been having trouble with it. Go on back to your office, and I'll call the repairman." Well I'd let him get back to his office, and then I'd put the grounds in! I'd make a pot of coffee and take him a cup. But you don't think I said, "Coach, you didn't put the grounds in." Oh, no!

In 1962 Alabama continued its unbeaten, untied streak until it reached 25 and went to Atlanta to play Georgia Tech. It was, in my opinion, one of football's greatest games. Tech edged the Tide 7-6 after a 2-point try failed, and Coach Bryant went into the Tech dressing room to congratulate Bobby Dodd and his players. Lee Roy Jordan recalls that game for us, and Benny Nelson talks about a memorable win at Tennessee in 1962.

BENNY NELSON

When I played high school football, we played out of the single wing. I always visualized myself as being another Johnny Majors. Somehow, Tennessee wasn't interested in me and I signed with Alabama. Tennessee was a really big game for me and a big game for Alabama, naturally. The game in 1962, I think, was one of the best games I ever had. That was the day they dedicated Neyland Stadium.

I'll never forget Joe Namath. I was playing what we called a strongback or wingback. Joe looked at me and said, "Okay, you're going to score on the next play." We ran what we called a "pass five X circle." That's where the tight end, Bill Battle, curled in and everybody went to him. I went out in the flat and turned it down. Namath put the ball right in my hands for about a 40-yard touchdown.

Coach Bryant always gave us some little incentive for RBIs, that sounds more like baseball terminology, for a big play. He would give you a plus for a good play. An RBI was an exceptional play. The first series they had the ball, their tailback dropped back to pass. I remember leveling off and Charley Stephens was up there in the flat also. Charley always says he got to the ball first, but we got our hands on it together and somehow I came down with the ball. Charley said I had taken it away from him. I got the RBI. Lee Roy (Jordan) had six in that game, but, of course, it wasn't hard for Lee Roy to get an RBI. I ended up getting five and I scored another touchdown on a pass from Jack Hurlbut. I caught two touchdown passes that day from two different quarterbacks.

After the game we started singing, "We don't give a damn about the entire state of Tennessee" and Coach started passing out cigars. You knew something big had just happened when Coach passed out victory cigars.

LEE ROY JORDAN:

We were No. 1 in the nation for most of the season, and we went over to play Georgia Tech at Grant Field. We just didn't play as well as we had or would against either Auburn or Oklahoma. Tech had an outstanding team, but we probably outcoached ourselves or outplayed ourselves. It was one of the few times I ever heard Coach Bryant second-guess his decisions.

We went to a new formation with two quarterbacks in the game thinking it would get us a quick touchdown. We had two near misses, too. I mean, it could have been two touchdowns, but on both occasions we threw the ball a little long.

In the second half, we went back to our old style of football and that was playing tough, playing hard, beat them in the fourth quarter. We got our opportunities to win it in the fourth quarter, but we missed a 2-point conversion that would have won it. Then we got the ball back and turned it over deep in Tech territory. All we needed was a field goal to win it, and we still had another opportunity late when we got the ball inside the Tech 50, but to their credit, they hung on and won it. We would have won back-to-back national titles, but we just didn't do the little things that would have won us the game. Instead we lost 7-6.

Although the heart-rending loss in Atlanta deflated the Tide, ending a cinch repeat at the national title, Coach Bryant challenged his squad to end its season by showing Auburn and Oklahoma the mettle of this squad.

A 38-0 rout of the archrival Tigers in a game that featured Butch Wilson's kickoff return for a score sent the Tide on a high into the Orange Bowl showdown with Big-8 Oklahoma, coached by the legendary Bud Wilkinson. It was to be the final game of the Lee Roy Jordan era, and what a way for Lee Roy to conclude it. His 31 tackles were a statistical reminder of why he became an Alabama folk hero, and he did it at the game President John F. Kennedy attended.

LEE ROY JORDAN:

Oklahoma had a lot of speed, and we knew we had to slow down their running attack, which was led by two big, strong fast backs, Joe Don Looney and Jim Gresham. Our objective that day was to stop Looney, and as a matter of fact, we may have held him to minus yards. But Gresham must have gained over 100 yards on us, although we did make him fumble twice and Oklahoma didn't score.

No linebacker makes plays without the help of the men in front of him. Players like Jimmy Sharpe and Jimmy Wilson were the ones who deserve the credit for any tackles I made that day or any that year.

Joe Namath was a dynamite sophomore, a great player on that team. I think Joe could have been a superstar in basketball or baseball or any other sport he chose. He was that talented. We did a good job of running the football on Oklahoma, and Joe ended up hitting my roommate Richard Williamson with a 25-yard touchdown pass.

President Kennedy was at the game that particular day, and he had visited the Oklahoma locker room prior to the game. He was pulling for Oklahoma because Bud Wilkinson was on his staff for the Physical Fitness Council. Coach Bryant used that as a motivating factor before the game and again at halftime. He didn't miss an opportunity to bring out a little extra emotion of his team. He mentioned several times that President Kennedy had ignored us and snubbed us and played favorites with Oklahoma.

Alabama's rise to the top of college football was evident by 1963 when fans were disappointed because the Tide was only 9-2 and the Sugar Bowl champs. That win was thanks to the gifted foot of Tim Davis, whose four field goals beat Ole Miss 12-7 in the New Orleans' Classic that may be best remembered for all the snow that fell on the Crescent City on the eve of the contest. Tim, who was the bowl MVP, recalls his famous day in New Orleans and Namath's probation before the season-ending finale against Miami.

TIM DAVIS:

Joe (Namath) got put on probation for a little escapade that we didn't think was that big of a deal and something minor compared with what some other kids would do on campus. He had come in a little late and maybe had a drink at a party. When he was kicked off the team, I think a lot of us were startled, but we were not too shocked. Coach Bryant was a man of his word, and he always preached, "It's my way or the highway." And when Joe admitted he had broken curfew, he was gone.

We moved the Miami game that year to the last game of the season for television, and I will never forget it. We got out to what we thought was a comfortable lead, something like 17-0 at the half, and we thought maybe we had done pretty good. But when you looked around the dressing room in the Miami heat, there was sweat running down the floor of the concrete dressing room toward the drain and into the drain. There were people sitting around losing fluids. It was half-time, and coaches were saying to just get people hydrated and hang on for the second half. It was hang-on time. George Mira, their quarterback, who we called the Matador, would get out there and start running around, throwing the ball, and before we knew it was 17-12. We were in a dogfight to hang on. One of our sophomore linebackers, Jackie Sherrill, intercepted a pass to clinch the win, saving the day for us.

That year we got the Sugar Bowl bid and I remember someone saying that Coach Bryant had been to a meeting before the Sugar Bowl and said, "We've got about as much chance of winning down here as it has of snowing." I woke up the day before the game and look out the window saw snow outside our hotel window! And I'm saying, gee whiz, this is amazing, snow falling down in New Orleans. We were going to practice at Tulane Stadium the day before the game, and there was a big snowman built on the campus.

Our defense played awfully well that day. There was one play Ole Miss ran that we had prepared for it in practice. It was a long pass play, and they had run it all year long. We were prepared for it, but they hit it twice on us, one for a score and one set up a potential winning touchdown for them. Our defense came up with a big play, though, and won us the game.

Ole Miss had a great quarterback, Perry Lee Dunn, and he drove them down to our 2-yard line. When it looked like they were going to score, Coach Carney Laslie turned to me and said, "Tim, get ready, we're going to have to kick another one!" Fortunately Bill Wieseman made a great stop on the 2-yard line, and and it didn't come down to that.

We started kicking field goals and got ahead by 3 and then 6 and then 9. I think, as the saying goes, both sidelines perked up when we got ahead 9-0. We tried a fourth field goal from 50 yards out, and we had a snap that put the laces back to me. Benny Nelson was holding it, and we kicked it plenty far enough, but it was just a foot or two to the right. It went over a snowbank behind the goal post.

I remember on the fifth attempt, Paul Crane was not snapping. You have to remember that in those days, whichever center was in the game did the snapping. There wasn't specialization in those days like now. Paul was an extraordinary snapper, and Benny would say you knew you'd get a perfect snap when Paul was in the game. He was an absolute genius at snapping. Well, we didn't get Paul into the game, and I told Benny, "Don't spin the ball. I'll just try to kick into the laces." And luckily I did from 48 yards out, and it had plenty of room to spare.

"I'll go to my grave knowing I scored. I have a sick, infuriating feeling."
— Joe Namath's assessment of his quarterback sneak against Texas in the 1965 Orange Bowl, an official ruled otherwise

1964 was Joe Namath's senior year, and he was on the Heisman track until he crumpled without being hit against North Carolina State and began the legendary saga of his knees. Nevertheless, a combination of Joe, when he could play, and Steve Sloan, when Joe couldn't, got Bama to the Orange Bowl against the Texas Longhorns. In a game of much disputed officials' calls (a split SEC and SWC crew worked the game), Texas won it. But Namath's gutsy and glittering performance captured American hearts.

GAYLON MCCOLLOUGH:

I learned a lesson from the 1965 Orange Bowl that I will carry with me for the rest of my life, and I will share that with you as I reflect on our game with Texas. First of all, it was a great gathering because of the great traditions of both Alabama and Texas and it was the first Orange Bowl played at night. We were already national champions because the final polls were conducted before the postseason games.

Joe Namath had been injured earlier in the year against North Carolina State, and he really had not played very much since he went down. Steve Sloan had filled in admirably, and we entered the game with Texas with what we felt was a sound game plan.

Right before halftime, with Texas leading 14-7, we sacked the Texas quarterback for a huge loss, and we would have gotten the ball back and gone into the dressing room trailing by 7. Well, way down the field, Mickey Andrews, who is now the defensive coordinator with Florida State, and a Texas receiver bumped into one another. Obviously no pass was ever thrown, but the official called pass interference. It turned out to be a 41-yard penalty, and Texas scored right before half to up their lead 21-7.

To Texas's credit, they had scouted us very well, and we went into halftime behind 21-7. Then Coach Bryant, as he often did, adjusted the game plan, and we started throwing on first and second downs. We also changed our snap count because we'd apparently been going on the first sound and I noticed Diron Talbert, who was their great nose guard, seemed to know the snap count as well as I did. He was on me about the time I snapped the ball.

Once we made the changes, we became more effective, and Namath came off the bench in the second half and directed one of the greatest comebacks that I think I ever was associated with while I was playing football. Toward the end of the game, I think there were just a couple of minutes left inside the Texas 2-yard line.

We ran the ball to about the 6-inch line. We had a timeout, and we called a quarterback sneak with wedge blocking. I remember going to the line assuming we would score and win the ball game. And then, just about the time the ball was supposed to be snapped, Tommy Nobis, Texas's All-American linebacker, came up into the gap and got right on my nose.

Well, the wedge blocking dictated that I was supposed to help Wayne Freeman block Diron Talbert, who had moved over into the gap. But Nobis moved up there and actually became like a nose guard. So I had to make a decision about which one to block. I went after Nobis, and Freeman had to take Talbert by himself. Joe plunged into the line, and then it was a big pileup, and we all started looking for the football. Joe happened to be lying right on top of me, and I was in the end zone and Joe was in the end zone, too. We jumped up and started celebrating.

Then we saw a conference among the officials because the one who had called it a touchdown was being talked to by another official. He asked, "Did he score?" While they were having this conference, either the referee or umpire came up, took the ball away from the other two guys, put it down on the 6-inch line, and whistled first down, Texas.

Of course there was protesting that went on, but he blew the whistle and started the clock. I remember going back to the sidelines and walking by Coach Bryant. He had been standing there and hadn't said anything throughout the whole thing. He hadn't come on the field or contested the call. But one of the players said as we went by Coach Bryant, "We scored." I'll never forget what he said at that moment. He said that if Joe walked into the end zone with the football, there could be no question about it, could there?

I've reflected on that statement ever since that night, and I think the lesson taught by Coach Bryant was this: If you want to accomplish something in life, don't do just enough to get the job done because the world's referees might not make the correct call, either. If you really want to do something, go beyond what is expected and leave no room for doubt.

A few months after the game, The Birmingham News *sports editor, Alf Van Hoose, was visiting with E.D. "Red" Cavette, the referee of that Orange Bowl game. Cavette, too, was none too pleased with what had transpired that evening. He acknowledged that on the controversial interference call a Southwest Conference field judge dropped the flag and told Cavette he had pass interference on Alabama. When Cavette informed the official that you can't have pass interference when no pass was thrown, the field judge changed his call and said Alabama was holding. Likewise on the Namath quarterback sneak, an SEC official was overruled by a SWC official, and the apparent game-winning score never occurred. Van Hoose noted that in all his years of covering college football, he had never witnessed a more obvious miscarriage of the rules than he did on the pass interference/holding play.*

The 1965 season has special significance to me because it was my first year of doing play-by-play on the Alabama Network. *Also it was a year Alabama won the national championship, but they traveled all the way around Aunt Nellie's barn to accomplish this.*

The season began with a visit to Athens and a game "Between the Hedges" with them Dawgs, always tough and ready. This was Steve Sloan's senior year,

101

and the Tide led 17-10 with just a few minutes remaining. Vince Dooley reached deep into his bag of tricks and came up with a "flea flicker" pass play to his All-American end, Pat Hodgson, who lateraled to a halfback named Bob Taylor, who outran the Bama secondary to score. The only problem was that the Alabama coaches thought Hodgson's knee was down before the lateral. Nevertheless, in the roar and pandemonium of Sanford Stadium, the Dawgs went for 2 and made it and, holding on for a thrilling 18-17 win.

The Sunday papers brought up the possibility of the downed knee, and from working the TV show with Coach Bryant, I know he looked at the film of the play several times but never commented on it. Honestly, I could not tell from the film whether it was illegal or not. When pressed for comments by the news reporters, Bryant's terse and laconic reply was, "You don't win games on Mondays."

Steve Sloan had one of his best games against Ole Miss a couple of weeks later in Birmingham, leading the Tide on an 80-plus-yard drive to win 17-16. Lady Luck smiled on Alabama here because Jimmy Keyes, the Rebs fine guard and placekicker, missed the only extra point of his career that night to enable Alabama to win.

The next roadblock to national championship hopes occurred the third Saturday of October against Tennessee at Legion Field. Late in the game it was tied 7-7, but the Tide was moving inside the Tennessee 20-yard line, certainly in Davis's field goal range. The stands were jammed and so were the sidelines as time ticked down. On a third-down play, Kenny Stabler, a brilliant sophomore quarterback, was trapped in the backfield but eluded tacklers and ran about 15 yards.

In all fairness to Kenny, he probably felt that he had run far enough for a first down and was anxious to stop the clock. The scoreboard showed third down, but the official on the sidelines adjusted his marker to fourth. To the astonishment and chagrin of Alabama fans, Kenny took the ball from center and quickly threw it out of bounds! The clock stopped all right, and Tennessee took the ball over and ran out the time.

Alabama and Mississippi State met in the night game of a doubleheader in Jackson's Memorial Stadium, and it was a bruiser. In the first series of downs, Ray Perkins made a couple of receptions, and a sophomore wideout from Muscle Shoals watched on the sidelines with interest. .

DENNIS HOMAN:

I was watching the Mississippi State secondary, and I said, more or less to myself, "It really looks like the post pattern would be wide open." I heard Coach Bryant's voice behind me say, "What did you say?" I swallowed and repeated that "the post looked open to me." He grabbed me by the shoulders and pushed me into the game. "Well, get your butt in there and run it." I went in and told Steve (Sloan), he hit me deep, and we completed a 65-yard touchdown.

> *That was Bama's only TD of the evening but we won 10-7. Alabama finished the 1965 season 8-1-1 and was ranked fourth, well away from the top.*
> *But some miracles were in store for the Tidesmen who headed down to Miami to take on Nebraska in the Orange Bowl. Tommy Somerville and Jerry Duncan remember that trip and what it took for Alabama to get the AP national championship when the smoke cleared after Alabama's 39-28 win over the giant Cornhuskers.*

TOM SOMERVILLE:

The 1966 Orange Bowl against Nebraska was probably one of Coach Bryant's most masterful coaching jobs because we were vastly outweighed by an undefeated Nebraska team. They were favored to win – I don't remember by how much, but I am sure they were favored.

It came down to a matter of the plan Coach Bryant worked out being just exactly right. And not just the plan going into the game but the way that we continued to play the game all the way through. I am sure Coach Bryant recognized that we had an advantage in speed and quickness. I remember before the game we came out and walked around the field. The Nebraska players were walking around, and they had smirks on their faces and were chuckling to each other. They were pretty confident when they saw how little we were. They were not nearly as big as the players of today, but their linemen were up there in the 250 range. Back in the 1960s, that was a huge player.

Coach Bryant told us to approach it as though we were behind the whole game, no matter what the score was. In the first half, we got ahead pretty decisively early, and we kept playing like we were behind. A vivid example is we were ahead 21-7 right before the half, and we on-sides kick. Think about it! We get the kick and score a field goal right before half and are up 24-7. Today you don't ever see an on-side kick until it's right at the end of the game, and it was pretty unheard of then to do on-side kicks in the first half.

Of course those tackle eligible passes to Jerry Duncan had Nebraska just absolutely baffled. I don't know how many passes he caught in that game, but I remember it was an important part of our offense. In the second half their offense clicked in pretty good, and they scored some points. Fortunately, we were far enough ahead to where they couldn't catch us, and we ended up winning 39-28.

I think it was probably the greatest single coaching job Coach Bryant did in the whole time I played, and I know it gave him great satisfaction to win the game.

"I didn't care if we ever quit practicing. I loved it. The only other guy I ever knew who loved it as much was Jerry Duncan. He would beg to practice even when he was hurt. I've actually seen him cry because the trainer told him he couldn't scrimmage."
— Coach Bryant on Jerry Duncan, his star tackle from 1964 to 1966

JERRY DUNCAN:

We got better and better as the season went along, and by the time we got to the Orange Bowl to play Nebraska, we had a pretty darn good football team. Nebraska was the biggest team I'd ever played against. I was going against Walt Barnes, who was 6-6, 280, and later was a first-round draft pick of the Redskins. Our whole offensive line didn't average over 190 a man. Cecil Dowdy was our biggest lineman, and he weighed about 205.

That day we really got the breaks because No. 1 Michigan State lost in the Rose Bowl to UCLA and No. 2 Arkansas lost to LSU, a team we had beaten 31-7 late in the season. Nebraska was No. 3, and we were No. 4, so it set up a national title showdown. Their quarterback was Bob Churchich, and they had Freeman White and a back named Lighthorse Harry Wilson. Going onto the field for the game was one of the indescribable moments — going on to the Orange Bowl field before 80,000 fans and knowing you're playing on national television for the national championship.

I'll tell you, Coach Bryant had us well prepared and ready to play people who outweighed some of us 70 and 80 pounds. All week long Coach Bryant and Steve Sloan had discussed opening the game with a tackle eligible pass to me, and the talk had gotten around to some of the other players. I was the only one who didn't know anything about it. We won the toss and got the ball, and Sloan calls the tackle eligible pass. Everybody broke the huddle except me, and I was just standing there. I was scared to death. I didn't know what to do. We opened up with it, and we ran it on the first two plays. Later in the drive, Sloan hit Perkins for a touchdown, and we were on our way.

I really believe it was one of Coach's most remarkable games. He was a conservative coach by nature, but he knew that night we had to play wide open if we were going to upset Nebraska. He told us he wanted us to play every play like we were 14 points behind. Everybody laid it on the line. I remember Frank Canterbury, one of our backs, was probably 5-7 or 5-8 and weighed 155 pounds drenching wet. He played a heck of a game, and so did Steve Bowman and Les Kelley. I don't know if I ever played in a game where I had nothing left to give at the end of it. I think our whole team spent all of its energy that night claiming another national title for Alabama.

The 1966 season began with a lot of enthusiasms and expectations on the part of the coaching staff, the team, and most assuredly the fans. Another national championship would make it three in a row, and most experts figured Alabama had the guns to get it done— two All-American receivers in Ray Perkins and Dennis Homan; a junior quarterback, Kenny Stabler, headed for All-American honors; a mobile offensive line with depth; a salty rugged defense; and good kicking. It appeared to be a team hard to beat during the regular season.

Alabama played Tennessee in Knoxville on October 15th that year. I still clearly remember driving over from Gatlinburg on a cloudy morning and hearing that showers were a possibility. This was one of the great meteorological understatements. Eating a hot dog in the press box a little over an hour before the game, I noticed a cloud in the west, no bigger than the proverbial "man's hand." Twenty minutes later a driving downpour began that was to last all afternoon.

Alabama won the toss and surprisingly elected to receive on this miserable day. They fumbled on about their own 20, and the alert Vols pounced on it and soon took it in and led 7-0. Alabama could do nothing, and Tennessee added a field goal to lead at intermission 10-0. At the half, the Crimson players were far from confident.

MIKE HALL:

Well, I was kind of frightened! I was a sophomore, and it was the first time I'd been in a big game-I didn't know what to expect, especially from Tennessee. When we went in at halftime, the offense went over what they were doing against us that hurt us. All of a sudden it got quiet for Coach Bryant to make his talk, and I just about crawled up under the bench — I was ready for some really harsh words! But he came through kind of clapping his hands and singing, "What a friend we have in Jesus." About that time the referee stuck his head in the door and told us 5 minutes to kickoff, and everybody got up and scrambled out of there. I felt like I'd dodged a bullet!

There were not many crimson smiles until the final whistle sounded in Knoxville on the third Saturday in October back in 1966. A deluge of rain cascaded down in East Tennessee but it didn't dampen what turned out to be an all-time classic. Many regard it as one of the greatest wins ever for Alabama and one of the most disheartening for Tennessee. The final score: 11-10 Bama.

Alabama's brilliant defense was tested early when fumbles set up a pair of first quarter Big Orange scores, the first coming on a pass from Dewey "Swamp Rat" Warren to Austin Denney and the second on a 40-yard field goal by Gary Wright. Shields-Watkins Field was rocking on mountaintop, and Bama appeared drowned by the noise, the Tennessee defense, and the increasing rainstorm.

Well if Tennessee had their Swamp Rat, Bama had its Snake, and he refused to lose. Trialing 10-0 in the fourth quarter, Stabler drove the Tide down the field, and his run to the 1-yard line, set up his own TD. Bryant opted for a 2-point try, and Stabler connected with Wayne Cook to make it 10-8.

Late in the fourth quarter and backed up on its 25, Stabler began another march. Thirteen plays later, Bama had it fourth and goal on the one. Steve Davis was sent in to try a field goal. Because of the inclement conditions, the snap was low, but Stabler, unbeknownest to most, made one of his spectacular plays, catching the ball and placing it perfectly for Steve Davis's field goal. It came with 3:23 to play, numbers that would take on even more meaning in Alabama's Crimson lore in years to come.

Tennessee wasn't finished, though. A halfback pass fooled Alabama, and with 0:18 to play, Tennessee was nestled at Alabama's 3-yard line. Gary Wright, a native of Alabama, missed his field goal attempt to the right and forever became known as Gary "Wide" Wright. Here are some memories of longtime Bryant aide Dude Hennessey and some of the players in that contest.

DUDE HENNESSEY:

Coach Bryant had an uncanny knack of *knowing* what was going to happen before it did. Before the game he had told us that it might come down to a field goal attempt, and if Tennessee was close to our goal line, they'd get a delay of game penalty to move the ball back for a better angle. He said, "If it happens, decline the penalty and make 'em kick at the angle." Well it did happen just that way, and the severe angle and Coach Bryant's prescience probably saved the day.

We were involved in a number of intense games, but I don't know if many matched that day in Knoxville. Tennessee had a great team, and so did we. Kenny Stabler was magnificent. I think the game typified our entire program.

Few people can imagine the coaching, the intensity level of football in the Southeastern Conference, the fierceness of the competition. In my opinion, only one man could ever have dominated over a 25-year stretch, and I believe he would have dominated over any 25-year period. That man was Paul Bryant.

Coach Bryant surrounded himself with winning people. Everyone in the athletic department was part of his family and contributed to the wins on Saturday – the assistant coaches, the office workers, the equipment managers, custodians, everyone. He made all of us believe we could win, not only the players but all of those other people as well. I don't know if any game measured up to Coach Bryant's spirit like that one in Knoxville.

He always stressed to all of us that we had to fight, and he didn't mean fistfighting. He meant when things were their bleakest, to suck it up and make something positive happen, and you could overcome the worst adversity. We did it that day in Knoxville.

"If he'd kicked it straight, we would have blocked it."
— Coach Bryant's remarks about Tennessee's missed field goal in the 1966 game in Knoxville, won by the Tide 11-10

STEVE DAVIS:

The center snap came bounding back through the mud, almost creating a wake behind it. Believe me, only a truly great athlete like Kenny Stabler could have fielded the ball and set it up for kicking. I just tried to keep my head down, and luckily it went through-Bama 11, Tennessee 10.

A little more than a minute remained, and all of us Alabamians there relaxed. Bad idea. Dewey "Swamp Rat" Warren rallied the Vols throwing to halfback Charlie Fulton for yardage. Fulton then threw to Austin Denney, and the Vols were inside our 10. Our great defense held them, and they had to try a field goal on the game's last play. Gary Wright from Heflin, Alabama, was their kicker, and he did have a difficult angle. His kick was sliced a bit (Bryant said Alabama would have blocked it if he had kicked it straight), and Bama won what I believe was the most exciting game I've ever seen. Poor Gary is forever remembered as "Wide" Wright in Tennessee annals.

The three top teams in the USA that year were Alabama, Notre Dame, and Michigan State, and unfortunately for the Tide, Notre Dame and Michigan did play each other. Their game finished in a 10-10 tie, and they ended up as co-national champs despite Alabama's thundering 34-7 win over a good Nebraska team in the Sugar Bowl. Just as Alabama had been unbelievably lucky in the way the bowl games fell the year before, they were unlucky in 1966 with what was probably Alabama's best team. Jerry Duncan remembers that 1966 team and the way he and his teammates closed one of the most remarkable years in Crimson Tide lore.

JERRY DUNCAN:

We went to New Orleans with every intention of demonstrating to the country just what a great team this was. We were the only undefeated, untied team in the country, but we were ranked third behind Notre Dame and Michigan State. I'm sure over the years, and at that time, I cussed and cried a lot about losing out on a third national championship because it was an unbelievable team we had in 1966.

On the first play of the game, Kenny Stabler went back and we had good protection, and he hit Ray Perkins on the sideline for a 45-yard gain. I really believe Ray would have gone all the way if he had a little more room to manipulate. Anyway, we jumped to a 24-0 halftime lead and fairly well coasted to the win over Nebraska.

I guess we will always be known as the "Uncrowned Champions" of Alabama football. I played on two national championship teams, and neither was as good as the 1966 team. It was one of those special groups. We gave up 37 points the entire season, and with players like Kenny Stabler, Ray Perkins, Dennis Homan, Cecil Dowdy, and Les Kelley, you couldn't help but have a pretty good offense.

As the tumultuous sixties reached its waning years, momentum clearly indicated programs within the Southeastern Conference were about to shelve the cloaks of segregation. Alabama's spring practice in 1967 featured Dock Rhone, Jr., a 5-8, 185-pound guard from Carver High in Montgomery. He is significant because he was the first black football player ever to try out for the Crimson Tide. Although he never played in a game, he set in motion the integration of the program.

Two years later, after the completion of the 1969 high school season, Wilbur Jackson from Ozark became the first black footballer to sign with the

University of Alabama, and soon at least some of the vestiges of segregated teams would forever end.

From a historical perspective, it should be remembered that while Paul Bryant was head coach at the University of Kentucky, he went to his president, Dr. Herman Donovan, and told him he could be the Branch Rickey of the Southeastern Conference if he allowed Bryant to integrate his football team. Donovan declined, and it would be nearly a score of years before blacks would be accepted for their athletic abilities.

On February 11, 1992, speaking before a packed audience in Birmingham, Penn State coach Joe Paterno fondly remembered Coach Bryant and his role in integration of the South. "In 1959 Coach Bryant brought his Alabama team to Philadelphia to play Penn State in the first Liberty Bowl. Not many leaders in the South had the courage to leave the South and play an opponent, much less one with a black player. He always wanted Alabama to be more than a regional team, and I think that is what separated him from his peers in his conference and why Alabama was a team with a national reputation."

Alabama also played integrated teams from Oklahoma and Nebraska in the 1960s, a time when most schools in the SEC still refused to compete against integrated squads. Slowly the mindset was changing, and it would swing dramatically in the 1970s. Before we move into that decade, let's remember the final three years of the 1960s, times that saw the Alabama program slump.

Dennis Homan, a returner from the 1965 and 1966 teams and an All-American to be in 1967, recalls that the preseason expectations were high entering his final year.

DENNIS HOMAN:

Entering the 1967 season, we were supposed to have one of the greatest defensive teams Alabama had ever fielded. It had been mentioned the defense would be comparable to the teams that Lee Roy Jordan played on.

We had Bobby Johns back as a defensive back. He was an All-American and had intercepted three passes against Nebraska in the Sugar Bowl. Another Birmingham boy, Mike Hall, was one of our linebackers, and Mike Ford was back at defensive end. We had to replace a lot of people from our 1966 offense, including guys like Cecil Dowdy and Jerry Duncan on the line, Ray Perkins at end, and Les Kelley in the backfield. We had some key gaps, but we felt optimistic entering the season we would be all right.

For whatever reasons the Alabama football program began to show a few chinks in its usual seamless armor as the 1967 season started. Maybe it was the sixties ambience, the flower child influence. Or as Bryant poignantly said, "We got complacent."

Alabama's opener was a wild and woolly affair with Florida State. Ken Stabler was a senior that year, and he had earned a spot in Bryant's doghouse during the spring. In fact, much was made of the fact that Stabler had been demoted to 6th team. In the first quarter, FSU ran a punt back 75 yards and scored with some nifty passes. The deeply underdog Seminoles led 14-0. Coach Bryant's innate forgiveness and compassion came out as Kenny made a significant, instantaneous jump from the 6th team to the 1st! The game ended 37-37, and Bryant wryly and wisely observed, "Some of my old teams wouldn't have allowed 37 points in a season."

Tennessee (in sweet revenge for 1966) got a narrow victory over the Tide, and Auburn looked forward to meeting Alabama that year. The game was played in even worse weather conditions than the 1966 Tennessee game, and Auburn dominated completely for three quarters but could only get 3 points on the boards. After a favorable punt exchange, Alabama had the ball around midfield. After a moment or so, Stabler veered to his right and ducked in a race through the gloom and the mire 47 yards for an undisputed Tide touchdown.

DENNIS HOMAN:

When we got to the Auburn game, the weather was horrible. I remember tornadoes were hitting all around the stadium, and the playing surface was 6 inches of mud. Of course, we were really fortunate to get away with a 7-3 victory, but I honestly feel if we'd played in better conditions we would have won easily. We couldn't throw the ball at all because of the weather conditions, but Kenny (Stabler) made the tremendous run in the fourth quarter for our only score.

You had to be on the field that day to comprehend how miserable the conditions actually were. I always kid Kenny about that game, telling him the only block I ever threw in my career was the one that helped spring him for the touchdown. It was an option play, and Kenny turned a routine play into a 47-yard score. Kenny was a truly gifted athlete, one of those rare players who had a flair for the dramatic and making the big play in the clutch. Certainly that dreary day in Birmingham, he made one of the single greatest plays in Alabama history.

KENNY STABLER:

Anytime you beat Auburn, anytime you beat the intrastate rival, it's the situation that we all have to live with — win or lose — that makes that game so important. The reason you have that kind of success, the reason you win is the lessons Coach Bryant taught: You refuse to lose, you have to find a way to win. Somebody will make a big play, but it's not only the run that I made. If you look back at the films, our tight end, Dennis Dixon, made a great block, and they said he was holding, which was crap! And Dennis Homan made a great block on the outside on the quarterback. That's the reason we have success — we are surrounded by a bunch of very talented football players.

That year Alabama went to the Cotton Bowl, where Texas A&M under Bryant's former star assistant, Gene Stallings, topped the Tide 20-16. Stallings recalls this memorable game.

GENE STALLINGS:

I'll tell you a story about when Alabama was playing Texas A&M in the Cotton Bowl, and every time I think about the Cotton Bowl, this is what I really think about.

It was a third-down situation, but Coach Bryant thought it was a fourth down. At that time the rules were that if you sent a player into the game, he had to play one down. Coach Bryant sent his punter in — I knew that he was confused. Nevertheless, he sent his punter in, so I sent in a safety who could only field punts — he wasn't a football player, but he could field punts pretty well.

Then I saw the Alabama coaching staff talking to Coach Bryant over on the sidelines, and finally he sent another player in and the punter came out. So I send my safety in so my other guy can come out, and the official over on the sideline says, "Whoa! You can't do that — he's got to stay in one play." So I said, "Now, wait a minute, fellow. I'm sitting right here watching Coach Bryant send his punter in, and then Coach Bryant took his punter out!" He looked at me and said, "You ain't Coach Bryant!" It nearly cost us the ball game because they threw a pass right down the middle, and this guy was just sort of flagging at everybody.

I'll tell you one other thing about that ball game. You know, Texas A&M won that game 20-16. Alabama had scored and went for 2, which would have made it 20-18. Then they would have gotten the ball down in field goal range and possibly won the game 21-20.

But it didn't happen, and after the game was over, Coach Bryant and I were visiting, and he said, "Gene, what's wrong with you?" I said, "What do you mean, Coach?" He said, "As long as you coached defense for me, you've always been in some kind of goal line out. So I knew that when we went for 2, you would be slanting your guys to the outside, and that little ol' play would go right up the middle, and it would work for a 2-point conversion. You've really changed!"

I said, "Coach, I'm fixin' to tell you something that's going to hurt you. We only had 10 men on the the field. My middle linebacker noticed that we didn't have a defensive guard, so he just jumped down in that spot. Now he didn't know what to do, so when the ball was snapped, he just ran straight ahead. He ran into your ball carrier! If we had had 11 men on the field, we would have been in goal line out, and you would have won the ball game 21-20!" So you can make all the preparations you want, and you don't always know how you win or lose a ball game.

Coach Bryant had the great knack of knowing how to win under all conditions. I used to hear him say all the time that you had to be able to win even when you're losing. Coach Bryant knew that when that game was over, all the writers would be in my locker room — they weren't going to be in his. I must have had a hundred or so writers doing interviews in there, and here comes the manager.

He was hyperventilating saying, "Coach Bryant's coming in. Coach Bryant's coming in." So I looked at all the writers and said, "Y'all are going to have to excuse me — Coach

Bryant's coming in, and I'm sure he wants to talk to me about something." Then I looked at Coach Bryant and said, "Coach, did you want to see me?" He said, "No, I want to see your players. I've seen enough of you!" That's one of the reasons I wanted my team at that time to play Alabama. I wanted my players to be exposed to Coach Bryant as much as they could.

One other story about that particular game. We did joint press conferences. They sort of liked the idea of Coach Bryant and me sitting beside each other and doing these press conferences. Well I got to the press conference a little late, and I just came right from the practice field. I had my coaching gear on, and Coach Bryant was sitting over there dressed up the way he could really do. When I walked in he looked at me, and everything sort of stopped. He said, "I refuse to have my picture taken with anybody who looks like that!"

Well I came on in and sat down beside him, and nobody asked me anything. It was all Coach Bryant, Coach Bryant, Coach Bryant. Finally he said, "Somebody ask Bebes something, will ya?" Somebody asked me a little old something that didn't amount to anything, and then it was Coach Bryant, Coach Bryant. He said again, "Somebody ask Bebes something." Well when the press conference was over, they decided that they wanted to do it again the next day. So I'm saying to myself, "I'm going to upstage Coach Bryant if it's the last thing I do — I'm going to that press conference in a tux!"

So I took a tux to practice, knowing that he was practicing before me and he would get to the press conference a little before I got there. I put that tux on as soon as practice was over, and I took off for the press conference. When I walked in, everybody was surrounding Coach Bryant. He had a cowboy hat on, he had an open shirt with some kind of scarf around his neck, he had his feet crossed, and he he had boots on – and the boots had Texas Aggies on them! Not one soul noticed that I had a tux on when I walked in!

It would be difficult to find a person who was closer to Coach Bryant and the Alabama athletic scene than sports information honcho Charley Thornton. A very popular guy all the way across the SEC and with many national media people, Charley was at the side of Coach Bryant for 14 years of his television show.

CHARLEY THORNTON:

During the summer of 1968, Frank Taylor called and asked me to meet him at Joe Namath's Tuscaloosa restaurant for lunch. Frank was the owner of the Frank Taylor Advertising Agency in Birmingham, and among other things, he produced and directed the *Bear Bryant TV Show*. When Frank arrived, he leaned over and whispered that he wanted me to host the *Bear Bryant TV Show*. "All I want you to do is open and close the show and get out of the way," he said.

I told him I didn't want to do anything that might hurt John Forney, who had been doing the show for years. "Don't worry about that," Frank said. "John is leaving the show because of his business interests, and he agrees with me and Coach Bryant that you should be on the show." I can tell you I was happy and a little scared. I had watched the show every week and felt that John and Coach had such a great relationship that it would be difficult to step in and fill John's shoes.

We never rehearsed or discussed with Coach Bryant what we were going to say or do on the show. We seemed to work better that way. As you know, he loved to "drop names" during the program, and it didn't matter if it was right in the middle of a big play.

"I saw Admiral Jackson from Mobile after the game yesterday, and he wanted to know why we didn't pass more. I told him it was because we were trying to win the damn game," Bryant said. He would talk about a letter he had received from a sick friend, and he wanted to wish him a speedy recovery, but most of all he enjoyed seeing his former players. He really got a kick out of them coming by the dressing room after the game, win or lose.

Surely you remember his famous "BINGO" saying. Anytime a Crimson Tide player made a big hit on defense, you could count on "BINGO" being heard.

He used the show to do a lot of coaching. The Alabama players would all be around television sets in Tuscaloosa watching, and I've heard there was a lot of razzing among players when Coach would say, "No, no, that's not the way we taught you to tackle," or "I know Jimmy's Mother and Father are proud of the way he improved his schoolwork" without any reference to his football ability.

The coaches used to watch, for sure. At the end of the program he used to show pictures of players who had played well and of a few coaches who had the game responsibility. Maybe the viewing public didn't realize it, but if a coach didn't get his picture on, he dug down and worked a little harder the next week!

During my years on the staff, Alabama won five national football championships and had a shot at as many as seven more, only to be outvoted in the final polls or to lose in a bowl game. Bama was on the top of the mountain as far as college football was concerned, and "our little offering" as Coach Bryant called the TV show, was consistently rated the No. 1 syndicated TV show in the country, based on ratings.

One year when we came in for the first program of the year, Frank Taylor walked up to the set and told Coach that our show was only the second-rated sports show in the nation. Coach asked, "Who in the hell beat us?" Frank told him that the *Bart Starr Show* in Green Bay was first, and we were second. "Well that's okay, Bart's one of ours," Coach replied.

A lot of things happened on the show over a 14-year period, including a lot of good-natured ribbing by Ronnie Long, who worked at the TV station but worse, was an Auburn fan. While Ronnie was reluctant to do anything that might upset Coach Bryant, often he pulled a prank on me. At the start of each week's program, I opened by welcoming the viewers to the show, then reached up and opened a bag of Golden Flake potato chips or corn chips, then reached over and took a big swig of ice-cold Coca-Cola.

Ronnie put scotch tape on the top of the bag once, so when I attempted to pop the bag open, the bottom burst and the chips fell out all over the set. Another time he put a miniature of vodka in my Coke, and it was all I could do to keep from laughing when I tasted it and knew what he had done. I did have the good sense to ask for another Coke just like that one.

Another time a cigarette that Coach had been smoking during the commercial caught fire in an ashtray underneath our set. As we came back on the air, smoke started filling the air. My knee-jerk reaction was to reach over, pick up my Coca-Cola bottle, take a swig, and then pour Coke on the fire. It quickly went out. I'll never know why I took a drink of the

Coke before I tried to put out the small fire, but I did. I suppose because that's what I always did when I picked up the drink from the desk. As I was putting the bottle back on the table top, I happened to casually say to Coach Bryant, "Coach, that just shows that Coke is good for a lot of things."

My most memorable part of each season was in late October through the early part of November, when the bowl pairings were put together. Coach Bryant was the all-time national champ in putting together bowl game matchups, and usually he was able to position the Crimson Tide in the bowl game he wanted to play in with the opponent he wanted. He carried that much clout during those years. Those Sunday mornings or afternoons Coach Bryant would only talk to other coaches, and he would be wheeling and dealing trying to help his people who were coaching. This went on a lot at night, also, with calls coming to the house. My bride Doris loved to be "in the know" on bowl game pairings. It was an enjoyable time to be working for the "king-maker" of bowl games.

Having been a part of the *Bear Bryant TV Show* along with Maury Farrell and John Forney was a part of my life that forever will be remembered as perhaps the highlight of my professional career. Oh, for the good ol' years again.

Alabama's lessening power carried over into 1968 and ultimately into (by Tide standards) a catastrophic 1969. Losses in 1968 to Ole Miss (10-8) and Tennessee (10-9) bumped Bama from the SEC Championship run, but even more disheartening was a Gator Bowl performance against Missouri that resulted in a 35-10 annihilation of the Tide.

While the 1969 squad ignited the scoreboard with record-threatening point productions, the defense ebbed to a point of futility. Head Coach Bryant indeed nodded his head in dissatisfaction as the decade neared its conclusion. Only a 33-32 win over eventual Sugar Bowl Champion Ole Miss in the spectacular Scott Hunter-Archie Manning shootout at Legion Field thrilled Crimson Tide supporters.

SCOTT HUNTER:

Coach Bryant was struggling with two tasks: keeping up with the increasing second-half pace and trying to light a soggy cigarette, sometimes by the filtered end.

Ole Miss quarterback Archie Manning was facing a third and impossible situation, so Coach Bryant was giving me the usual what-to-do-next when Manning rolled out and completed a 40-yarder. Coach Bryant (never will I refer to him as Bear, or Bryant, or just Coach, and that's that) turned crimson, forgot the what-to-do-next, and charged by me hollering, "What coverage were we in?" Defensive coordinator Ken Donahue was shell-shocked and looked it.

His mumbled reply proved it. Coach Bryant fired him right then, right there. I turned to Jimmy Sharpe, running the offense on the sideline with side duty as my defender and protector from Coach Bryant's blowups and exclaimed, "He just fired Coach Donahue. Don't worry about it. He's already fired him twice."

Since 1969 maybe 150,000 people have told me they were there. Legion Field held about 72,000 or so. The rest were watching it on television with such intensity I guess they thought they were there.

Our ho-hum 14-7 halftime lead didn't foretell the second-half fireworks. We'd score and go up, then I'd go to the sideline and Jim Goostree and Sang Lyda would give me a cup of water. I'd look up, and we'd be behind.

I have a hundred memories of the second half. Here's one: We're up by 5, and they have a third-and-goal near our 5-yard line. Coach Bryant squeezes my arm and says "If we can hold 'em here, then I think..." Well before he finished I had the silliest thought. "Shoot," it flashed, "that's a gimme." As it passed my mind, Manning skipped untouched around right end for 6. I looked up, we were behind again.

Another memory: As the Rebels lined up for an extra point, Coach Bryant turned and roared, "Get Frankie McClendon in there." Frankie McClendon? McClendon had apparently been a good kick blocker, but he was on the 1964 team. Sharpe discreetly informed Coach Bryant that McClendon had been gone for five years. I'll forever remember Coach Bryant shaking his head and with a chagrined look, muttering "Aw, hell, I knew that!"

When we were down 32-27 and the quarter fading away, I strangely thought of the immortal Don Hutson standing in the pregame locker room with Coach Bryant. I remember thinking to myself, "That all-time great has come from California to see this game and his Rose Bowl teammate. Dammit, we just can't lose this game." Corny, it was, but it was 1969, and I believed it — and still do.

David Bailey, George Ranager, Bubba Sawyer, and others were catching everything, and I was throwing tight spiral strikes. Sure Archie was working on our secondary, but hey, I owned his.

Danny Ford, Charlie Ferguson, Kenny Wilder, Alvin Samples, and Richard Grammer wouldn't let them touch me. They knew it and began to blitz. It came down to this: Down 32-27, facing fourth and 18 at their 20, and the clock closing. If they get it back and score, it's over.

I called time-out and went over to ask Coach Bryant what he wanted to do. He began to growl at Sharpe, who began to yell into his headset at Steve Sloan in the press box. No answer. As the time-out expired, the referee was waving me back on the field, "Time's up, Alabama captain, commercial's over, let's play." I heard the familiar gravelly voice, "Run the best thing you've got." It was the best sideline advice I ever received.

"Red right, 56-Comeback-In," I called while looking into wide-eyed, sweaty faces of Ford, Ferguson, Grammer, and the rest. I followed up again with, "Watch out for the blitz!" as I glanced over at Ranager. If they come with them all, I was going to him. They came with them all!

One of Alabama's greatest football players then made one of his greatest plays, without the football or any prospect of getting it. Johnny Musso stepped up for his primary blitz assignment, the weak outside linebacker. Somehow he saw that Ole Miss had sprung one free up the middle. Musso forgot his less-of-a-threat linebacker, corkscrewed from his planted stance and into the legs of the getting-bigger-in-my-face rusher, and chopped him down 6 feet and a half-second from the game-winning sack.

Ranager was just into his plant, and all I saw was the 88 on his back as I let go before being drilled. We'd run it a thousand times, I knew where he'd be. George turned, came back, pulled in a low but accurate throw, scrambled away from the desperately grabbing Ole Miss defensive back, and rolled in to the EZ for the TD.

When I saw no signal for a TD, I got off my butt and started running in the direction of Ranager and the official. There was a flag on the ground. When I heard him say pass interference on the white, I started to say, "We'll take the..." The referee said, "Yeah, I know, you'll take the play," and he raised his hands for the TD.

Manning quickly drove the Rebs to a fourth-and-a-foot at our 35-yard-line. Another gimme? Nope, not this time. Paul Boschung slashed between the guard and center and torpedoed Manning for no gain.

We ran some off the clock, Frank Mann dropped an eight-iron punt on their 5-yard line, and the clock expired after Manning completed a long pass to Floyd Franks.

Archie had completed 33 of 52 for 436 yards, and he rushed for 104 more, for 540 yards. I was 22 of 29 for 300 yards. Most important, we won.

I received a letter the next week that read: "They voted me Back of the Week, but you deserved it, you won." It was signed: Archie Manning. It's the classiest gesture and compliment I've ever seen or had.

Oh, you should have seen Coach Bryant and Don Hutson grinning at each other in that loud, celebrating, hot locker room. And that congrats kiss from that wrung-out cheerleader, Debbie Thomas (now Hunter), gave me a grin, too.

In the closing seconds of the game, Manning completed a pass to Floyd Franks that reached the Tide 35. Franks was tackled in bounds, and he tried to signal time-out to the official who just looked at him and watched the final seconds tick away. Franks said he was miffed at the official until years later he found out that the Rebs had no time-outs left, and thus the inaction of the official.

After that, it was all downhill-losses at Vanderbilt, Tennessee, LSU, Auburn, and Colorado in the Liberty Bowl. Needless to say, there was muttering aplenty among the Alabama faithful, Paul Bryant included. On his television show he said not to write him letters, he was aware of what was going on. As an alumnus, he, Paul Bryant, was not happy with the football situation or the coach, Paul Bryant, and he intended to do something about it.

The record books illustrate, despite the spiral downward at the end of the sixties, Alabama's rule of the college world. Overall the Tide was 90-16-4, with three national championship trophies on its mantelpiece and Bryant named Coach of the Decade.

"Coach Bryant pays me to have players on the practice field not in the training room feeling sorry for themselves."

— Coach Jim Goostree's explanation to a reporter who remarked that Alabama's training facilities were not as large or plush as the other SEC schools

"We were in the first meeting with Coach Bryant, and he told us that in four years if we believed in his plan and dedicated ourselves to being the best we could be, we would be national champions. He was right."
— Billy Neighbors remembering Coach Bryant in 1958

"They play like it is a sin to give up a point."
— Paul Bryant before the 1962 Sugar Bowl talking about his defense, which had yielded only 22 points during the regular season

"No, man, I majored in journalism. It was easier."
— Joe Namath responding to a reporter who asked him if he majored in basketweaving at Alabama

"Give all the credit to Ray Perkins, Dennis Homan and the offensive line. All I had to do was get the ball near them. With receivers like that you throw it out there and when the line gives you as much time as I have, how can you miss? Everything I've got belongs to my teammates."
— Kenny Stabler after leading Alabama to a 34-7 win over Nebraska in the 1967 Sugar Bowl

"It's the greatest football team I've ever been associated with. It's the greatest football team I ever saw."
— Coach Bryant on his 1966 team

"Coach, don't feel sorry for me. I have had a wonderful 29 years."
— Pat Trammell talking to Coach Stallings in 1968

"This is the saddest day of my life."
— Coach Bryant on hearing the news Pat Trammell had died in Birmingham in December 1968

"George Bush could walk in the door and it wouldn't bother me because once you've worked for Coach Bryant, you can handle anything."
— Linda Knowles, longtime University of Alabama athletic department secretary

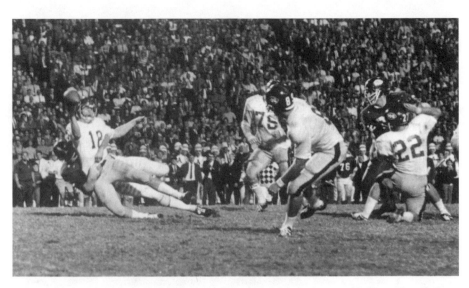

Alabama 33, Ole Miss 32, right before halftime. QB Archie Manning being tackled by unidentified UA player.

Benny Nelson

1967 Alabama - Auburn — Kenny Stabler's touchdown run.

Jerry Duncan's (77) halfback catch.

Coach Paul Bryant and Coach
Dude Hennessey.

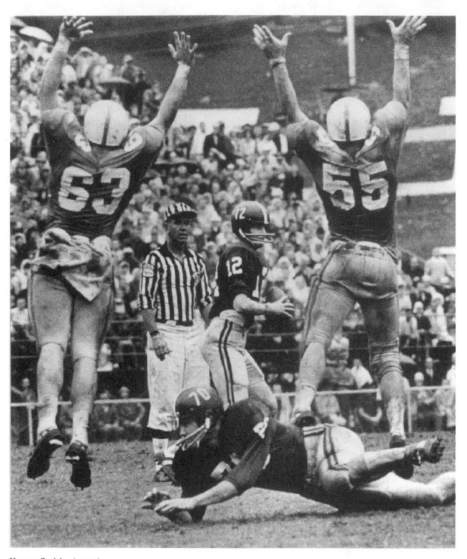

Kenny Stabler in action.

THE SEVENTIES
Reassessment and Rebirth

The dawning of the 1970s paralleled the conclusion of the sixties, not only in the turbulence of societal discontent but also on the hallowed playing fields of the Alabama football team. Athletic Director Paul Bryant admitted candidly he was displeased with the performance of his football coach. His self-critique of himself and his beloved program boded incisive decisions needed to be made — and quickly.

After another 6-5-1 season, culminating in a 24-24 tie with Oklahoma in the Bluebonnet Bowl, Bryant was seen doodling on a pad en route home from Houston. A cursory glance at his pad revealed the venerable coach was searching for a more productive direction for his 1971 team, specifically a way to control the tempo of a game and strengthen his defensive troops. An uneventful spring session for the offense portended another less-than-average fall. Renowned sportswriter Alf Van Hoose remembers that trying time for Coach Bryant.

ALF VAN HOOSE:

The prevailing talk on the streets was that Bryant had grown too old for the job and his mastery had faded into a memory of the glory days of the sixties. Paul Bryant was never inflexible when it came to changing with the times, and that's just one of the marvelous traits that separated him from the ordinary. He was a liberal thinker when it came to football and the motivation of people, and when he told me in 1971 that he was determined to move Alabama back to its accustomed slot in college football, I never doubted he would do it.

By early summer Bryant indeed dramatically turned a new direction, deciding to scratch his pro passing attack and instituting the wishbone. A telephone call from Bryant to Texas head coach Darrell Royal, whose Longhorns were trampling opponents with its option offense, and the subsequent meetings with his staff, forever altered the flow of the Tide and college football for the 1970s.

Alabama was set to travel to Los Angeles, Caliifornia, to meet top-rated Southern California for a Friday night matchup. The date was September 10,

1971, a day before Bryant's 58th birthday. Bama entered the game as a double-digit underdog, and who could ignore the oddsmakers since the mighty Trojans of John McKay had trounced Bama 42-21 a year earlier in Birmingham. It would be an epic evening for Alabama football, one of those rare moments that will forever be suspended in time.

One of the coaches who masterminded the upset was the ever-popular Dude Hennessey.

DUDE HENNESSEY:

There are no words that can describe Paul Bryant's unique talents, but I would be remiss in not taking you back to 1969 and 1970 when we were coming off 6-5 seasons and folks were writing off Coach Bryant. Our defense wasn't very good, and we had been throwing the ball 30 to 50 times a game on offense. I honestly believe Coach Bryant would have resigned after the 1971 season if we hadn't turned it around.

During our summer high school clinic in 1971, Coach met with Darrell Royal to learn all he could about the wishbone. When Coach called a secret meeting with his staff to tell us we were going to the wishbone and we were going to keep it quiet until the night we played Southern Cal, there was no question the commitment to return to the top prevailed in the room. He closed the meeting by saying, "We're going to sink or swim with the wishbone." We knew it was time to swim.

We were determined to have an Alabama defense again — I mean a tough, hard-nosed unit that punished offenses. We hadn't done that in quite a while. People remember the switch to the wishbone, but they forget the recommitment on defense. Coach Bryant knew a controlled offense would do what he wanted done — win games.

Sworn to secrecy, our August practices proceeded as planned with no one being aware of the change. Even when the Skywriters came to Tuscaloosa for practice, our squad practiced out of the split-back set.

I've never been around a more intense team than the one that went to Los Angeles. Coach Bryant said a team shared the same heartbeat — and on a Friday night in Los Angeles, we all did. No one knew we were going to unveil the wishbone, especially Southern Cal, a team that had thrashed us 42-21 the year before. At the Coliseum, both teams came down the same ramp, and our players were quiet. USC came out for its pregame walk, and their players were in a festive mood, talking loud, with their radios blaring.

We won the toss, drove the length of the field, and Johnny Musso scored a touchdown. We moved ahead 17-0, and won it 17-10. The victory symbolized the reemergence of Alabama football to the level it had enjoyed in the 1960s. We went 11-0, and even though we lost to a great Nebraska team in the Orange Bowl, Alabama was back — mainly because the Chief had made a strategic maneuver that defied logic.

Terry Davis, the deft quarterback, whose sleight-of-hand with the ball and quick feet ignited the wishbone, and Johnny Musso, the gifted All-American runner, also recall that special moment in Tide history.

TERRY DAVIS:

Going to the wishbone, obviously suited my abilities best. We did a great job of hiding the fact that we were going to the wishbone. Whenever anyone seemed to speculate we might be making some changes, we were able to disguise what we did in practice, and no one ever suspected.

When we went to the West Coast to play Southern California, they had no idea we were coming out in the wishbone. When I think back to that night, I think it was a monumental evening for me as well as for the Alabama program. I was a scared little country boy from Bogalusa, Louisiana, when I got off that bus at the Los Angeles Coliseum. After we won, I certainly gained a lot of confidence in myself, and the team did in itself.

What I remember most about the game was our offensive front, people like John Hannah, just pushing those guys back 3 or 4 yards a lick. There was so much daylight between me and the offensive line that we were gaining 2 or 3 yards before we even saw a USC player.

"Johnny Musso typified our program. He just chewed up opponents, wanted to kill them off, with his running and blocking. He always gave total effort which makes him one of my favorite former players, and he did it without regard to the punishment he was taking."
— Coach Jim Goostree talking about the Alabama star in 1971

JOHNNY MUSSO:

The first time we learned Coach Bryant had decided to switch to the wishbone offense was when we returned for August practice. Talk about top secret! It was. We had run the wishbone in 1970 but only on short yardage and goal line situations, and it was not really a true wishbone.

Coach Bryant told us we could be good with our old pro-type offense or great with our new wishbone attack. We were shocked with this radical change. We were coming off a 6-5 and a 6-5-1 season, and Coach Bryant had decided for us to return Alabama to its accustomed spot in college football. He had to do something radical.

Terry Davis was our quarterback. He was an outstanding athlete, super quick with the special gifts to run an option attack. In my opinion he was the greatest wishbone quarterback Alabama ever had and maybe the best one anybody ever had. He was just perfect for the wishbone.

The change really made us even more intense for our season opener against No. 1 Southern California in the Los Angeles Coliseum. It was a Friday night game, and I remember how well prepared we were mentally to play against USC. They had beaten us 42-21 the year before in Birmingham, and I don't know if we were out for revenge or just for redemption of what they had done to us.

On our first drive, we went the length of the field for a touchdown. I think Terry made a key third-down run to sustain the drive, and I scored a touchdown that put us ahead 7-0. I think that touchdown not only set the tone for that game but for our entire season — perhaps for the entire wishbone era of Alabama football. Our confidence level skyrocketed when we scored, and whatever doubts we may have had vanished.

I remember practicing the night before we flew out to California. It was a Wednesday practice since the game was played on Friday night, and Coach Bryant wanted us to work under the lights because the game was going to be played at night. There was a pep rally on the quad that night, and since we were too busy practicing to be at the pep rally, all of the students decided to come over to the practice field. Coach Bryant had wanted everything so secretive for the game and to keep Southern Cal from having any hint we were installing the wishbone, that he had ordered a wall of tarps put up around the practice field. The students tore down the tarps and came on the field and watched the practice. You could feel the electricity growing, and we could sense the excitement of the students when they realized they were in on the "big secret." The players also sensed their enthusiasm, and it fired us up even more.

The Southern Cal game was the most exciting I ever played in during my Alabama career. At one point I came out with an injured finger. Coach (Jim) Goostree was flexing it around, and my running back coach, John David Crow, came over and asked Coach Goostree how bad I was hurt because they needed me back in the game. I knew how badly Coach Bryant wanted the game because he came over to check me out, too. He rarely, if ever, did that. Coach Goostree said, "Aw, he's only got a hurt finger." And Coach Crow repeated that to Coach Bryant, who told them to get me back in the game.

We went ahead 17-0, but Southern Cal, being the gifted and great team they were, rallied back to make it 17-10. That was the halftime score and the final score. Both teams made some huge plays defensively in the second half. I remember Robin Parkhouse repeatedly outfighting bigger USC linemen to make tackles. It was a gratifying experience to win that game. It was truly a big one.

Alabama's wishbone debut season concluded with a regular season 31-7 romp over Auburn on national television. Legendary Crimson Tide trainer-administrator Jim Goostree, who served at the University from 1957-93, remembers events leading up to that historic showdown at Legion Field.

JIM GOOSTREE:

Most people remember the significance of that game because it is the only time both Alabama and Auburn entered the contest unbeaten. We were 10-0 and Auburn was 9-0. A couple of nights before the game, Auburn's Pat Sullivan had been announced as the Heisman Trophy winner. I don't think we needed any additional motivation, and I don't think that played any part in the game.

The biggest factor from our end of it was the status of our All-American running back

Johnny Musso. He had been hurt pretty badly in the LSU game, spraining a big toe joint and suffering damage to the arch of his foot. At the time it didn't seem possible that he would be able to play.

He underwent therapy three times a day. We started with some ice treatments, cold-water immersions, and massages. We also installed a metatarsal bar on all of his shoes to elevate his toe so it would not bend. At that time Johnson and Johnson had a relatively new product called orthoplast, a plastic that would mold to the form of the body. We used it like a body splint on his foot.

The week of the game he still had a tendency to walk on the side of his foot, which indicated it still had not healed. It worried me because of the damage it could do to his lower back.

To make a long story short, he tried to run on Thursday before the game, and you could tell he was in a lot of pain. He didn't look functional at all. But I had no doubt, never did, that knowing the type of person he was, that he would endure the pain and play against Auburn. We strapped his foot and arch to keep it in a rigid postition with the orthoplast splint.

His participation in the game was a demonstration of want-to and guts. He knew the importance of the game to the University of Alabama, the football team, and to himself. There have been many others who had a lot of determination, but to me Johnny Musso symbolized what a barrel of guts on a football field meant. For him to go out there that day and play was amazing, but what he accomplished was even more amazing. He rushed the ball 33 times for 167 yards and scored 2 touchdowns. We won the battle of unbeatens 31-7.

"I know one thing. I'd rather die now than to have died this morning and missed this game."
— Coach Bryant after Alabama's 31-7 win over unbeaten Auburn in 1971

Almost forgotten in the transformation of the Alabama football fortunes in the early 1970s was the significant, and in Bryant's words, "long overdue" integration of the team. Dock Rhone and several other black athletes had attempted to break the color barrier by walking on back in the late 1960s, and Wilbur Jackson's signing in December 1969 forever set in motion the razing of the segregated structure.

The next September at Legion Field, Southern California's Sam Cunningham ran all over the Crimson Tide, creating a quip attributed to Coach Bryant, "Sam Cunningham did more for integration in one night in Alabama than Martin Luther King accomplished in all of his life." Bryant later said a former assistant made the remark. It wasn't knock on Dr. King but rather a tribute to how much Alabamians admired and appreciated their football. In essence it paved the way for more blacks to follow and succeed Jackson at the Capstone.

While Jackson was serving as a backup in the wishbone backfield in 1971, the first black starter came to Alabama via East Arizona State Junior College —

John Mitchell. Actually it took a rather odd set of circumstances for Mitchell to arrive at Alabama.

Bryant was visiting with his old friend USC head coach John McKay at a hotel in Houston, and along with them was one of Bryant's cronies from his Texas A&M days, ironically named Johnny Mitchell. Coach Bryant was showing McKay a recruiting list of prospects on the West Coast, and the USC coach mistakenly remarked, "The best one out there is not even on your list, and he has the same name as your buddy here and is from Mobile."

McKay planned to sign Mobile's Mitchell, but Coach Bryant immediately went to work. He was on the phone with Mitchell two hours later, recruiting him to Alabama. Not only would Mitchell enroll at the Capstone, but he would become the first black starter, All-American, and captain for the Crimson Tide.

JOHN MITCHELL:

I was interested in Alabama because I had grown up in Mobile and had followed the Crimson Tide football, just like every other kid did back then. All the kids loved Alabama football and were aware of all the success the team had enjoyed under Coach Bryant during the 1960s.

I think the thing that impressed me most, or at least left the most lasting impression on me, was how big Coach Bryant actually was. When I went to Tuscaloosa on my official visit, I was surprised at how big a man he was. He had huge hands that just wrapped around mine. He was a real gentleman to me and my mother and father. I knew I wanted an opportunity to play for the Tide.

Wilbur was the first black signed at Alabama, and I was the first one to start. Coach Bryant and the staff treated all of us fairly, and I don't think any of us really thought about a race issue.

We started my junior year off against Southern California in the Los Angeles Coliseum, and I had moved into the starting lineup. There had been a couple of injuries, and I was at right end. It was quite an emotion-packed night for our entire team. Alabama had been down the past couple of years, and USC had beaten us pretty soundly in 1970.

My first game at Alabama, I guess still ranks as one of the high points in the school's football history. I remember we were expected to lose. My attitude that was I was going to try as hard as I could and hope that the team and as I could play well enough to compete. We won it 17-10, and for all intents and purposes, Alabama was back as a national power.

To be really honest, I had a much better junior year than I did a senior season, so I was fortunate enough to make some All-American teams in 1972. Whatever success I had, I owe it to Coach Bryant. He was such a great motivator. He taught us that all players have peaks and valleys, and you'd have them in life. Coach taught us you could have more peaks if you worked hard and dedicated yourself to being better than average. I attribute everything I have accomplished in football, both as a player and as a coach, to Coach Bryant.

Being named captain was the biggest honor I ever received as a player, much more so than being chosen All-American. To be honest with you, I didn't even attend the meeting when they voted on who would be captains of the team. About 5:30 that night I was walking into the dorm, and one of the players told me I had been elected defensive captain. I didn't believe him — I thought he was joking. Then Coach Jack Rutledge told me it was true and said Coach Bryant was mad at me because I hadn't attended the meeting so I'd better get my fanny over to his office and talk to him.

It is special for any player to be elected captain by his teammates. That's why it was my greatest honor because my peers, not the media, chose me for that type of recognition. For my teammates to have that much faith and trust in me certainly made me proud and is something I will always cherish.

Even a humbling loss to a superior Nebraska team in the national championship showdown in the Orange Bowl hardly dampened the intensified optimism that Alabama was rolling again. In 1972 Alabama claimed another SEC title, but an inexcusable loss to Auburn in the blocked-punt game haunted an otherwise outstanding year. The sun did shine brightly on the Tide, though, on the third Saturday in October when Alabama rallied for a stunning 17-10 win over Tennessee in Knoxville. Defensive end Mike Dubose was one of the heroes that afternoon, and he vividly remembers that improbable win.

MIKE DUBOSE:

Tennessee led the entire game, and it was 10-3 with less than 3 minutes to go. Terry Davis completed a long pass to Wayne Wheeler, Steve Bisceglia broke a run to the Tennessee 2-yard line, and Wilbur Jackson scored to make it 10-9.

The next sequence really won us the game. Coach Bryant decided not to go for 2 but elected to kick instead. He knew we had the wind to our back and Tennessee would be forced to throw the football. I think he felt confident we would get the football back and have an opportunity to win the game. Coach Bryant had the courage to make that decision, and it was the right one. We won because of it.

After we tied it at 10-10, we kicked off and had Tennessee backed up (on the Vols' 12). Their quarterback, Condredge Holloway, started scrambling, and I reached out to sack him and knocked the ball loose. John Mitchell recovered it up field, and one play later Terry Davis ran about 21 yards for the winning touchdown.

That win proved to us what Coach Bryant had told us and preached to us: If you keep playing good defense and hang tough in the fourth quarter, something good is going to happen to you. We had the type team that really never thought it was going to lose, and I doubt if any of us thought we were going to lose — even though I'm not sure how any of us figured out how we would win it!

Some of the truly unsung heroes of Crimson Tide football efforts over the years are the student trainers and managers. These young men accomplish back-breaking tasks in unusually short time frames and, during fall and spring training, routinely work 50 and 60 hour weeks. I recall being on a bus headed for an enemy stadium right after the NCAA's edict that prevents scholarshiped players from being occupied with football more than 20 hours a week during the season. The obviously weary student manager sitting by me sadly said, "I just wish they would come out with a shorter week for us, but there's no chance of that."

Kirk Wood, who ran Host Communications' University of Alabama operations for three years before opening Collegiate Sports Partners, was one of a number of outstanding young men who served in the capacity of student manager during the Bryant era.

KIRK WOOD:

There are now NCAA rules and regulations about how many hours an athlete can participate in a sport. When we all get together, one of the things we laugh about is it's too bad they didn't apply that rule to student managers because I don't think we would ever have been able to complete our jobs. And I'm sure the managers today probably spend pretty close to the number of hours we did.

One year I kept up with it during the football season, and each of our managers invested at least 70 to 80 hours a week doing the things you had to do as a manager. Under Coach Bryant it was considered a very important job, and it was fairly well organized, but we were left with the responsibility of making sure all the equipment and administrative activities happened. That meant we loaded the trucks, we drove the trucks, we ordered the drinks and the ice — actually they were ordered by the University, but we had to make sure that they were in there and all those things happened.

So for a road trip, we spent 2 or 3 hours on Wednesday night rechecking equipment and cleaning helmets and items — because after Wednesday you wouldn't have a contact practice. Thursday night about 3 or 4 hours were spent literally packing the truck. Then sometimes — depending on how far away the game was — a manager and Mr. Willie Meadows, or a manager and a guy named Davis would drive the truck, leaving either Thursday night right after the truck was packed, if it was a distant trip, or 3 or 4 o'clock Friday morning so they would be there and have the truck unloaded when the team got in to practice on Friday afternoon.

As managers we took our jobs very seriously and probably were more concerned about keeping the football team happy and Coach Bryant happy than we were about our grades and academics, which the NCAA didn't seem to care about.

The managers had different jobs. I was not head manager in 1972, but one of my jobs was to go to the locker room when there were only 3 minutes to go in the game and make sure certain things had been completed — make sure the door was unlocked and open, the showers were turned on so they would be heated and hot water coming out, get out the towels and the ice and drinks, clean things up from halftime, and so forth. It was a real important thing, because nobody wanted the game to be over and the team to be standing there wondering where the guy was with the key to the door. So you would always leave at least 3 or 4 minutes before the end of the game.

When we played Tennessee at Tennessee in 1972, Terry Davis was the quarterback. We had a great team that year, but we had a very bad day that day. When I went into the locker room, we were losing 10-3, and I wanted to be doggone sure all my stuff was done correctly because there wouldn't be a lot of happy guys coming in the door and I didn't want them to be upset. I wanted it to be as pleasant an experience as possible so I could drive home in peace. So I had the showers running and was moving trunks and getting everything ready. I could hear the roars of the crowd, but I didn't know what was going on because I was back under Neyland Stadium. All of a sudden the game was over, and the guys were coming in. I was expecting some real sadness, but they were yelling and screaming, and whooping and hollering, and jumping up and down.

Coach Goostree (the Tennessee game was always a big one for him and Coach Donahue) is climbing up on the trunk to do his traditional Tennessee trunk dance. Everybody's going crazy, and I couldn't figure out what was going on.

Another thing you also did as a manager for the Tennessee game was to have cigars in the trunk. Coach Bryant handed out victory cigars when we beat Tennessee — it was the only game he would do that. Of course, the cigars were buried deep in the trunk because I sure didn't think we were going to need them. One of the head managers came in trying to make me understand that I needed to get the cigars and get them very quickly. I finally got someone to tell me that we won, but it wasn't until the next day when I watched Coach Bryant's TV show that I could figure out how we won.

The other side to that story is that in the later part of that same year, we had a very famous game with Auburn where they blocked two of our punts. And it was the same story again — I was in the locker room with just a few minutes to go, we had had one punt blocked, but we were still beating Auburn. And we had played pretty well, so I said to myself that we would beat them again.

I was standing there with a big smile on my face waiting for the players to come into the locker room under Legion Field, and people were throwing things at their lockers and not saying pleasant things, and there were a lot of unhappy faces. Again, I had to grab somebody and ask what happened, and they told me that Auburn had blocked the punt. I said, "Yeah, I know — I was there when they blocked the punt. But what happened?" They said that Auburn had blocked *another* punt. Again, it was Sunday or Monday before I had a chance to see the film of what happened.

So it was interesting to be the manager. You never really knew what went on during the game. You were busy doing a lot of different things, and you never had a chance to really understand, except by looking periodically at the scoreboard to see what was going on. A little while after that 1972 season, we began putting a radio in the locker room so we could listen to the play-by-play and at least have some indication of how to receive the team when they came in.

Alabama's series of postseason frustrations continued to torment Bryant and his teams through the early 1970s. Practically invincible in the regular season, bowls were anything but rewarding experiences for an 8-year period.

Particularly excruciating were extremely close back-to-back losses to Notre Dame in the 1973 Sugar Bowl (the game was contested December 31, 1973) and the 1975 Orange Bowl, a pair of setbacks that wiped out perfect seasons and prevented universal acclamation of the perennial goal of the Tide to secure the national title. Both the 1973 and 1974 teams were 11-0 in the regular season, but while Irish eyes may have been smiling, Bama fans were crying crimson tears after those 24-23 and 13-11 losses.

Richard Todd, a sophomore in 1973 and the backup to starting quarterback Gary Rutledge, remembers the Sugar Bowl that turned sour, and Ronnie Robertson, a linebacker on the '74 team, recalls the Miami showdown.

RICHARD TODD:

The 1973 Sugar Bowl against Notre Dame occurred in my sophomore season. We had already won the UPI National Championship going into the game because at that time they cast their final vote before the bowl games.

I guess I remember the excitement of the game as much as anything. Gary Rutledge was our starting quarterback, and I split time with him. I did score our final touchdown, which put us ahead 23-21 in the fourth quarter on a halfback pass from Mike Stock. The play was one Coach Bryant used every few years, and usually when he called it, it worked. I just pitched the ball to Mike, and he ran to his right. I ran to the left, and it worked effectively for the touchdown. I think it was about 25 or 26 yards.

It was one of those games where we never seemed to be able to get momentum. We went ahead 7-6, and on the next kickoff, they ran it back for a touchdown. While those plays were big, the pivotal play came late in the game when we had them backed up on our goal line. It was third and eight. They ran out of a tight formation, a running formation, with two tight ends. They made a gutsy call, a play action deep pass to the tight end, Robin Weber, and their quarterback Tom Clements made a great throw to get them a first down, and they ran the clock out.

It was a heartbreaking loss, but what made it worse was when we watched the films of the pass from the end zone. Leroy Cook, our great defensive end, actually was blitzing on the play, and he tripped coming through. No one touched him. He still hit Clements just when he released the ball. If Leroy hadn't tripped, he would have gotten a safety, and we would have won the game.

RONNIE ROBERTSON:

Alabama's 1975 Orange Bowl press guide says, "Alabama's Orange Bowl Training Plans: The Crimson Tide planned to return to the practice field on Monday, December 3rd, to begin working on its plans against Notre Dame. Final exams in mid-December made it necessary to have a late starting date. The Tide will train in Tuscaloosa until Monday, December 30th, when it will fly to Miami and hold a 4 p.m. workout. Bama also will work at 4 p.m. on December 31st, both times at the Orange Bowl Stadium. No player interviews will be allowed in Miami."

So you can see that Coach Bryant had us pretty well confined to the Tuscaloosa campus until the last moment. And once we got to Miami, there were going to be no player interviews. He didn't want us having any publicity or joining in any of the hoopla that went along with the traditional bowl trips.

Word had gotten back to us in Tuscaloosa that Notre Dame had gone down a week early and they were on the beach, enjoying the sunshine and pretty girls. We were in Tuscaloosa practicing. But we were not questioning why we weren't down in Miami. We were just intent because we had all been in the game the year before, the Sugar Bowl, when they beat us by a point. So we had our minds set that we were going down there and beat Notre Dame. Whatever it took to do it, we were willing to pay the price.

We didn't play particularly well in the Orange Bowl, especially early in the game when we got behind 13-0. Actually Notre Dame missed a field goal, and we would have gotten the ball back, but we were offsides and they ended up getting a touchdown out of that sequence. We cut the lead to 13-3 at the half, and in the fourth quarter we got back in it when Richard Todd hit Russ Schamun for a touchdown. We went for 2, and George Pugh scored the conversion to make it 13-11. That was the final score.

Coach Bryant, like all of us, was very disappointed that we had lost the game. He told us after the game to hold our heads high, show our class, show our pride, we had nothing to be ashamed of. It was sort of like we had lost the game, but we didn't get beat.

For whatever reasons during my years at Alabama, we didn't play our best in the bowl games. We were 43-1 in the regular season and 0-4 in bowl games. Coach Bryant took the blame himself for the losses saying he hadn't prepared us well, but everyone knew that wasn't the case. If there was a problem in the 1975 Orange Bowl, it may have been we were a little tired and mentally we were trying to overcome the albatross of losing all the bowl games before this one. I think we were a little tight going in and made some mental mistakes early that ultimately cost us the game. It was also Ara Parseghian's last game at Notre Dame, and that certainly didn't hurt their motivation any.

Sylvester Croom, who played for the Crimson Tide during the 1974 season and was a Tide coach until 1986, remembers Coach Bryant from an All-American's perspective.

SYLVESTER CROOM:

The biggest thing when you play for Coach Bryant are the lessons, the things he said over and over again. When you're that age and he's telling you about discipline, he's telling you about hard work, he's making you work hard, he's talking about cooperation, and having guts and hanging in there when it gets tough. You hear it over and over again, but you really don't understand it.

Finally, about your junior year, maybe you start to relate it to what's happening on the football field. But you don't really understand until you start making house payments, you get on the job and you lose a job, you get in a situation where you don't know where your next check is coming from, you're having problems with your kids or your wife or things are just going tough in general. That's when you find out what he was really talking about.

To me, that's what the goal line stand represents. You've got your back against the wall, and you've got two choices: You hang in there tough and get the job done or you quit. Once you quit, you die. So many times those lessons have come back to me. It's those lessons that you learn while playing for Coach Bryant that you remember when the going gets tough. You always remember, if I did it one time, I can do it again.

Very few of Coach Bryant's teams matched up with other teams physically, but they always played better than they were capable of. I think one of the great things he did was to get individuals to sacrifice their own egos for the good of the team. He'd get them so centered on one goal that they were willing to literally lay their lives on the line.

Coach Bryant was the central figure of it all. Either you did things out of fear of him or to prove to him that you were better than what he thought. How can a man affect so many different personalities in that way? He was the only man I knew that could kick you in the behind and make you like it.

After playing a couple of different positions, I dodged playing center for two full years, and that was the only regret that I have about my career at Alabama. It wasn't that I didn't want to play center, but I thought by moving to center that I was a failure at the other things I was trying to do. But Coach Bryant called me in one day and asked me if I would consider playing center. That's something I always appreciated. He didn't say I had to move. He said he felt that it would be good for me and it would be good for the team. When we got through talking, I asked him one question, "Coach Bryant, do you think I can play center and be good at it?" He said, "Yes, I do." I said, "That's good enough for me."

While Bryant no doubt had a legion of friends, one he entrusted and confided with frequently was Aruns Callery, a member of the Sugar Bowl Committee. After the celebrated Sugar Bowl contest with Notre Dame, Bryant growled to all who dared to listen that he had played the game in New Orleans and not in the Orange Bowl for one reason: to support his friend Aruns Callery, who had been beset with personal problems and had been treated unceremoniously by some of his peers.

"I have to think about what's best for the rest of the conference."
— Coach Paul Bryant telling his his close friend and Sugar Bowl official Aruns Callery that Alabama would vote for an SEC tieup with the bowl in 1975

Bryant's unyielding loyalty to Callery dated back to the Bear's days at Kentucky. Callery recalls some of the more intricate behind-the-scenes activities that molded much of the bowl dealings during those glorious days of the 1970s.

ARUNS CALLERY:

My friendship with Paul Bryant dates back to his days with the University of Kentucky, and I am lucky enough to say that over the years we became closer than brothers. I have been fortunate enough to know some of the most powerful individuals in the world, but none matched Paul in charisma and talent. He was the best leader I ever knew.

There are numerous poignant moments I will never be able to forget involving Coach Bryant and his Alabama teams, including a Sugar Bowl Alabama didn't play in and some they did. During 1971 both Alabama and Auburn were unbeaten and headed for a showdown Thanksgiving weekend. The Sugar Bowl already had a commitment from Oklahoma, also unbeaten at the time and destined to play unbeaten Nebraska on Thanksgiving Day.

We apparently had some miscommunication among our members because I was assigned to try to lock Alabama up for a match with Oklahoma. I was with Paul, and we talked about the Sugar Bowl game, which would have been a rematch of the previous year's Bluebonnet Bowl. Alabama and Oklahoma had tied 24-24. Well Paul committed to play in the Sugar Bowl. He felt it would afford Alabama its best opportunity of winning the national title because Oklahoma was hosting Nebraska that year and I guess he felt the homefield advantage would be the difference in the game. Of course, ultimately, it didn't matter because Nebraska won.

Anyway, I was elated to get the commitment from Alabama and felt we had an opportunity to have a national title game. But while I was getting a commitment from Coach Bryant, another one of our members was getting one from Coach (Shug) Jordan at Auburn, and when I called to relay the news about Alabama, I was told Auburn was already a lock.

You don't know how difficult it was for me to call Paul and tell him the Sugar Bowl already had a deal and it was with Auburn. To be perfectly candid, I'm not much of a drinker, but I had a stiff one before I called him and told him the news. There was a long pause on the phone, and he told me, "You go back and tell those Sugar Bowl people that Alabama is going to beat the hell out of Auburn and they picked the wrong team." He was right, too. Alabama beat Auburn 31-7. Unfortunately, both the Sugar and Orange Bowls turned out to be anticlimatic with Nebraska and Oklahoma both winning easily over Alabama and Auburn.

Before the 1975 season, I was with Paul. He told me point-blank that if he had a decent team he wanted to play in the Sugar Bowl because it was going to be the first one ever held in the Louisiana Superdome. When he said something he meant it, and I knew Alabama was going to be an awfully good team that year, but it didn't start off that way. Missouri upset Alabama on Labor Day Night in a nationally televised game. After the game I was with Paul, and he said it looked like we'd have to get another team because Alabama wasn't good enough to go to any bowl.

It was the only loss for the Tide that year, and by season's end, Alabama was 10-1 and headed for a matchup with Joe Paterno's Penn State squad. You know Paul was often accused of making the bowl matchups, and to say he didn't cast a large shadow would be a lie. He respected Joe and wanted to play Penn State, figuring it would be a heck of a matchup between the premier powers in the East and the South. Alabama won 13-6 in a hard-fought contest, and it broke a string of losing bowl appearances by Alabama that dated back to 1967. I remember Paul didn't wear his hat that night, and when the press asked him about it after the game, he told them his mother always told him never to wear a hat indoors. Paul wanted to play in the first Sugar Bowl in the Superdome, and he did.

The Orange Bowl had signed a contract with the Big-8 champion, and there was pressure for the Sugar Bowl to try to do the same with the SEC. Alabama was the dominant factor in college football at that time, and it really was not in the best interest of Coach Bryant or the Crimson Tide to be locked into having to go to the Sugar Bowl. His teams every year were so dominant that he could literally pick which of the major bowls, with the exception of the Rose Bowl, he wanted to play in.

The Sugar Bowl approached the SEC about the champion automatically going to the Sugar Bowl, and my dear friend and Commissioner Dr. Boyd McWhorter said it would never pass, because Coach Bryant would never agree to it. I talked to Paul and let him think about the proposal. He mulled it around and said, "You know this is not the best thing for Alabama, but it is the best thing for our conference, and I have to think about what is best for the league. I can't be selfish about it." I think that really shows how magnanimous a person he was. He told me he'd go to Johnny Vaught, the great Ole Miss coach who was retired from coaching but serving as AD at Mississippi, and the two of them would get it passed. It did.

With Alabama already locked because of the champion rule, Paul told me he wanted to play Ohio State and his good friend Woody Hayes in the 1978 Sugar Bowl if the Buckeyes didn't go to the Rose Bowl. Those two had a tremendous mutual respect, probably because they believed in the same principles of football, on and off the field. We weren't making much progress with Woody, but Paul said he'd handle it, and he did.

One of the great scenes in sports was at the press conference in the New Orleans' Fairmont a few days before the game. The two coaches were there, and Paul said, "I'm sick and tired of you media guys trying to make this a game between Woody and me. It's Ohio State and Alabama. I can assure you I'm not going to play a down, but I hope like hell Woody does 'cause he's too old to do much of anything."

The Sugar Bowl had distributed a poster of Coach Bryant and Coach Hayes. The media people had copies, and they all went up there to get Paul and Woody to sign them. It really was an unusual scene, watching all these writers and television newscasters asking for autographs. I had never seen it before or since.

> *Alabama fans reveled in the machine-like efficiency of the wishbone, and while running the ball was certainly vogue, the element of surprise from the passing attack created a plethora of big plays. Adding wings to the wishbone in the most prodigious as well as graceful style was the wonderful Wizard of Oz, No. 82, Ozzie Newsome, whose 1974-77 career earned him century-long accolades as one of the best 25 players in Bama history.*
>
> *In that 1975 Sugar Bowl, once again played on New Year's Eve, Alabama's Richard Todd completed 10 of 12 passes for 212 yards. His passes were*

generally targeted for the gifted Newsome, who recalls that win over Penn State that snapped an 8-year drought of bowl miseries.

OZZIE NEWSOME:

We opened our 1975 season with high expectations because we felt we had a really good football team. But we lost to Missouri on national television in a Monday night game, and we didn't play well at all. We came back to win our next 10 and get the invitation to play Penn State in the Sugar Bowl. At that time Alabama had not won a bowl game since 1967, and we were determined to break that streak. It was my sophomore season, and the year before we had lost to Notre Dame in the Orange Bowl. Not only were we intent on breaking the losing streak in the bowls, but it was also to be the first Sugar Bowl ever played in the Superdome.

There is one play we ran against Penn State I'll never forget, mainly because we had used the same play against Tennessee earlier in the year. The pass pattern is what I call a "slant and go." In the Tennessee game I was wide open and dropped the ball, and it may be the only touchdown pass I dropped in my life. But we came back with the play against Penn State, and it ended up setting up the only the touchdown in the game.

Richard Todd was our quarterback. He hit me on the pass, and it went for 55 yards setting up a run by Mike Stock for the TD. One of my coaches at the Cleveland Browns had a son on that Penn State team, and he was the only one who tackled me. The coach would always kid me about his son catching me, but I'd always remind him who won the game. That game started a bowl winning streak for Alabama that lasted until 1982.

Winning that game was certainly important for Coach Bryant. He had accomplished everything in coaching, but he had an albatross on his back about winning bowl games. I'm proud to have played on the team that finally got us back on track.

Besides the disappointing debut of the decade in 1970, the only other "bad" year came in 1976, when the Crimson Tide's record ebbed at 9-3. However, a 36-6 rout of Pac-10 co-champ UCLA in the Liberty Bowl escalated the expectation level for the final drive of the decade. Bob Baumhower, another player destined for exclusive membership among the legends in Crimson, remembers that night in Memphis at the Liberty Bowl, his final game as a Tider.

BOB BAUMHOWER:

I played pro ball in Buffalo, New York, Foxboro, and Minnesota — I've played in every cold place you could play. But never in my life did I play in a place as cold as the 1976 Liberty Bowl in Memphis. We played UCLA, and it was one of those strange, strange times when the cold weather got all the way down to Memphis. To this day, it's the coldest I've ever been in my life.

Usually when you get into the now of the game, you'll overcome that feeling of cold and that shivering feeling, but that never happened in that game. As bad it was for us, I think the UCLA Bruins had it worse. I tell you it was so cold I think it even affected Coach Bryant. He was an amazing, amazing man. He never let on to any of us that he could ever not be invincible, but I believe the cold really hurt him that night. He was bundled up just like a big, no pun intended, bear. It was a miserable night.

It was a strange year for me and the rest of the guys on the Alabama team. We had just come off a great year when we went 11-1 and lost the season opener to Missouri in a game we played about as poorly as we could. We won our last 11 and beat Penn State in the Sugar Bowl. We had a great defensive team in 1975, but in 1976 we returned only Charlie Hannah, Gus White, and me on the defense. We lost to Ole Miss in the opener and Georgia a few weeks later, but we got better as the season went along. I seriously believe the night we beat UCLA, we could have beaten anyone in the country. UCLA had been ranked No. 2 until its last regular season game, and they were still in the top five. We just whipped them good that night, 36-6.

Defensively we had a good game, and Barry Krauss, who was a sophomore and just coming into his own, won the MVP honors. I can still remember him being all over the field. One of our other linebackers was Dewey Mitchell. Dewey cut his hand very badly. I mean it was a terrible gash, and it was so cold that he didn't bleed! The blood just congealed immediately once it hit that cold air. It was so cold that the drinks on the sidelines froze!

For me it was a great way to conclude my college career, and I think that win propelled Alabama to a great run at the national title in 1977. Of course, the next two teams won it all. It boosted me for a decent professional career with Miami.

Facing one of its most challenging schedules ever, the 1977 team descended in the rankings after losing the second game of the year, a 31-24 decision to Nebraska in Lincoln. Slowly, though, the team began its rise up the polls. The game that cemented the greatness of this unit in Bryant's mind was a 21-20 thriller over top-ranked Southern California in the L.A. Coliseum.

When the season concluded with the Tide rolling impressively to a 35-6 win over Ohio State on January 2, 1978, in the Sugar Bowl, Alabama fans were delirious in their jubilation. It lasted only a few hours, for 5th-rated Notre Dame jumped to No. 1 in the polls after the Irish pummeled Texas in the Cotton Bowl, and the 1977 team proved an awfully attractive bridesmaid, a team Bryant rated with his 1966 squad. Murray Legg, a junior safety in 1977, remembers that fateful day in California when the tide of fortune turned a resounding crimson tint.

MURRAY LEGG:

The fourth quarter was a great one for the spectators and certainly an exciting conclusion to a great game. The Coliseum was packed, and the game was just back and forth, up and down the field. Both teams were super offensively.

Like most big games, there are several plays that really stand out in my mind. Southern Cal had the ball down on our goal line, and it was third and one. It was crucial for us to stop them. They called a sweep to our right side — their left side. We had a cornerback named Mike Tucker, one of the captains of our team. Mike came up, fought through a block, and made a spectacular play in the backfield, throwing their running back for a 4-yard loss.

If Mike hadn't made that play, USC would have scored a touchdown. Instead, they were forced to kick a field goal, which made the game 7-6 in our favor.

Another pivotal play came with the score 14-6 in our favor when Wayne Hamilton made an interception. It was a tremendous play on Wayne's part. He was rushing the passer, and the ball was tipped. Wayne fell flat on his back and caught the ball. That set up our final touchdown.

In the final seconds they scored to make it 21-20, and they decided to go for the win. We had a blitz call on the 2-point conversion. I was blitzing, and Wayne, I think, had three blockers on him. He fought through every single one of them. He caused their quarterback to rush his pass — actually he had their quarterback on the ground when he released it. The play should have been stopped there. Their quarterback threw it and Mike Tucker stepped in front of the receiver and tipped the ball upward. Barry Krauss got the tipped ball and the interception, and we won the game.

By season's end there was little question of Alabama's dominance as a team, and it clearly showed in the surprisingly sweet Sugar Bowl demolition of Woody Hayes's Ohio State Buckeyes. It was the only time the two fabled coaches encountered each other on the gridiron. Two of Bryant's more brilliant stars back from 1976 to 1978 were a pair of Birmingham natives, quarterback Jeff Rutledge and halfback Touchdown Tony Nathan. Here are some of their memories of the Bryant-Hayes faceoff.

JEFF RUTLEDGE:

Looking back over my career, I think some of the greatest moments and things I remember most were the games that we played against Auburn. Just being a native of Birmingham and growing up with Auburn fans made playing those guys a big thrill. I remember Coach Bryant used to say that we had braggin' rights for a year as the winner of that ball game. It was always a tough ball game, and once in a while I look back and say that Auburn never beat Alabama while I was there. I think I had some of my better games against Auburn — the only game we rushed for 100 yards was against Auburn, and I wasn't known too much for my running ability.

I also think the Penn State game in the Sugar Bowl and winning the national championship has to be a highlight. Going after it was one of the reasons I went to Alabama, to hopefully win a national championship. To finally have a dream come true like that was a big thrill for me.

I guess, too, I'd have to say the Ohio State game my junior year was great too — with Woody Hayes and Bear Bryant face to face, two of the best coaches in college football going against each other. Winning the MVP for that game was a great thrill for me, also.

"Woody is a great coach, and I ain't bad."
— Paul Bryant after the Tide beat Ohio State 35-6 in the 1978 Sugar Bowl

TONY NATHAN:

One of the things I remember most about the 1978 Sugar Bowl game against Ohio State was the preparation going into the game. Coach Bryant totally surprised everybody on our team by the way he prepared us for the game. We didn't work out in pads all week, which was strange because of the way Coach usually practiced us for games.

There was quite a bit of hype about the Sugar Bowl matching the two winningest active head coaches, Coach Bryant and Coach Hayes. Coach Bryant downplayed that aspect of the game, and when the media would try to make something of it, he would tell them the game was between Alabama and Ohio State — not between him and Coach Hayes.

Actually we played one of our best games of the year and won easily 35-6. That was the good part. The bad part was we finished No. 2 in the final rankings to Notre Dame. We went into the Sugar Bowl ranked No. 3, Oklahoma was No. 2, and Texas was No. 1. Notre Dame jumped us, which caused us a great deal of disappointment. We really had a great team that year. Our only loss came in the second game of the year at Nebraska, and we were a team that got better each week. When we beat Southern Cal, they were ranked No. 1 at the time. Out in Los Angeles, we really gained momentum, and it carried with us the rest of the way.

Coach Bryant liked to play a lot of people, and I'm certain Ohio State had to be somewhat shocked by the number of full units we would run in there on them. Jeff Rutledge was our starting quarterback, but his backup, Steadman Shealy, led us to a couple of scores. Jeff was the game's MVP, and I think he threw a TD pass to Rick Neal. I scored one early in the game, and we got ahead 13-0 by halftime and fairly well dominated them in the second half.

While the Tide crested near the top throughout most of Bryant's illustrious 25-year career, there is little doubt the 1964-66 and 1977-79 years surpassed all others in success on the field and in the balloting boxes of the polls selecting national champions as well.

As 1979 opened, Alabama's football team, ranked No. 2, prepared for a New Year's showdown with top-ranked Penn State, coached by Joe Paterno. The driving rainstorm that cried all day on New Orleans may have hindered Sugar Bowls of the past, but the Superdome eliminated the weather as a factor in a game forever termed in Bama Country as "The Goal Line Stand."

In his melodious voice, Keith Jackson, the ABC megagiant announcer, called the action this way: "Fourth down and a foot separating top-ranked Penn

*State from a possible national championship. Fusina hands to Guman —
He didn't make it! He didn't make it! What an unbelievable goal line stand
by Alabama!"*

*One of the members of the goal line crew, Rich Wingo made the pivotal
stop on the third-down play.*

RICH WINGO:

Don McNeal made a fantastic play on the 1-yard line on a second-down pass play from (Chuck) Fusina to (Scott) Fitzkee. Don was really about 8 yards deep in the end zone covering the wide receiver when he looked back and saw, at the last second, the ball being thrown to Fitzkee. Don came up and tackled him on the 1-yard line. Just a fantastic play.

On the third-down play, they lined up in an I-backfield, two tight ends, and came up the middle with a lead blocker on Barry Krauss. Barry and I were the two middle linebackers, and Byron Braggs and Marty Lyons were the tackles. David Hannah was in the middle. Their job was to get on their all fours and basically submarine to get as much penetration forward as they possibly could, allowing the linebackers to step up and try to make the play—if the play came up the middle, which it did. They led with the lead blocker Mike Guman, and Barry hit Guman head on and stopped him in his tracks. Matt Suhey, who ended up playing for the Chicago Bears, was the ball carrier.

Because of all the penetration, Matt tried to go over the top, and I got the tackle. The key effort came from David Hannah. David was able to penetrate, submarine through, and basically clip Suhey at the chin, making him go up in the air when he was trying to get up over the goal line. I was so nervous on the play, I stumped my toe and fell forward and was lucky enough to run into Suhey and stop him short of the goal line.

So then it was fourth down and less than a yard to go. Penn State called time out. Murray Legg and I called our defenses. We would have the linebacker call the front alignment, and the strong safety, who was Murray, call the secondary coverage. Murray and I went over to the sideline, and we were standing there between third and fourth down. We came back in, and it was very quiet. They were measuring the spot, and Marty (Lyons) was standing there when Fusina looked back at Joe Paterno and put his hand up in the air, signaling how much they needed for a touchdown. Marty looked at Fusina and said, "You'd better pass." He told him that he wouldn't be able to run it in.

We got back in the huddle and all looked at each other. We always held hands on either side of us, in sort of a circular unity. Murray spoke up first and said, "This is we what worked so hard for." The other seniors — Barry, Marty, and I all said something.

I remember it very plainly in the huddle, it was like time sort of froze. We were saying, "This is what we're here for, this what we paid the price for all these years, all the lower gym workouts, all the summers, all the pain that we had to go through to get to this point, it's up to us." We had the feeling in the that huddle we couldn't be beaten. That's what Coach Bryant was always trying to teach us. You hope and pray that one day it comes down to you and you are the ones who have the opportunity to make it happen. Here's a moment you dream about happening, and here it was staring us in the face. Gut-check time.

We broke the huddle, and they came out in a two tight set. The call from the sidelines was what we called a bruin. That's where the corners pinch. If they had passed the ball to the tight end on either side, they would have scored a touchdown. We basically knew they would run because the people coaching us, starting with Coach Bryant, had us prepared for what Penn State did in those situations. Our defensive coaches, Ken Donahue, Brother Oliver, and Jeff Rouzie had studied their thoughts, their mentality, and they knew what they were going to run.

Mike Clements was on the end at one corner, and Clemmy came from his right corner slot. The lead blocker came and I didn't know if he had the ball or not. It was Suhey. So they just switched Guman and Suhey. Now Suhey was a fullback and Guman was the tailback. Same play, same cadence, everything, except the two backs had flip-flopped. Suhey came right at me, and all I remember is just hitting him head-on. Coach Donahue taught us that if you stop the lead blocker, the tailback's got to do something other than come right behind him. He's got to go over the top or to his right or left, but he can't go where the hole is supposed to be. And my responsibility was to stop Suhey in his tracks. I just remember hitting him as hard as I could.

Guman then came right into where Barry was coming, and Barry just made a perfect tackle. Barry didn't take a chance of missing the tackle. The pictures of the play show that. He put his face right on Guman's. You put your face helmet to helmet, like Coach Bryant would say, jaw to jaw, cheek to cheek, and the man isn't going anywhere.

Another Tide all-timer, Marty Lyons, gives his insight into the plays on the goal line.

MARTY LYONS:

We were well-schooled at that time. Coach Ken Donahue knew exactly what they were going to run. He always had their tendencies down inside the 5, inside the 10 and the 20, and he had schooled us well before the game.

On a goal line situation, Coach Donahue wanted us to submarine underneath the offensive lineman, try to take his inside knee off, or outside knee, depending on where we were lining up, so that he couldn't scoop off and hit the linebacker. I believe on both plays, the defensive line got enough penetration, so the offensive back had to jump, which gave our linebackers some momentum to come up and stick him right on the line of scrimmage.

During the timeout before Penn State's fourth-down play, Fusina came to the line of scrimmage to see how much they needed. It was inches, and I told him, "You'd better pass." They didn't, and the rest is history.

Don McNeal made the play on second down, Rich on third down, and Barry (Krauss) on fourth down, but it went deeper than that. We were a very close team. We played as a team. There was no person hungry for individual stardom. We shared it. There is enough glory when you win for all the players. I think after that game we knew everyone on the team had earned his glory.

I will always remember Coach Bryant saying, "A winner in the game of life is that person who gives of himself so other people can grow." I think you can take all the awards you win and all the championships you win, and you can put those in the closet compared to what Coach Bryant taught you off the field. I think the one thing Coach Bryant did was make you believe in yourself. He believed in his players, and by having him believe in you, it made you believe you could accomplish anything on and off the football field.

I remember after my first year in the pros, I saw Coach Bryant. I had grown a beard, and the first two questions he asked me were: "When was I going to come back to school and graduate and when was I going to cut that crap off my face!"

1979 epitomized the iron resolution of its leader Paul Bryant. That team won all 12 games with a defense that yielded but 6 points a game and an offense that bewildered defenses with its incessant pounding. Along the way the only real scares came against Tennessee, LSU, and Auburn. In the end, in true Bryant fashion, the Tide won the fourth quarter and prevailed against all three time-honored foes.

One of the stalwart's during that season was big Byron Braggs, whose giant image on the defensive front certainly was a discouraging reminder to opponents of the dominant and irrepressible stance of Alabama during that generation. During his 1977-80 career, Braggs played on teams that chalked up a 44-4 worksheet. He remembers those days well, particularly the Tennessee game of 1979 and what tradition at Alabama is all about.

BYRON BRAGGS:

When I played professional football (for the Green Bay Packers), it was nothing compared to what we did at Alabama. I'm saying the practices were brutal, but Coach Bryant was preparing us for more than just football. Game days were when everything came together. You had an opportunity to execute what he taught you, what was honed into you and defined in practice.

When we played Tennessee my junior year, we were down 17-0. Prior to the half, Major Ogilvie scored a touchdown to make it 17-7. Tennessee hadn't beaten Alabama in 8 years, and they were really fired up. There was one thing I always remember about playing for the University of Alabama: We had an inner strength, a tenacity, an arrogance that we would find a way to win.

We really didn't talk about such things, but Coach Bryant instilled this factor into us. A lot of teams we played against, even though they may have been ahead of us and had better players than us, well they really weren't sure if they could beat us. There were a lot of teams that played us tooth and nail in the first half, and in the second half we'd wipe them out.

We came in at half of the Tennessee game, and we were somewhat mystified. It was one of those days when it was dangerous to have a wishbone offense. We were just fumbling it around.

Defensively, we prided ourselves in not giving up many points, and we had given up

17 in the first half. Coach Bryant came over, and he was not hysterical. He was very calm, and I remember him saying, "Everything will work out for the better. We have nothing to worry about. We have them just where we want them."

When he made that statement, several of us just looked at one another. I was looking at Warren Lyles, and we shook our heads and thought, "Yeah, it's time for Coach Bryant to retire. He doesn't know what he's talking about."

But he did, and we won 27-17. Coach Bryant always looked at the Tennessee game as a measuring stick, and that's sort of been entrenched in my psyche. I really focused toward the Tennessee game. Playing at Alabama, it's a big game. Auburn is always a big game, but I never smoked a cigar after an Auburn. We always smoked a cigar after the Tennessee game.

You can't inherit tradition. Tradition is like a book that's being written, and the people that are at this place in their particular time write their own chapters. Whether they carry the tradition on or not is left solely up to them. Tradition to me is like the old Pony Express. When you're delivering the mail, you change horses, and that horse picks up a beat like the other horse did. You ride it until you exhaust that horse. You get to the next station, and you change horses and ride on.

So when Johnny Musso stopped running the ball, he handed it to Wilbur Jackson; Wilbur handed it off to Calvin Culliver; and Calvin handed it off to Tony Nathan; and so on. Tradition is based on great players like this and to me these are people who are willing to die for the program.

We have had great athletes, but what separates us is the category Coach Bryant loved: The Winners. He wanted people who wanted to sacrifice and play for team championships. Those were the gold medals, the championships. Coach Bryant had an uncanny knack of making you better and really if you weren't a part of it, it is hard to describe his impact.

I remember the Wednesday night before the 1980 Tennessee game. Coach Bryant told the team a story about the difference in winners and losers, and I promise you there wasn't a dry eye in the audience. It scared me to death because I thought we were going to go out and kill people at practice. His story carried over to Saturday and we beat Tennessee 27-0.

I was a member of the 1978 and 1979 national championship teams, and it's interesting. You're happy, and then it's kind of depressing because when you wake up, you become the defending national champions.

It is understood at Alabama that you are to be in contention for the national championship. The SEC Championship was an understood goal that you didn't even mention — it was an unwritten rule that we were going to win it.

Another one of the stars who radiated brightly in 1979 was halfback Major Ogilvie, whose MVP performance in the Sugar Bowl against Arkansas capped the most productive decade any team had ever enjoyed. For the record, Alabama, including that win on January 1, 1980, rolled to a 103-16-1 decade, winning 8 SEC and 3 national titles.

MAJOR OGILVIE:

Our 1979 team was by far the best team I ever participated on. I don't mean to be derogatory toward the other three teams I played on at Alabama, but our 1979 team had been playing together for three years, and we had a certain bond that separates really great teams from good ones. We went 12-0 and won the Sugar Bowl with a 24-9 win over Arkansas.

We ran a lot out of a double wing in that Sugar Bowl game. We had used that formation a little during my freshman year in 1977, but in the Sugar Bowl it was a secret weapon that caused Arkansas quite a bit of trouble. First of all, the double wing helped us significantly in terms of giving us a chance to get ahead. We had not been a great first-half team that year, but the double wing worked for us. I believe we got ahead 17-3 at the half.

We had the nation's best defense that year with people like Thomas Boyd, Byron Braggs, E.J. Junior, David Hannah, Randy Scott, Don McNeal, and Ricky Tucker. They were all top-notch players. Our strength offensively was having one of the best offensive lines in the country with Tim Travis at tight end, Buddy Adyelette and Jim Bunch at tackles, Vince Boothe and Mike Brock at guards, and Dwight Stephenson at center. Steadman Shealy was our quarterback, and of course, we had Steve Whitman, a great wishbone fullback.

One thing we did during that game that was rather unique for us was the implementation of the quick kick. It was one of those plays that Coach Bryant wanted to run, and we put it in on Christmas Day. We practiced that morning, and he pulled Joe Jones, Billy Jackson, and me off to the side, and we practiced quick kicking.

Coach was determined to use it, and I guess I won the honors of being the quick kicker by default. Everybody had gone inside when we started our punting drills. None of the other guys knew what was going on, but they knew Coach was up to something. We used it in the bowl game, and it worked to get us out of the hole!

"I thought Nebraska was the most football-crazed state until I came to Alabama. Coach Bryant got up and introduced members of the 1925 Rose Bowl team, and he got teary-eyed, and so did all the people in the audience who welcomed the team with an absolute admiration that is hard to describe."
— James Michener in 1975 when he was writing his book *Sports in America*

"You're a great athlete with a great arm. It's a shame you don't have time to use it."
— LeRoy Cook talking to Tennessee quarterback Randy Wallace after sacking him in the 30-7 Bama win in 1975; it was 1 of 4 for Cook that day and one of 13 for the team

"You'd better pass."
— Marty Lyons's admonition to Penn State quarterback Chuck Fusina when he walked to the line of scrimmage to see how far the football was from the goal line in the famed 14-7 Sugar Bowl win in 1979

"Fellas, I've been in football all my life and there has never been a better defensive team anywhere, anyplace than the one Alabama has. It strangles you. We've played both USC and Alabama and there is no doubt in my mind Alabama is No. 1 because of that defense."

— Former LSU coach and Paul Bryant pupil Charley McClendon after the 1979 Alabama-LSU game, won by the Tide 3-0

"Plow, Bear, Plow."

— Auburn students yelling at Bryant before the 1979 game in response to Bryant's remarks he'd have to go back to Arkansas and plow if his team lost to Auburn

"Our winning drive (13 plays, 82 yards) was one of the finest I've ever seen. We had to have it. I'm just thrilled to death with the win. We've got some mighty fine plow hands on this team."

— Bryant after the 25-18 win over Auburn in 1979

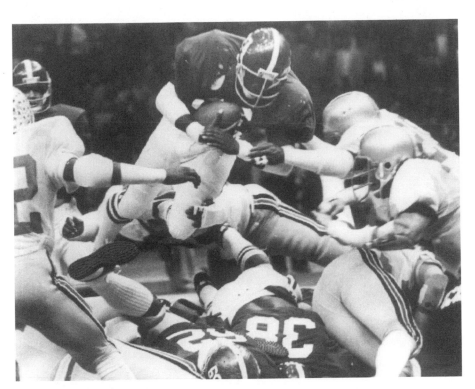

Tony Nathan triumphs.

Ronnie Robertson gives an autograph.

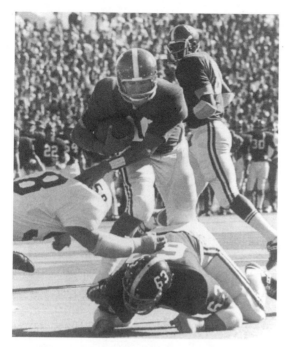

Terry Davis and #80 Wilbur Jackson.

The great Ozzie Newsome.

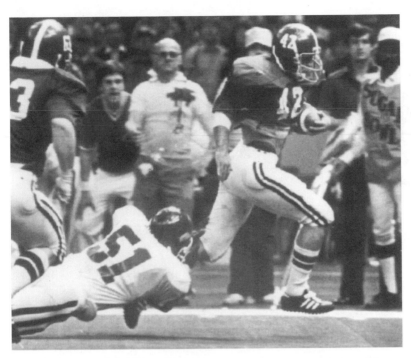

Alabama's Major Ogilvie (42) streaks down the sidelines as Arkansas' Ozzie Riley (51) tries to bring him down.

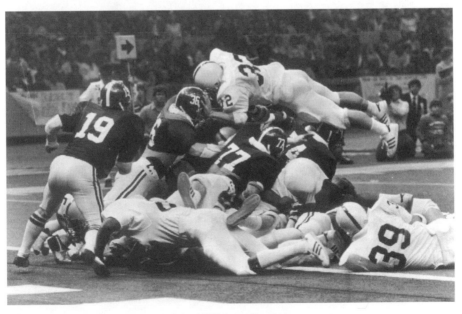

Third-down play of the goal line stand — 1979 Sugar Bowl.

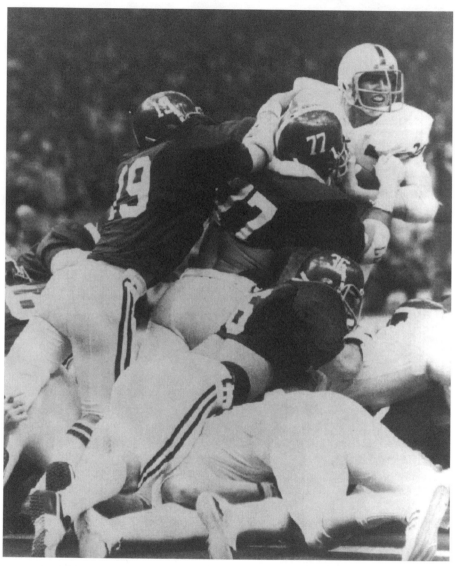

One of the greatest plays in Alabama football history sees Murray Legg (19), Barry Krauss (77), and Rich Wingo (36) stop Penn State's Mike Guman on fourth and goal inside the 1-yard line. The Tide won 14-7 and the National Title as well.

THE EIGHTIES
The Agony and the Ecstasy

Alabama's rollercoaster ride through the 1980s started with the sentimental journey of Paul Bryant toward the all-time winning record for major college coaches. It concluded with suspense in the air on the status of the third mentor of the decade, Bill Curry, who was being courted by the University of Kentucky for the void left with the retirement of Jerry Claiborne.

After a 10-2 1980 season, Alabama rolled into the 315 season a favorite to compete for the national title. An early season loss to Georgia Tech and a tie with Southern Miss not only dampened those spirited talks of No. 1 but also delayed the opportunity for Bryant to tie and break Amos Alonzo Stagg's record. Season-ending games against Penn State and Auburn respectively emerged as the dates with destiny for Bryant and the Tide.

One of the stars of that era and those two games in particular was the gifted Walter Lewis, who engineered a 31-16 win over Penn State and a 28-17 victory over Auburn. The talented quarterback remembers those two November afternoons that placed Bryant on a pedestal above all his peers.

WALTER LEWIS:

In 1981, everyone was talking about Coach Bryant's age, but I didn't really think about it. Our coaching staff did a good job of making us play hard. To tell you the truth, our biggest concern was who would be the starting quarterback. There was never a hint of Coach Bryant retiring.

When we went to Penn State, it marked the first game of a 10-game series. We really didn't know what to expect when we went up there. We had watched some of the 1979 Sugar Bowl film to get some tendencies, but overall we had a lot of questions.

The game was played in mid-November and each team had 1 loss. We were both ranked in the top 10. I remember us hitting some long passes against them, and Jesse Bendross and Joey Jones had outstanding days. We were up 24-3 at half, and to start the second half we had an unbelievable goal line stand that had a major impact on the rest of the game. Our defense held them one set of downs. Then there was an interference call in the end zone that gave them another set of downs, and we held them again.

I guess the most memorable scenario came when our defense came off the field, and

Coach Bryant tipped his hat to the players. We didn't really realize the significance of it being his 314th win. We just went out there to play and have fun.

I don't guess I realized how influential Coach was, but I remember people just standing in lines on the field as he was walking on. They were just trying to get a glimpse of him. They were more in awe of him than we were of playing on Penn State's field. They really respected him.

In the Auburn game, I remember us not playing very well at the start of the game, but as the game progressed we started playing better. Winning 315 really wasn't the focus of the game, but playing well was. All the players were relieved when it was over, and we knew we had been part of a historical victory. I think it was great that the 315 game came against Auburn. When I was being recruited, I remember coaches saying Coach Bryant would not be there much longer. But one coach from Alabama told me that I could be the player to throw the winning touchdown pass. I did throw a touchdown pass (to Jesse Bendross) in that game. That touchdown put us ahead to stay.

Perhaps nose guard Warren Lyles summed up the euphoria for Alabama that day, and even a telephone call from President Ronald Reagan could not have touched Paul Bryant more than the words of one of his stars. In reflecting on the win Lyles emotionally remarked, "I wish I could tell you how proud I am to be an Alabama football player, but I have no idea how to do it. I feel as rich as Howard Hughes. I feel like I share that pedestal Coach Bryant stands on tonight."

Humbled by the victory and relieved the long trek had ended, Bryant praised his players. "I ought to be carrying my players off the field on my shoulders. And I would if I were strong enough. I'd take them one at a time if I had to stay until midnight."

Despite finishing in a tie for the SEC Championship with Georgia, the Sugar Bowl opted for the Dawgs and Herschel Walker over Bama. Longtime Bryant colleague Aruns Callery, who passed away in October 1992 at the age of 84, shares his memories of that selection and some of his final days with Bryant.

ARUNS CALLERY:

It became obvious that because they didn't play one another, Alabama and Georgia were both going undefeated in the conference, and the Sugar Bowl was going to have to choose between the two schools. That was the year Paul was chasing Amos Alonzo Stagg's record, and Georgia had Herschel Walker.

Paul really wanted to play in the Sugar Bowl. He knew he wasn't going to be coaching that much longer, and he wanted to play Pittsburgh in the bowl. At the time of bowl invitations, Pitt was undefeated and ranked No. 1 in the nation, and Alabama was coming off a 31-16 win over Penn State. The Sugar Bowl committee was split, and of course, I wanted Alabama. There was a strong sentiment that if it had not been for Coach Bryant, the Sugar Bowl would have fallen on hard times. He had taken his team to New Orleans back in

1973 to play Notre Dame when he could have played them in the Orange Bowl for substantially more money. Of course, without his support the SEC tie-up would have never occurred. Despite these arguments, the committee opted for Georgia because Georgia was No. 3 at the time of the invitations and Alabama No. 4. Paul was disappointed, and he never had the chance to play in the Sugar Bowl again.

The summer before he died, I was with him. I knew he wasn't feeling well. One time he was just sitting there, and he asked me to come over and cross his legs for him because he couldn't do it. I loved Paul Bryant, and I love Alabama. One of the most special moments for me was when he made me an A-Club member and gave me a national championship ring.

One night after the 1979 Sugar Bowl, the goal line stand game, we were having a victory party in his suite at the Hyatt. Paul had on a t-shirt, a new one but it had a hole in it. One of the guests said, "Coach, your shirt has a hole in it." He said, "Yea, I know. I always tear a small hole in my t-shirts so I'll never forget where I came from."

Another time we were trying to get Paul through the lobby of the Fairmont a couple of nights before Alabama played Arkansas in the Sugar Bowl in 1980, and it was a mob scene like you see for a President or entertainer. There was a little boy, no more than five or six years old with his father over in the corner and obviously disappointed because there was no way he'd ever get to Coach. I pointed him out to Paul, and he made his way through the crowd and talked to the little boy. It was a touching scene. He had an uncommon goodness about him, and he never forgot his roots.

Alabama's unexpected downslide in 1982, especially successive losses to LSU, Southern Miss, and Auburn, expedited the retirement of the legendary Bryant. Word leaked out on December 14 that an announcement was imminent. It came a day later from Memorial Coliseum. The following is Coach Bryant's speech, announcing his resignation.

PAUL "BEAR" BRYANT:

There comes a time in every profession when you need to hang it up, and that has come for me as head football coach at the University of Alabama.

My main purpose as director of athletics and head football coach here has been to field the best possible team, to improve each player as a person, and to produce citizens who will be a credit to our modern day society.

We have been successful in most of those areas, but I feel the time is right for a change in our football leadership. We lost two big football games this season that we should have won. And we played in only four or five games like Bryant-coached teams should play. I've done a poor job coaching.

This is my school, my alma mater, and I love it. And I love the players, but in my opinion they deserve better coaching than they've been getting from me this year. My stepping down is an effort to see that they get better coaching from someone else.

It has been a great job for me, personally, to have the opportunity to coach at my alma mater. I know I will miss coaching, but the thing I will miss most is the association I have had with the players, the coaches, the competition — all those things that have made such a strong tradition at Alabama.

Two weeks later in the Liberty Bowl against Big-10 rival Illinois, Alabama survived in a 21-15 thriller. The game, of course, will be indelibly locked in the minds of Bama fans as the finale for the incomparable Bryant. Here's what Coach Bryant had to say after the game.

PAUL "BEAR" BRYANT:

I told the squad before the game that whether I liked it, whether they liked it, this would be a game all of us would remember the rest of our lives. I think it'll make my future years, or year, more pleasant. I'm thankful to have been associated with top-notch people throughout my career. I've been fortunate in that those people have reached most of the goals we've set throughout the years.

I'm tremendously proud of the the team for winning. I'm flattered the team responded tonight like they did — I think they wanted it for themselves and for me.

I've looked at the last roundup forever, too, and this will make my memories a lot more pleasant.

Players Walter Lewis, Steve Mott, and Russ Wood reflect back on that night in Memphis that sealed the final chapter of the most remarkable era in the history of college football.

WALTER LEWIS:

That season we lost 4 games going into the Liberty Bowl, which was more than a lot of guys had lost in their entire careers. The game was one of the most emotional I've ever been a part of. Jeremiah Castille and Eddie Lowe got up and gave a speech before the game in the locker room. After that, I couldn't even talk I was so shook up.

I remember it was really cold that night, but you couldn't really tell it because the emotions were just flying. It was an unbelievable game and, of course, a most satisfying victory.

STEVE MOTT:

Everybody on the team realized Coach Bryant was coaching his last game, and that intensified our emotions. Obviously we went to Memphis determined to win that final game for Coach Bryant. It was an extremely emotional time for all of us because we realized how much Coach Bryant cared about us and all of us former players. Everybody loved Coach Bryant, and it just raised the emotions of our team against an awfully good Illinois team.

After the game, I think it took a big load off everybody's shoulders. It was a really important game for all of us to be part of a win in Coach Bryant's final game. I know it entered every player's mind that heaven forbid what it would be like to have to live with having lost Coach's final game.

Another thing about the game was the cold weather. You know at bowl games, they give the players different souvenirs and things like that from the game. One of the packages we had had a number of different things in it. I think it was toiletries and things like that. And they had a pair of panty hose in them. I don't know what we were supposed to do with those, but a lot of the guys ended up cutting them off at about the knees and wearing them to keep warm at the game!

RUSS WOOD:

The final practice under Coach Bryant was the most emotional I've ever been through. To have been a part of the last practice and hear Coach Bryant's last talk to one of his teams is really special to me. We had our last practice in Memphis before the bowl game.

I bet there were 85 of us in a room, the projector room. We always viewed films on our last day. Coach said a few words. Everybody, managers, trainers, players, were all crowded together trying to hear him. He got to talking, and he got choked up, tears started rolling down his cheeks and everything went quiet.

He went over the game plan format like he always did, but all of a sudden he got off on football, told us how much he loved it, and how much he cared about us. He told us he wanted us to do well in the game for ourselves and Alabama and not for him. He got choked up, and his mouth was moving, but no words were coming out and the tears were flowing.

It seemed like an eternity, but it was probably just eight or nine seconds. Finally somebody turned off the lights and started the projector. I bet 85 of us were sitting there sniffing and crying while we tried to watch Illinois film.

When we went out to practice, it was like a numb feeling among us. Usually on the day before the game, everybody's kind of loose and fired up, but after that meeting, nobody seemed energetic. Everybody was going through the motions, and I bet the concentration level was probably about 50 percent.

Tony Eason, the Illinois quarterback, said he'd never seen a whole team hit as hard as Alabama did. Late in the game, we were up 21-15 and holding them off. Illinois was driving but we had made a pretty good play on first down, forcing a second and long. One of their guys missed a block on me, and I got a good lick on Tony and knocked him out of the game. His backup (Kris Jenner) came in, and Robbie Jones intercepted his pass to preserve the victory for us. Coach Bryant made a comment in the paper that it was one of the greatest plays he'd ever seen. You can't imagine how proud that made me feel.

Several months before the final cheers echoed in the caverns of the Liberty Bowl Stadium in Memphis, Tennessee, Paul Bryant, the venerable legend, expressed some rather candid points in an interview with some old media friends. Here is one of the last in-depth talks by the Coach.

PAUL *"BEAR" BRYANT:*

The same things win today that have always won, and they will win years from now. The only difference is the losers have a whole new bunch of excuses why they don't win or can't win. I don't know if I'm smart enough to know how to describe a winner, but I guess I've been wise enough or maybe just lucky enough of being able to spot one. I know a winner has dedication and pride and the will to win, and he'll do a little bit extra every day to improve himself and his team. A winner is worried about his team and his school, and he'll outwork people, and he'll sacrifice.

I've always looked at myself as being the champion of those little rascals that didn't have a whole lot of talent but didn't know they didn't have any talent. Those are the types of young men that I always liked to coach. See them put it on the line every Saturday and see them grow as players and people. I've always tried to stress to my players that they need to grow each day of their life in three important ways: mentally, physically, and spiritually. If they'd do that, they'll be all right.

Over the years, I don't know if I mellowed any or not, but I think I've done a good job of adapting to the changes in our society and in the game of football. I know back in the late 1960s and early 1970s, the long hair business became important for the players. I didn't like it, but when I realized what a big deal it was to the athlete, I know I had to do some adjusting. I think it is important to be a listener in order to understand the mood of your people, and I have always tried to surround myself with good people.

I used to be a pretty good coach, but the assistants do all the work now. I'll just go out there and try to give them a hint or two every once in a while.

I have said it many a time, I do love the football. I really do. Lord knows where I'd be without it. Probably back in Arkansas pushing a plow. You know on those August days when the players are out there sweating and stinking and wondering what the heck they are doing out there, I think back to when I was in their shoes and I knew I didn't want to go back to plowing. Football has been a road out of poverty for many a young man. When you don't have anything to go back to, then by gosh you're going to work a little harder. I think you can trace the history of athletics, particularly football, and most of your players have come from your poorer backgrounds.

Some people say there is something inherently bad about football. I guess they have to find something wrong. I think you can ask any young man who has paid the price and stuck it out four or five years here and ask him if it weren't worth it and he'd tell you, "Yes."

You learn a heck of a lot about work ethic, working with your fellow man, sacrificing, being a better person right out there on that practice field and in their meetings with their coaches and hopefully every once in a while from me. Coaches are teachers, and they teach many an important lesson to these young men. I've seen many a boy grow into a man by playing football. As far as the critics, well, they don't know what the hell they're talking about. Most of them have ridden their daddies' coattails and haven't done a thing on their own anyway.

I have always tried to teach my players to be fighters. When I say that, I don't mean put up your dukes and get in a fistfight over something. I'm talking about facing adversity in your life. There is not a person alive who isn't going to have some awfully bad days in their lives. I tell my players that what I mean by fighting is when your house burns down, and your wife runs off with the drummer, and you've lost your job and all the odds are against you. What are you going to do? Most people just lay down and quit. Well I want my people to fight back. Don't quit. I just hope a few of them learned that over the years, and I think they have. I look at all those young 'uns who played here and sacrificed to become men, and they have gone on to be doctors and lawyers and stockbrokers and businessmen. You don't know how proud I am of those men.

I also want my players and coaches and all my staff to learn to develop to have a plan — have a plan in your life and be able to adjust it. Have a plan when you wake up, what you're going to do with your day. Just don't go lollygagging through any day of your life. I hope I have had some luck in my life because I have planned for the good times and the bad ones.

I don't know if I'll ever get tired of football. One time I thought I might. If I ever get that notion, I think back to one day I was out there on the practice field wondering about whether I'd get tired of the sport then I heard the Million Dollar Band playing over there on the parade grounds. When they started playing "Yea, Alabama," I got goosebumps all over me. I looked out there at those young rascals in those crimson jerseys, and I just wanted to thank God for giving me the opportunity to coach at my alma mater and be part of the University of Alabama tradition.

I've been awfully lucky over the years to be surrounded with great people. I don't know if I ever did much for them, but they sure as the heck have done a lot for me. When people ask me what do I want to be remembered for, I have one answer: I want the people to remember me as a winner 'cause I ain't never been nothing but a winner.

Four weeks later on January 26, 1983, in Druid City Hospital, located within seeing distance of Bryant's office, the Coach's heart stopped beating for the final time, and the skies cried on Alabama.
Linda Knowles, Bryant's secretary, remembers the great Coach.

LINDA KNOWLES:

His last year he was a very sick man, and he willed himself to live — that's exactly what he did. What was driving him to stay alive was to complete the season, to get things in order. I don't know if he himself knew how short his time was, but I think he had the drive and will to complete that season and to have things in order before he died.

Coach Bryant was a very compassionate and caring man. He did a lot of things for people that are not known. We had an old janitor in what we call the "old building" from back in the early sixties, and his name was Hooch Man. He was an elderly, black gentleman, and Coach Bryant gave him a room in part of our office building to live in, bought him a TV, and gave him a monthly check out of his personal bank account for his expenses. Coach Bryant looked after him until he died.

Coach Bryant visited sick children, and one of his biggest joys in life was his players bringing their families back to visit him. He'd get those kids in his lap, and just the joy and satisfaction of seeing a young man who had gone on and been successful and knowing that he'd taught him something more than football – the values of life. The joy would be written all over his face, a big old smile – he loved it.

Tears and tributes marked those dreary January days. This tribute from the President of the United States, Ronald Reagan, personified the overall emotions of the Alabama family.

"Today we Americans lost a hero who always seemed larger than life. Paul 'Bear' Bryant won more college football games than any coach in history, and he made legends out of ordinary people. Only four weeks ago we held our breath and cheered when the Bear notched his final victory in a game named, fittingly, the Liberty Bowl. Paul Bryant was a hard but loved taskmaster, patriotic to the core, devoted to his players, and inspired by a winning spirit that would not quit. Bear Bryant gave his country the gift of a life unsurpassed. In making the impossible seem easy, he lived what we strive to be."
– President Ronald Reagan on January 26, 1983, upon learning of Paul Bryant's death

In late January 1983, I was at a client's office talking about an ad campaign for that spring. The receptionist stuck her head in the door and said, "Mr. Forney, I'm sorry to interrupt. You have a phone call they said was urgent." I picked up a phone just outside the door, and it was a friend of mine, Bob Esdale.

"John," he said, "he's gone." I did not know what he meant and stammered something. "Coach Bryant," he said in not too steady a voice. "He just died."

Someone at Druid City Hospital had called one of Bob's children who had called Bob. I was shocked to say the least. Everybody knew he was in the hospital, but he was supposedly doing fine. I went to my car and turned the radio on. In about five minutes, a bulletin came on the air confirming the awful news.

I went to Tuscaloosa and stayed at the Bryant house for awhile. I saw and visited with the luminaries of the sports world who had come to bid farewell to one of the brightest stars in its constellation.

The next day I walked a mile or so to Elmwood Cemetary to be near the gravesite. I waited on a little knoll with Jimmy McDowell, of the College Football Foundation and Hall of Fame, and Mickey Herskowitz, of the Houston Post, *who had flown in with a man who had played for Coach Bryant at Texas A&M. This big, rugged former Aggie brought his 13-year-old son to the funeral.*

Before long we could see the bright lights of the police escort flashing distantly through Elmwood, and soon the tremendous cortege pulled in front of us. We walked forward to get a bit closer, and I noticed that Grafton Hocutt from the funeral home in Tuscaloosa had driven the hearse himself. A 78-year-old

Alabama fan, Grafton has watched several thousand Alabama practices, many of them from just below the Coach's tower. I deduced that Grafton would have considered letting no one else bring Paul Bryant to his final rest. (Grafton passed away in the summer of 1993 at the age of 88.)

I felt a strong hand on my arm and turned to see Sergeant Bobby Hayes, the Birmingham Police Department Traffic Control director, looking at me through dark glasses. "You need to be closer, John," he said, and steered me part way up the little slope to be near the grave. Bobby, too, had performed countless tasks for Alabama and Coach Bryant, escorting the Tide through Birmingham for Legion Field games, meeting opponents' planes, getting coaches and bowl representatives and assorted press and broadcast types through heavy game traffic for close deadlines, and handling dozens of other such problems. Bobby was not far from retirement, but no one else was going to be in charge that day.

The ministers were properly brief. As I looked at the casket and the youthful football player pallbearers, I thought sadly that his strength and power and force were now still. And I hoped there would be others possessing these qualities when the country needed them. He was a hell of a man.

The service was over, and I walked with the crowd out through the iron gates of Elmwood. It was journey's end.

During the Bryant era, his trainer-coach Jim Goostree proved to be an extension of the head coach, particularly in the organizational and disciplinary areas. Being in charge of travel, Goose arranged the final trip for his mentor.

JIM GOOSTREE:

There are so many joyous memories for me and my tenure at the University but the most empty feeling was those January days in 1983 when Coach Bryant died and that final trip to Birmingham.

Coach Bryant's family rode in cars ahead of the bus caravan. There were six buses with the staff and players, and the most eerie and ironic event occurred. Coach Bryant always rode in the front right seat, and I always sat across from him on the aisle.

Coach Ray Perkins and his wife, Carolyn, boarded the bus and took the seat right behind where Coach Bryant had always sat. No one sat in Coach Bryant's seat. It wasn't planned that way. It's just the way it happened, but nobody sat in Coach Bryant's seat. That's the way it should have been, too.

I will always remember the thousands and thousands of people who lined up by the interstate and on the overpasses to say their final good-byes to Paul Bryant. I will always remember Coach Bryant as a teacher. He taught his coaches how to teach and let them teach.

Paul Bryant prepared his team physically and mentally and expected 110 percent effort from everyone on his staff. He remembered those who laid it on the line for him. When I was asked why I stayed at Alabama, I have two reasons. I didn't like to lose and I knew we weren't going to lose very often, and I didn't have enough nerve to tell Coach Bryant that I was leaving for another job.

The heavens did not smile kindly on Ray Perkins's first team. The Crimsons finished 8-4, but the 4 losses were all agonizing experiences, including a debatable 34-28 defeat at Penn State and a fiercely contested 23-20 loss to Auburn. Salving the wounds of a year that could have easily been a perfect one was a stunning 28-7 victory over SMU in the Sun Bowl, in a game that marked the end of the careers of Walter Lewis, Joey Jones, and Jesse Bendross, among others. The popular Jones recounts his final game as a Crimson Tider.

JOEY JONES:

It was my last football game at Alabama, and the guys I had played with for four and five years were determined to end our career on a high note. I know the SMU players had talked all week about the game, and they felt like we were an inferior opponent. It was Coach Perkins's first year, and we had gone 7-4. Really, we had lost 4 tough games. SMU was 10-1, and they just talked about how bad they were going to beat us.

I was fortunate enough to catch a touchdown pass from Walter (Lewis) from about 19 yards out. I just dove, closed my eyes, and the ball landed in my arms. Actually Walter did a great job of avoiding a blitz. One of their players came in clean, but Walter was so quick, he just side-stepped him, laid the ball up to me, and I was able to get it.

We went on to win 28-7, even though SMU had been heavily favored. One of the keys to our win was our freshman center Wes Neighbors, who got the offensive MVP award for his play that day, which is really unusual for a lineman, but Wes did a great job of blocking Michael Carter and that really keyed our offensive effort. Ricky Moore had a great game for us, too. He wasn't very tall but he was powerful. I remember on one of our touchdowns, he carried about four or five of their players into the end zone with him. Two of his runs that day were among the best I ever saw while I was playing. They rank up there with the two Linnie Patrick had against Auburn in Coach Bryant's 315 game in 1981.

For the first time since 1957, Alabama suffered the agony of experiencing a losing season. There were disappointing losses and sinking spirits in Tuscaloosa in 1984, but a season-ending 17-15 victory over Auburn elicited a twinkle of hope.

Remembering those days well are quarterback Mike Shula and center Wes Neighbors, who carried on his family tradition of bruising opponents during his tenure at Alabama. An All-American in 1985-86, Neighbors started all four years of Ray Perkins's tenure as head coach at Alabama. In his senior year in 1986, Neighbors was elected by the SEC assistant coaches as the winner of the Jacobs Trophy, signifying him as the best blocker in the conference, an honor his father had won 25 years before. They are the only father-son tandem to be so honored.

Wes Neighbors remembers the 1984 Auburn game and how it reverberated around the South and jump-started Alabama's return to prominence in college football.

WES NEIGHBORS:

The one thing I remember most about the 1984 game was sitting in a team meeting when Coach (Ray) Perkins came in and told us we were going to beat Auburn and we were going to do it by running it right down their throats. We looked at one another like he was crazy. Auburn had the No. 1 rushing defense in the country, and they were No. 3 overall in defense. Well Coach Perkins was right — we won it by running right at them and playing an outstanding defensive game.

People remember the last sequence when Robert McGinty missed the field goal on the last play. We had stopped them on the goal line moments before that, when Rory Turner tackled Brent Fullwood, but we controlled the entire game, though, and it shouldn't have come down to those plays.

Our defense shut down Bo Jackson that afternoon. He had one run of 15 yards, but on that play Cornelius Bennett caught him from behind. I'll always remember that as one of the best plays I've ever seen.

Coach Perkins, in my opinion, pulled one of the best motivating tactics I ever saw. He brought in about 20 former players to talk to the team. Major Ogilvie talked to us, and he started crying, and so did Joey Jones. Joe Namath was there, and so was Lee Roy Jordan and my dad. Tommy Lewis told me that he was supposed to be one of the former players talking to the team, but when he got there, he turned around and left. He said, "I couldn't talk to the team because I knew I would get so emotional, I'd cry and not be able to say anything."

One of the things I remember most was the postgame bedlam. Man, it was wild. I was running around and felt someone jump on my back, and he was screaming and cheering. I was shocked when he got off and I saw it was Joe Namath.

Paul Ott Carruth was the SEC Player of the Week. His best run came in the second quarter when he just ran over Kevin Porter on about the 2-yard line and scored a touchdown for us. Mike Shula played really well that day, too. I really believe having the former players talk to us carried over into our performance on that Saturday and into the next year.

All year long we turned the ball over and had breakdowns that cost us games. That big win over Auburn was satisfying not only because of who the opponent was but also from a confidence factor — I believe that win paid untold dividends for the future of Alabama football.

Indeed, the confidence level among the Tide players and fans alike escalated with the unexpected victory over Auburn and regenerated enthusiasm for 1985. When the Georgia game was switched to Labor Day night to accommodate the ABC cameras, Bama fans approached the game "Between the Hedges" with cautious optimism. It would be the Tide's first sojourn to

Athens since the 1976 team was ambushed 21-0.

MIKE SHULA:

We had come off a difficult year, and here we were back again, behind at the end of the game. We just knew we had to get it done, and there wasn't a whole lot of time to really think about being down and being behind. We just went out there, and everyone concentrated in the huddle.

Boy, I had some good receivers — Al Bell and Greg Richardson — I just threw it out there, and they were the ones who pulled it down. They did a great job, and before we knew it, we looked up and were ahead!

The crowd over there in Athens was pretty quiet. All you could hear were the Crimson Tide fans in the corner of the stadium shouting, "Roll, Tide, Roll!"

Wes Neighbors remembers that particular evening and the impact it would have on an even more entertaining and heartstopping season-ending game against Auburn.

WES NEIGHBORS:

We'd never played "Between the Hedges," so that was a motivating factor. We remembered from the year before how the Georgia players would get in your face after they had made a big play. It's funny the little things you remember, but on a lighter side I'll never forget Larry Rose before the game. Gary Otten had gotten injured, so Larry, a true freshman, was starting on national television against Georgia. I thought, "My God, he'll never make it. He's scared to death." His eyes were huge!

In a way, it was a very frustrating game because we dominated Georgia but we never could put them away. I felt we played way too conservatively, but I knew the reason why. Coach Perkins had been haunted by all the mistakes and turnovers we had made in 1984, and he just didn't want us to be giving the game away. He felt our defense was too strong for Georgia to beat us.

Late in the game, I don't even know if there was a minute left, they blocked a punt and scored to go ahead 16-13. My first thought was, "Here's last year all over again." But I'm telling you, that didn't last long. When we got into the huddle, there was a feeling we were going to make something happen. I looked in Mike Shula's eyes, and I saw determination and a calmness I hadn't seen before. We believed we were going to win, at least 10 of us did. One player said, "A tie is better than a loss." Meaning, of course, if we could get close enough, Van (Tiffin) could kick a tying field goal. We all looked at this player and said, "Tie, hell, we're going to win this game!"

Shula was sensational on the drive, hitting about four or five passes, to get us to Georgia's 16-yard line. Larry Rose was next to me in the pass protection, and we saw Al Bell break wide open in the end zone. We were yelling at Mike to throw the football. When we saw Al catch it, there was absolute bedlam again.

The 1985 season was my favorite because it had a team that didn't think it could lose. We had fun playing together, and the most fun was the season finale against Auburn. It was not only the greatest game I ever played in, but it was also the greatest game I ever saw!

The personnel on both sides of the field were just unbelievable. It was a game that the team who had the ball last was going to win. It was such a draining game, hard-fought, clean-played game that I actually felt sorry for the Auburn players when it was over. They had fought just as hard as we had. It was a game that seemed like it lasted five or six quarters. You know it is a game that starts in the afternoon, and by the second half, it is completely dark, nighttime. That made it even more unique.

I wish I could tell you what I did after Van (Tiffin) kicked the field goal, but I can't. I remember just going blank.

"I love you, Van Tiffin, I love you."
— Coach Ray Perkins after Tiffin's 57-yard field goal beat Auburn 25-23 in 1985

The man who kicked his way into the hearts of Bama fans remembers that famous moment.

VAN TIFFIN:

The last few seconds of the game, we were behind by 1 point, and it looked like there was no hope in sight. The offense really did a spectacular job of getting the football down the field in hopes of getting a field goal, which was a lot to hope for at the time. However, they did, and I realized that it would be a difficult field goal because we didn't have time to get down far enough to make it a short one. Finally Greg Richardson got out of bounds. The first thing that happened (after Coach Perkins called for the field goal unit) was my stomach went up into my throat. After that, it was like something took over, and we ran out on the field.

We had a hurry-up call just to get everybody on the field faster than normal. I ran out and set up my tee, but I really didn't get lined up properly. It was basically just a shot in the wind — just kick it and hope for the best. So that's what I did, and it sort of surprised me that I made it. I'd never had a kick quite like that one!

Actually, I didn't feel anything — that was what was so unusual about the kick. I looked up and said, "This must be a dream — it's going right down the middle!" That's the kind of kick you always miss, but I didn't. That was what was so great about it.

And when I made it, I didn't realize what it meant — I didn't realize it was the game-winning field goal. I had never had a game-winning field goal, so I was ready to just go back into the dressing room. Then everybody went wild, and I realized exactly what had happened. That was one of my greatest moments in any game or as a player.

Alabama concluded its 1985 season with a 24-3 victory over Southern California in the Aloha Bowl, capping a 9-2-1 season. Even higher expectations arose for the 1986 squad, which faced a schedule that included non-conference foes Ohio State, Notre Dame, and Penn State.

Tragedy struck that team in August when budding star defensive lineman Willie Ryles collapsed on the practice field and later his heartbeat stopped at University Hospital in Birmingham. Not only would Ryles's death leave a glaring hole in the starting line, the emotions of the team were severely tested for a second time in a matter of months. Back in April, Alabama fullback George Scruggs had been killed in a car accident, which also severely injured stellar defensive back Vernon Wilkinson.

WES NEIGHBORS:

There is really no way to measure the impact of the loss of a teammate to an injury. If you could and then multiply it by about an infinite number, you might not come close to feeling like we did after having two players die and another one critically injured.

You could classify the season as disappointing because we finished 10-3 and should have been better. There's no question about that. I really believe we played so many emotional games early in the season — the Ohio State, Florida, Notre Dame, and Tennessee games — that we didn't have a lot left for the stretch drive. In retrospect, playing Ohio State in the Kickoff Classic was a mistake. We were mentally and physically drained by the midway turn of the season.

Of course the win over Notre Dame in Birmingham gave our team a great deal of satisfaction. I was happiest for Sylvester Croom, who was one of our assistant coaches. I'll never forget him crying in the dressing room after the game. He'd been a player and coach on the other Alabama teams that had lost all those close games to Notre Dame, and I guess he felt some redemption.

All my life I had wanted to play against Notre Dame, and I'll never forget my first impression when they came on the field — I couldn't believe how big they were. The guy I was blocking was so tall that I could have run through his legs and jumped on his back. They had great talent, but they really couldn't move the ball on us.

They played most of their defense close to the line of scrimmage, which gave us an opportunity to throw the ball on them. When we got ahead 28-10, we got conservative, feeling it would be impossible for them to come back unless we turned the ball over.

Cornelius Bennett made one of the most memorable plays in Alabama history, and I didn't even see it. I was sitting on the bench, and I heard a roar from the game and asked Coach (Jimmy) Fuller what everybody was yelling about. He said, "Biscuit just knocked the crap out of one of their players." Greg Richardson ran a punt back for a touchdown, and I'll never forget Cornelius wiping out one of their players for one of the best blocks I'd ever seen.

I really credit the Alabama crowd for helping us that day. They were all pumped up before the game, but like most games there was a lull — until Cornelius made his tackle. That fired the fans up, and they inspired us the rest of the afternoon.

After painful losses to Penn State, Auburn, and LSU (all top-10 teams), Alabama accepted an invitation to play Pac-10 co-champion Washington in the Sun Bowl. An air of controversy enveloped the El Paso scenario with the rampant rumor that Ray Perkins was about to bid adios to the Tide and accept a position with the Tampa Bay Buccaneers. Perkins emphatically denied the rumor when he was asked by Associated Press writer Herschel Nissenson if it were true that he was to be the next head coach at Tampa.

The Crimson Tide players seemed disinterested in the rumblings and appeared totally relaxed after a few weeks off from the gridiron strife. On Christmas Day 1986, Alabama played perhaps the most complete game of the Perkins era in a resounding 28-6 thrashing of the powerful Huskies.

"He knocked me woozy. I have never been hit like that before, and hopefully, I'll never be hit like that again."
— Notre Dame quarterback Steve Buerlein after Cornelius Bennett tackled him in the 1986 game

Superstar Cornelius Bennett, the defensive MVP that day and Lombardi Trophy winner that season, recalls his Christmas in El Paso and his move to linebacker at the Capstone.

CORNELIUS BENNETT:

It was Coach Perkins's last game at Alabama and my last game at the University. My senior class wanted to go out winners, and I guess we had just a little extra incentive going into the game against Washington. We wanted to be remembered as a good football team.

When I had first signed with Alabama, Coach Perkins had told me he would let me try three positions. Believe it or not, he was going to try me at linebacker first, then running back, and then tight end. But the day after the first practice in helmets and shorts — and I don't know how he saw the talent or whatever — he's qouted in the newspaper as saying, "Cornelius Bennett is going to be the next Lawrence Taylor."

That was like "Wow!" How can he say this when I've only practiced one day at linebacker? And so that was it as far as running back was concerned, but I wanted to be a tight end more than anything else.

For the four years I was at Alabama, I would go to Coach Perkins and bug him about letting me play tight end. I wanted to play both ways because I had played both ways in high school, and I thought I could handle it. But we had such fine tight ends while I was at the University that I was never needed. But every day in drills in those four years, I would practice catching the football with the receivers whenever I wasn't practicing as a linebacker. I would go to Coach (George) Henshaw and work with the receivers and run pass routes with them so I was always ready and keen on playing tight end in case Coach Perkins might need me!

The play I'm most remembered for is the hit against Notre Dame. You know, that's probably one of the greatest honors that a human being can get — being immortalized in a painting (referring to Daniel Moore's print "The Hit") or a statue. It's something I enjoy seeing. I have one in my office at my house, and my mother has one in her den. And when I go through the shopping malls and look into the stores and see one, it makes me feel good. Until this day when I see the art work or photo, I see a fumble, but I guess it happened so fast the referees were caught by surprise. I still say the play was a fumble.

During the week after the bowl, the sun certainly began to set on the Perkins regime as the apparent rumor of his return to pro football became more than just idle street talk. By January 4, 1987, Perkins was traveling to Florida, and Bill Curry was being ushered in as head coach of Alabama.

At his final Alabama press conference, Perkins publicly stated: "I can't begin to tell you how tough the decision was because of all the people involved. I'm talking about my coaches and the players who I've fallen in love with since I've been at Alabama. I'm talking about our administration, the trustees, and our fans. But there comes a time in your life when you can't make a decision based on how you feel about other people. For the first time in my life, I felt I had to make a decision for myself and my family. And I think I've done that now."

Bill Curry tried his best to soften the discontent among his detractors by making these remarks at his announcement press conference: "I realize I didn't play at Alabama or coach at Alabama, and for that reason I'm not considered one of the family. I accept that. That's how it should be. But I'd like to earn a spot in the Alabama family, and you do that by what happens on the field."

During his three years at the Capstone, Bill Curry posted a 26-10 record, including a trio of wins over Penn State and its legendary coach Joe Paterno. In 1987 Alabama rollercoasted to a 7-5 season with the high mark coming in the 24-13 upset over the Nittany Lions in Happy Valley. Penn State was defending national champion and a 23-3 winner over the Tide the year before in Tuscaloosa. It was a night that belonged to Bobby Humphrey but also one that began to showcase the extraordinary talents of Derrick Thomas, a linebacker deluxe who was expected to try to alleviate the loss of Cornelius Bennett.

In 1988, in perhaps one of the most incredible individual performances in college football history, Derrick Thomas penned his own name in the legendary column in an 8-3 win over Penn State in Birmingham. There were no touchdowns by either offense, just three field goals and a safety registered by Thomas. In a season in which the Sack Man bagged 27 quarterbacks and 12 other runners for losses, there was no afternoon like October 22, 1988. Derrick remembers that incredible day at Birmingham's Legion Field.

DERRICK THOMAS:

I remember not doing a whole lot in the first half—I wanted to have one of my best games, and here I was doing nothing at all. Penn State was doing things to keep me out of the offense, so Coach (Don) Lindsey made some adjustments at the half, and I was intent on making some things happen for us defensively.

I knew it would be one of those games where points would be hard to come by, and I remember when I tackled Tony Sacca for the safety, I felt that those 2 points may win us the game. We had a great defensive effort for the entire game, and while I may have gotten a lot of recognition, my teammates were making things happen all game.

I don't remember how many yards Penn State got, but it wasn't much. I do remember the game was on CBS, and announcer Brent Musburger said that my performance was the most dominating and best held ever seen by a college player. That made me feel proud.

For the record Thomas had 3 sacks, 1 pass knocked down, 8 solo tackles, and perhaps most incredibly, he was credited with forcing Sacca to pass early on eight other occasions, including the last play of the game when his hurry caused an interception for Lee Ozmint. After the game, these remarks were made about Thomas.

"I thought Derrick Thomas played the game of his life, and that's saying a lot. When Derrick Thomas is flying around, all kinds of things happen. They start looking for him and start to compensate. It's a real nightmare when there's a player like that on the other team."
— Alabama head coach Bill Curry

"I play tackle now, and I know how it is to try to block Derrick Thomas. It's like being on an island. I'd never want to be in an opponent's shoes and go against Derrick Thomas."
— Alabama tackle John Fruhmorgen

"Derrrick Thomas was everywhere. He had a dominating-type game. We just couldn't handle him at key times."
— Penn State fullback John Greene

For his efforts, Thomas was the national player of the week, and that inspirational outing certainly elevated him to the status of being the best linebacker in college football, an honor he would win in December as the Butkus Trophy recipient. Thomas would end his college career by blocking two field goals and being named the defensive MVP in Alabama's 29-28 win over Army in the Sun Bowl. Thomas's teammate and fellow captain of the 1988 squad, quarterback David Smith, the game's outstanding player after completing 33 of 52 passes for 412 yards, remembers the finale in El Paso that marked the end of a 9-3 season.

DAVID SMITH:

Our 1988 season got off to a rocky start because of some injuries, including my own. I hurt my knee in practice the week after the Temple game and didn't come back until we beat Tennessee in Knoxville. I had some pretty good games, but it was capped off for me when we had a great win over Army in the Sun Bowl. Everybody played really well, and I was lucky enough to play the best game of my career in my final game.

Going into the game Coach Homer Smith had told us we might have to pass more than we ran because he felt Army would do everything possible to stop our running attack and force us to pass the football. So I felt we had a really good game plan to move the football on them. We thought we could run the ball, but we knew that if we couldn't that we would adjust and throw the football.

Army proved early they could move the ball equally well out of their wishbone, and they scored a couple of quick touchdowns. We trailed almost the entire game.

Derrick Thomas, who was just a phenomenal player, made a couple of critical plays for us, blocking a couple of field goals that ultimately won us the game. His blocks of field goals and a couple that Philip Doyle converted for us were really the turning points of the game.

The Sun Bowl really was a great bowl to go to. Army is a unique school to play. They are a little bit smaller than most of the teams we played, but they played as hard as anybody I had ever seen. It was a great game from a competitive standpoint.

Shining brilliantly on and off the field during that era was tight end Howard Cross, whose superb blocking skills earned him a starting spot for the New York Giants and one Super Bowl ring. Cross never earned all-star accolades at the Capstone during his 1985-88 career, but he produced on the field and no doubt was an all-leaguer in the eyes of his coaches. Big Howard remembers some of his more forgettable as well as unforgettable days on the Bama practice and playing fields.

HOWARD CROSS:

My favorite memory is about one day when I was outside practicing catching footballs. They were throwing long balls to me, and they threw about 25 to 30 to me in a row and Ozzie Newsome was up in the window watching. There was one I didn't reach for — I didn't dive for it although I could have. When I went inside, Ozzie came up to me and said, "Look, kid, if you want to be a successful football player, you've got to dive for those, too!"

Another forgettable moment came in a practice session. Coach Perkins used to have us practice at night once a week in the summertime drills. It was always exciting. They had the lights on, and everybody was screaming and yelling. We had this one-on-one drill — this happened my freshman year, and I remember it clear as day. I weighed 205 pounds, and I got really excited because everybody was screaming and challenging each other.

I yelled, "Yea, I want to hit Cornelius!" Uh-oh!! Man, it was dark outside, but it got real bright. Boy, I messed up. Well, Cornelius picked me up and brought me to the line first of all, and he kept saying, "Boy, do you know what you just did?" I remember what his shoes looked like when he was stepping on me! He ran over me a couple of times that day. But after that? He graduated!

Even the loss of such luminaries as Derrick Thomas, David Smith, and Howard Cross along with Bobby Humphrey's decision to enter the NFL draft hardly derailed the 1989 Crimson Tide team. It won its first 10 games, cresting at No. 2 in the nation. But a 30-20 loss to Auburn in the first ever Iron Bowl contested on the Plains left a bitter taste that even a Sugar Bowl date with eventual national champion Miami couldn't sweeten.

Despite losing those final two games, Alabama claimed a share of the SEC title with Auburn and Tennessee, the first time in eight years the Crimsons had garnered some conference hardware. It was a team of improbable heroes, most notably junior quarterback Gary Hollingsworth, who had been relegated to a role of a scout team thrower for his first three years before being forced into action due to a knee injury to starter Jeff Dunn. By season's end, the Hamilton, Alabama native would be the SEC Player of the Year and somewhat of a folk hero to Bama fans. Even in the defeats to Auburn and Miami, he was sensational and almost flung the Tide to the winner's circle.

"The best I ever hoped for was to have my picture hanging up in a Hardee's in Hamilton."

— Quarterback Gary Hollingsworth when asked if he had ever expected to have his picture appear in *Sports Illustrated*

Gary remembers his junior season game with Miami in the Sugar Bowl.

GARY HOLLINGSWORTH:

We knew that being up against a tough Miami team, we were going to have to do some things differently. I think we stayed in the shotgun about ninety percent of the time that night, because of the superior defense they had. Fortunately we were able to complete some passes and stayed in it. We gave them a run for their money before we lost it 33-25.

We knew going into it that it was going to be a great challenge, and I think we accepted that challenge and went down and did our best. I don't think we have anything to be embarrassed about because I think they were by far the best team in the country that year.

I think that particular game you'd have to give credit to the whole offensive line for the job they did all night. They were going up against four guys who were drafted in the top one or two rounds.

Lee Ozmint had an interception, and I think John Mangum played exceptionally well in that game. Keith McCants came up and played well, and Willie Wyatt. and heck, you could just name off both sides of the ball and in the special team. It was truly a team effort that night. I don't think there was one particular person who stood out as playing exceptionally well. We pretty much all had to to be able to stay close with them.

It was a super enjoyable time because once the season starts, during the off season, that's your goal, that's your driving thing, that's what you're working for — to make it to New Orleans, to make it to the Sugar Bowl. To be able to do that, was one of the most rewarding things that happened to me while I was at the University.

Perhaps the most memorable win of the season came in Happy Valley, Penn.sylvania, home of Joe Paterno and his heralded Nittany Lions. Evenly matched, the two prolific football powers battled to a 17-16 score when the Lions roared down the field to within 6 inches of the end zone and seemed positioned to secure a cinch victory. With 13 seconds left to go and no timeouts, Paterno sent in kicker Ray Tarasi for a chip shot attempt. Defensive tackle Thomas Rayam joined the ranks of Crimson Tide fabled heroes late that afternoon when he blocked Tarasi's field goal to preserve the 17-16 win.

THOMAS RAYAM:

That was the last time Alabama was scheduled to go to Penn State. We had beaten them in my sophomore and junior seasons, so we were really up and optimistic going into the game. Since we were undefeated entering the game, we thought we could beat them to death, but they really surprised us. They were playing us tough.

I was playing on an injured ankle. I had hurt it in practice the Monday before the game, and the coaches had taken me out of the game six or seven times because of the pain I was in. The game actually reminded me of an old-timer's game — there was mud everywhere, and we were all so dirty.

On the last drive I was on the sidelines, and I wanted to go in so badly. Two plays before the kick, Coach (Larry) New put me in for Derrick Rushton, and I'll never forget him saying, "Let's see what you can do."

On the next play Willie Wyatt stopped their running back Blair Thomas inches from the goal line. They almost scored, and he bounced into the end zone and apparently a lot of the fans thought he did score, but he didn't. Penn State lined up to kick a field goal, and I was thinking, "We've got to believe." I nominated myself to be the leader of those 11 guys. I made everyone hold hands, and we all believed they were not going to score.

The play was called, and it was "desperation block." My job was to make a hole for Mike Ramil, but instead I just crashed through my man. I wasn't even thinking of my ankle. To be honest, I don't even remember the guy in front of me because I hit him so hard. I just remember my hand stinging. I knew I had hit something, but I didn't know if it was the ball or someone's helmet. We were all just lying on the ground, and Efrum Thomas had the ball in his hands. I couldn't believe it — I just couldn't believe I had blocked the kick. You couldn't believe how high I had jumped and how fast I had run. I just totally forgot my ankle. It was so swollen.

I've played for three seasons in the pros, and I even played in a Super Bowl for the Washington Redskins, and to this day, Alabama-Penn State is the most exciting game I've ever played in. We never stopped believing we would win. We proved ourselves. There are still paintings around from the game. It is such a thrill to come back to school and have people still remember that game. I will never have another game like that one. Nobody believed in us, but we did. We proved to everyone we were good. It just goes to prove that if you believe in yourselves you can do anything.

After the game Tarasi, who had kicked three field goals, including a season long 46-yarder, remarked, "When the kick left my foot, I felt like it was good. Then I felt the block. It was a sickening feeling."

Alabama Coach Bill Curry commented: "Our team, even when Penn State was ramming it down our throats on that last drive, felt they would find a way to win the game, and they did."

The decade of the 1980s dawned in New Orleans on New Year's afternoon when the 1979 team clinched a national title. Probably none of the celebrants that joyous day would have dared forecast it would be a decade before the Tide rolled back into the Crescent City to participate in the Sugar Bowl. Worse yet, the union of the program would be split asunder in the 1980s.

Ironically, in the same locker room where the last team of one decade celebrated being No. 1, the last team of another 10-year cycle listened intently as Bill Curry stood before his team and implied he would be examining several job opportunities in the next few days. In that first week of 1990, Curry would accept the position of head coach at Kentucky, and Alabama would be seeking his successor.

For the decade of the 1980s, despite an endless litany of complaints and disillusionary moments, Alabama finished with a record of 85-33-2, not bad by most standards but inadequate in the eyes of the beholders of a school traditionally destined to vie for No. 1. Some men may not be intimidated by treading on the shadows cast by titans. Yet their intrepidness does not necessarily merit them a sacred spot in the hearts of the idolators of the giants whose silhouettes are still considered hallowed territory. Perhaps that is how fate frowned on the first two successors to Paul William Bryant, whose down-home charisma forever left an imprint on the psyche of his followers.

Here stood a man who defied all the national pontifications that the people of Alabama were destined for the inferior bottom-rung ranking. Coach Bryant preached to his people to believe in themselves, pay the price with dedication and pride, and the fruits of victory would arrive. Vicariously, his legions of followers found comfort in his exploits and the resounding successes of his crimson gladiators, and to the detractors, his people could shout to the rest of the nation, "We are No. 1."

His retirement and death dealt a crushing blow to the minds of the Alabama family, folks who could identify with houndstooth hats and talk of mamas and papas and impending national championships but who weren't accustomed to descriptive speeches and guarantees of a promising tomorrow. The heck with delayed gratification.

So when the search began for a coach to guide Bama into the future with a gentle reminder of its gloried past, Cecil "Hootie" Ingram, director of athletics, chose a man who would not only reinstill the charm of the Bryant era but who also had the ability to lead Alabama football into another distinctive age of its own. The man who would get the anointment, Gene Stallings, happened to be an out-of-work, twice-fired head coach with an overall losing record. Yet his mere presence instilled a calming confidence in the Alabama people that he could escort them down a fresh pathway of champions while never traversing on the footsteps left by his own beloved instructor.

"Let's face it. Alabama just likes to hit you. They are the hardest-hitting team I've ever played against."
— Illinois quarterback Tony Eason after Alabama beat the Illini 21-15 in Paul Bryant's final game

"I don't know how long I'll stay on as athletic director. I want to be out before next football season. I don't think there is any way I could be around and not hurt the team."
— Coach Bryant after the 1982 Liberty Bowl win

"A lot of success Alabama has enjoyed through the years is related to tradition. Prestige and that sort of thing make good boys want to play football at Alabama. They want to win championships. Tradition is a rich asset for Alabama football. To my way of thinking, there is no other school, with the possible exception of Notre Dame, with such tradition."
— Wallace Wade discussing the Alabama program some 50 years after he left the Capstone

"I just waxed the dude."
— Defensive back Rory Turner's explanation of his game-saving tackle of Auburn's Brent Fullwood in the 17-15 1984 game

"Folks, this is the greatest individual defensive effort I have ever witnessed."
— CBS announcer Brent Musburger talking about Derrick Thomas in the 1988 Penn State game

"My gosh these Alabama people sure love their football team"
— Assistant coach Homer Smith's admiration of Bama fans after seeing them lined up to wave at the team buses on the highway from Tuscaloosa to the Mississippi line before the 1988 Mississippi State game

"I just want to thank God for blessing me with some athletic talent and letting me play for the University of Alabama."
— Derrick Thomas in accepting the Butkus Trophy in 1988

A jubilant Thomas Rayam after he blocked Penn State's field goal and won Bama a game-saving 17-16 triumph in 1989.

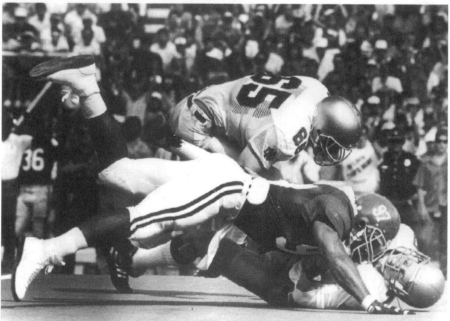

"I've never been hit like that before." — Notre Dame's Steve Beuerlein on Cornelius Bennett.

Derrick Thomas vs. Penn State, 1988.

#54, Wes Neighbors.

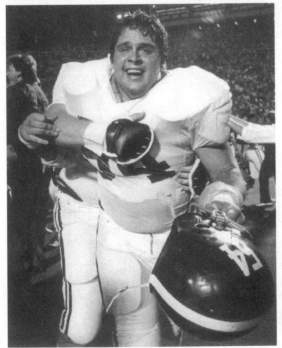

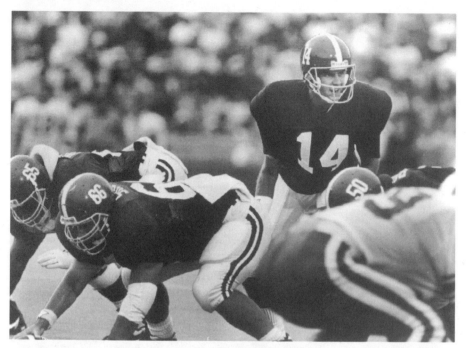

Gary Hollingsworth (14) and center Roger Shultz (66) are all-time nominees.

The great coach says good-bye. 1982 Liberty Bowl.

174

Bama's defense celebrates after Rayam's blocked kick in 1989 against Penn State. To left is Mike Ramil (92); to right is Thomas Rayam (95).

Cornelius Bennett (97) and Derrick Thomas (55).

Announcing Ray Perkins as new head coach, Dec. 15, 1982.

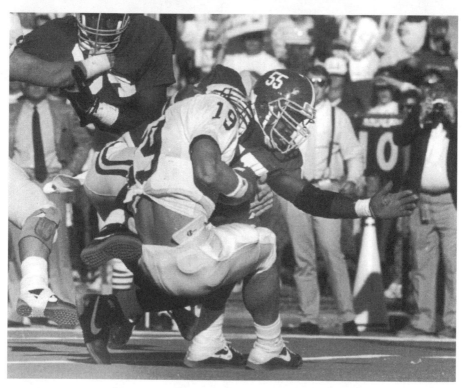

"Folks, this is the greatest individual defensive effort I've ever witnessed." Brent Musburger on Derrick Thomas in 1988 Penn State game.

THE NINETIES
The Tradition Rolls On

Perhaps the most poignant moment of Gene Stallings's earliest days as head coach at the University of Alabama occurred in the office of Hootie Ingram, director of athletics. It was a winter's morn, January 11, 1990, to be exact, and Stallings was waiting his cue to exit the office and enter the media room for his official coronation as the leader of Crimson Tide football fortunes. Dramatically, Paul Bryant, Jr., walked into the room, and as the two old friends embraced in tears, Paul proclaimed: "This is what Papa always wanted."

The media room overflowed with former players who wanted to be there to pledge their support. Former stars Bart Starr and Lee Roy Jordan were there to voice their opinions. According to NFL Hall of Famer Starr, "Gene Stallings is a very special person. He will earn the respect of the alumni and fans of the University, and he'll do it quickly."

Jordan emphasized, "Gene Stallings was Coach Bryant's selection when he retired. It didn't happen at that time, and that may have happened for a reason. We may not have been ready for it. I think the University of Alabama, the fans, and the people are ready for Gene Stallings now."

All Alabama fans were not convinced, citing Stallings's age (he was 55 when the season started) or his losing record at Texas A&M and the Phoenix Cardinals. And after an 0-3 start when inexplicably all breaks bounced in the wrong direction from Alabama's perspective, some alarmists reacted with I-told-you-so attitudes. A few years later they'd be impossible to find. Stallings's secretary, Linda Knowles, remembers his entry into the program as head coach.

LINDA KNOWLES:

You could probably call any coach or player or staff member who has ever been at the University and ask where they would like to be, and once you've been associated with the football program at Alabama, it gets in your blood and just becomes "home."

Coach Stallings just came home, the way I looked at it, and it was awfully good to see him.

One player, center Roger Shultz, had a unique role of playing for all three coaches who followed in the shadow of Paul Bryant. Always quick with a quip, Shultz commented the day Stallings was hired, "I heard him on the radio, and it sounded just like Coach Bryant. I believe this man is going to make things happen." I.

ROGER SHULTZ:

Coach Perkins recruited me to come to Alabama, and he was a good coach and a good teacher. I was just at Alabama for four months before he left to go to Tampa Bay. I wasn't expecting him to leave, but I didn't attend Alabama because of who the coach was and I don't think many players do. I was just thankful to have a scholarship to Alabama.

The transition to Coach Curry was a feeling out process. Alabama was still new to me, but the off-season went well, and for me the transition was smooth. Coach Curry got enough out of us to win, but we were never in the upper echelon. There were some games that we should have won that we just didn't.

The transition from Coach Curry to Coach Stallings was a little more difficult for me. I was a fifth-year senior, and it was hard because I thought I knew what I could do and couldn't do. We were just set in our ways. But it was just another change for us, and one we had to adapt to. We had become used to changes. I had been through three head coaches and four offensive coordinators.

I had high hopes for our team entering the 1990 season. We were coming off a co-championship and a Sugar Bowl game against No. 1 Miami. But we got off to a horrible start, losing our first three games. All of them were close, and we should have won all three of them. If we would have won those three games, and like I say we should have, just think of what Coach Stallings's record at Alabama would be.

I realized after the first three games that we were simplifying things and were moving toward the power running game. We went from a so-called "finesse blocking" to "power blocking," and it was just different for us. It would be like a traditional passing team, like a Brigham Young, changing to the running game.

The two key games for us in 1990 were the win over Tennessee in Knoxville and, of course, the 16-7 whipping of Auburn in the Iron Bowl. Both of them were gratifying, and I guess I was the first one who said, "We own Tennessee," after we beat them in Knoxville. They were the huge favorites. The amazing thing about the game was that they just had unbelievable field position the whole game, and we were back up on our own goal most of the afternoon.

That win elevated our confidence level, and it should have. Tennessee was extremely talented, unbeaten, and sure they were going to beat up on us. They didn't. Everything had gone wrong for us in the first three games, but we got a break when Stacy Harrison blocked the field goal attempt, and the ball rolled back about 20 yards to get us in position for Philip Doyle's field goal.

The Auburn game was even more intense for us because they had beaten us four straight years. On the first play when Byron Holdbrooks slammed Stan White down for a sack, the tone was set. Some of the Auburn players were saying there was a different look in our eyes than in previous years. They felt we had been intimidated before. I don't know if that is accurate or not, but we were a determined team in 1990.

We had endured quite a few injuries to our key skill people in those first three losses, so they pretty well knew we were coming right at them. After Efrum Thomas intercepted the pass to set up our touchdown, we just kept pounding away at them.

When we got the ball back on the final time, I grabbed the game ball and headed to the locker room. It was a crazy scene, the fans were jubilant. We were, too.

Certainly there are special autumn afternoons that forever embedded a crimson tint in the memory banks of Alabama's ardent followers. One that will never fade was that October 20, 1990, game against Tennessee in Knoxville.

No one, sans a few coaches and 70 players dressed in their road whites, even hinted at the Tide having a chance of rolling out of Tennessee with a victory. ESPN analyst Lee Corso asserted his opinion that it would be like a high school team against a college team and rout no doubt lingered on the horizon for the Crimsons. Undaunted by such declarations and perhaps inspired by them, Alabama played football reminiscent of the halcyon days of Bryant by physically standing toe-to-toe with the double-digit favored Vols and leaving Knoxville with an improbable 9-6 victory.

Heroes abounded, and one of the most touching scenes occurred in the delirious dressing room when reporters interviewed defensive coach Bill Oliver. His tears of exultation earned him a Sunday morning headline sobriquet of Weeping William.

One of Coach O's shining lights that third Saturday in October was safety Stacy Harrison, whose determination to make the desperation block literally turned the possibilities of the agony of defeat into the ecstasy of victory. Moments after the win, Stacy declared, "I wasn't going to let Alabama lose." A few years later and with well-earned glee, he recalled that victory that began to turn doubters of Gene Stallings and his regime into believers.

STACY HARRISON:

When we went to Tennessee to play them in 1990, no one gave us a chance to win the game. For me it was an especially memorable day because it just so happened I was the player that made the difference in the game.

We were tied at 6-6 real late in the game, and it was one of those desperation situations. Tennessee was lining up for what would have been a game-winning field goal. I knew somebody had to make a great play, and I was fortunate enough to make it. We had a play called Desperation Block, and the coaches told us that one day somebody would make that play. A hole just opened up for me, and I got through to block it.

We were sending all 11 players, and they couldn't block everybody. I was the one who had the opening and came away with the block. That sort of put my name on the map.

Not to sound cocky about it, but once I saw the ball cross the 50-yard line, I knew we were going to win the game. I knew Philip (Doyle) was capable of kicking the ball 100 yards. That's how much confidence I had in him. There was no doubt he was going to kick the field goal to beat Tennessee.

Going into the game, no one in America had any faith in us. The odds were against us, but we stuck together as a team. That's the main thing — we got a victory from having a team concept. Lee Corso had gone on ESPN and said it would be like a high school team playing against one of the three best teams in college football. I don't know if that motivated us any more than we already were. We felt like we had a good team and had given our first three games away.

We were playing in a hostile environment in front of 97,000 fans, and all odds were against us. That's when you get your spirits uplifted by your teammates, that's when you come together and lay it on the line as one team with a common goal.

Basically the game was just as the final score of 9-6 indicated—a defensive struggle. The previous week Tennessee had beaten Florida 45-3 and ran up over 400 yards in doing it. One thing different about Alabama was we had a mastermind on defense in Coach (Bill) Oliver, and he put together a game plan that completely puzzled the Tennessee offense. We kept them off guard by playing a lot of different sets with a lot of defensive backs. Tennessee had a fantastic receiving corps, which included players like Alvin Harper and Carl Pickens and I don't think any one of them caught a pass that day. *(EDITOR'S NOTE: During that game Tennessee quarterback Andy Kelly and Sterling Henton were 9 of 25 for 51 yards passing with two interceptions, Alvin Harper didn't catch a single pass, and Carl Pickens caught a single pass for only 7 yards.)*

Our entire defense just dominated the entire afternoon, and there were just so many big plays. Antonio Langham and George Teague each had an interception, and George Thornton, Byron Holdbrooks, and John Sullins shut down Tennessee's running game. We played without Eric Curry, who had gotten hurt a couple weeks before.

One huge play that set up the blocked field goal came on a third-down screen pass from Kelly — Efrum Thomas made a super play to stop them for a loss. That block will always be something special for me. It was a do or die play for us, and I wasn't going to let Alabama lose.

After the abysmal start of the Stallings era, the Tennessee victory signalled hope. By season's end, the Tide eagerly awaited its appointed date with Auburn, victors for four straight years over the Tide. When All-American Philip Doyle connected on his third field goal of the day to secure a 16-7 victory, Alabama fans initiated their celebration that would last well into Sunday morning. Even a dismal performance against Louisville in the Fiesta Bowl hardly dampened the expectation that 1991 would be special.

With the return of Siran Stacy, who severely damaged a knee in the 1990 opener, hope for a brighter 1991 prevailed on the Tuscaloosa practice fields. Even Stallings's best efforts to temper the enthusiasm by reminding the few who would listen that Alabama's inexperience, particularly at quarterback, hardly classified the Tide as a contender for conference and national honors.

Optimism diminished quickly and realism set in after a 35-0 blowout loss to Florida in the second game of the year and the first conference matchup. Assistant coach Jimmy Fuller once marvelled at Stallings's unflappable attitude. "You know you hear coaches talk about playing one game at a time, but most of the time that's just a bunch of talk. Well Coach Stallings literally takes them one at a time. When we lost to Florida, we didn't dwell on it. We just got ready for Georgia."

The 10-0 win over Georgia started a modest 1-game winning streak, and the Tide's victim list continued to grow one a week for the remainder of 1991 and throughout the centennial 1992 season. An 11-1 record, blockbuster victory over Big-8 co-champ Colorado, and a 5th place national finish were a few of the accomplishments of Stallings's second team. He was quick to point to his leaders on the field for the remarkable turnaround from the disastrous night in Gainesville.

Senior captains Kevin Turner, John Sullins, Robert Stewart, and Siran Stacy, reflected on that season and their careers and reported these Crimson memories at the A-Day game in 1992.

KEVIN TURNER:

I've been looking at those names in the Walk of Fame for a long time now, ever since I was small. Just to be in the same place with them is unreal.

I don't think anyone last year in their wildest imagination figured we were a team that would go 11 and 1. And I don't think anyone could really feel how good that team was because nobody really knew. Every week we were getting tested, and every week we wondered if it was another fluke — we'd barely won that time again. When we first went out there in August, we had a lot of young guys and no men. Siran and I were the only two seniors on the offense, and we looked around and said we kind of wished we were going to be here for a few more years.

JOHN SULLINS:

As far as me being the leading tackler, it's a team effort all around, and our defense played outstandingly all year. To be a co-captain with Robert, Kevin, and Siran is a dream come true. To actually put my hand and footprint in the cement — it was great. Not a lot of defensive stars get a lot of credit, but at this University — Linebacker U, with McCants, Bennett, and everybody else — it's a great place to play ball, especially if you're a defensive player. That's one of the reasons I came here.

When you come in as a freshman, and you look at the older guys, you want to learn something from them because that's who's going to leave the program and leave it intact. You are the future coming through as a freshman, and you want to do your best to contribute to the team, to look up to a junior or senior upperclassman and get a few fine points from them, a few hints here and there.

I know some of the offensive linemen give the younger guys lessons on holding. Every freshman who came in as an offensive lineman last year held me to death! And I think that's contributed to Tobie Sheils and Roger Shultz who left that advice to them. So I try to help the younger players. Mike Rogers, a young guy who came in and played a lot for us last year, is a prime example of someone who wants to get better. He was always bugging me to death about what do you do here, what do you do there. He's going to turn out to be a fine football player, and I just try to help him. Just like Willie Shephard, Greg Gilbert, and all those guys before me helped me.

ROBERT STEWART:

When we went out for spring training, we knew that we had a lot of defensive guys coming back. Even though we didn't have any idea we would go 11 and 1, we knew we had the potential to be one of the top teams in SEC football. With all of the guys pulling together through spring practice and all the hard work, we could see that we were going to be a good football team. But it was beyond my wildest dreams that we would be 11 and 1.

We have some pretty decent names stepping into my spot. James Gregory has done real well, and today we can see how he's made it. As far as anchoring the defensive line and running the 3-man front, I think James will come in and do well. He has some weaknesses and there are some things he still has to work on, but I feel that when the season kicks off next year, he'll be where he needs to be. I think our defense will compete as well as we did last year.

SIRAN STACY:

We have outstanding talent at running back. I know that Kevin and I are leaving, but I think we've left the running back position in good hands. The guys have really worked hard — they've been working hard for three years, and Derrick (Lassic) is going to get his opportunity to go out and perform, and not only him, but the rest of the guys.

Going back to this past season, I think the turning point for our football team was the Florida game. We won the Temple game by a large margin, but we didn't know exactly how good we were. When we went out against Florida, we just weren't ready to play. The next week of practice and preparation for Georgia, with Robert, Kevin, John, and I sitting down for a team meeting and talking with the guys, we got everything back on the right track. We got out minds set, and we just put it all together. That really was the turning point of our season, and I look back and realize we learned so much from that Florida game.

Coach Stallings is the kind of coach who used to come up to us after the game and say, "Well, we just got beat. It's just one of those things — it's going to happen. We've got to come back and work next week. We've got another SEC game, and we can't go cry in a corner."

You lose one game in the SEC, and you figure you can't lose another one and be in contention. So we had our backs against the wall after the Florida game, and we came out fighting the rest of the season. That was our attitude — no matter what it took to win, we would just go win the game.

There are two days that I can pinpoint that were very important to me. One was in 1989 when I first came to the University. It was the game with Memphis State played at Legion Field. I recall I had four touchdowns that game. No one really knew anything about me then, and I had so much fun. It was my first time to put on the Crimson jersey, and I felt like I was a god.

The other game was my last game — I'm going to leave out the Tennessee game — against Colorado. So much had been written about how we were the worst team in America and how we were lucky, and I think in that game we went out and proved to America just how good a football team we were. As seniors, we went out in style.

Alabama's Centennial season dramatically dawned on an April morning when more than 500 legends of the past returned to the sites of some of their most memorable days. Led by the Million Dollar Band blaring "Yea, Alabama" to the heavens and marching through a mass of idolizing fans, the stars of yesteryear paraded through campus to the Quad. Standing on the library steps, applauding them, and admittedly with a tear in his eye and goose bumps on his neck, was head coach Gene Stallings. "You know this is really special being the head coach at the University of Alabama in its Centennial year," whispered the tall Texan to a few media folks watching the ceremonies.

Often throughout the year, Stallings reminded his team what a privilege it was for him and them to be the principals in Alabama's celebratory season. Week by week the Crimson Tide flowed upward toward the charts of the polls, setting in motion the tension-packed SEC title win over Florida and the calming of the Hurricane in the Sugar Bowl. Throughout the final week of 1992, Alabama players had been subjected to an endless litany of bashes from Miami players whose proclamations of superiority only inspired the Tide to reach a higher crest. In defeating Miami, led by its Heisman Trophy winning quarterback Gino Torretta, and winning Alabama's 12th national title, the 1992 team had more than lived up to the "Century of Champions" theme of the Centennial. And when thousands flooded T-town January 30-31, 1993, for the official celebration of the champions, they heard Gene Stallings, humble as ever, make these remarks.

GENE STALLINGS:

Only in Alabama could you fill an arena with 15,000 for an award banquet or draw 70,000 on the quadrangle to honor a national championship team. I have said it a jillion times, but I am honored to have been the coach at the University of Alabama in its

Centennial season and to be the coach of a team that responded week after week. To win 13 games, to be in the first-ever SEC Championship game, and then win the national championship is really gratifying.

All great teams have a common thread that links them together, and I have thought often what that common denominator was for our team — I really believe it was the fact that every player on our team truly loves the University of Alabama. All of them wanted to play for the Alabama Crimson Tide, and man is that important.

Our team played under constant pressure week after week, and I don't mean just the games against Florida and Miami. We opened the season with a conference game against Vanderbilt and that's not easy. Each week the pressure mounted — going to Arkansas to play them in their first-ever SEC home game and going to Knoxville to play Tennessee. I really believed that after we won that game we had a pretty good football team.

I told our players before Ole Miss that we didn't have anything to prove but we had a lot to play for. You don't have to flaunt your success, but you don't have to apologize for it either. Well that was a big game against a really tough opponent, and so was that trip to Mississippi State. It was a pressurized situation, especially when we had so much going against us in the third quarter. I remember after that game thinking how that third quarter may be the best thing to happen to us all year — facing adversity and overcoming it. But while it was going on, I wasn't enjoying it a bit.

Then we had to play Auburn, and it was an emotional day for them with Coach Dye retiring. We won that one and were 11-0, and we really hadn't won anything yet. As strange as it may sound, Florida losing the week before they played us took some pressure off them. I really felt we played a little tight in the SEC Championship game, but Antonio Langham made the big play. We won that one and went to New Orleans for the Sugar Bowl with Miami.

I'd go to the press conferences down there, and they'd all ask me, "How does it feel to be such an underdog?" I'd tell them I didn't think we were underdogs and that I wouldn't trade our team for theirs. You're only an underdog if you think you are, and our team never thought it was.

We took 145 players to New Orleans, and we didn't have one player get in trouble the whole time we were down there. We had 11 p.m. curfews for four straight nights and not one player was late. I know I've said this a jillion times, but you could take 145 Sunday school teachers to New Orleans and leave them for a week, and some of them are going to get in trouble.

I always tell our players to have this goal in mind: You play 55 to 60 plays for the privilege of making three or four plays that determine the outcome of the game. All year long different players kept coming through making those big plays. This was a totally unselfish football team. I think that about two great football players like John Copeland and Eric Curry. When Eric would win an award, no one was happier for him than John. That epitomized our football team.

I've often said and I mean it, the University of Alabama's coaching staff is the best in the country, bar none. They are all outstanding teachers and outstanding people. They absolutely did the best job of getting players to perform to the best of their abilities each week.

Sir Isaac Newton once said, "If it seems I can see farther than most people, it's because I stood on the shoulders of giants." In my case I sat on the shoulders of giants. I am grateful to have a staff with coaches like Mal Moore, Larry Kirksey, Jimmy Fuller, Woody McCorvey, and Danny Pearman on offense, and Bill Oliver, Jeff Rouzie, Mike Dubose, and Ellis Johnson on defense. To have an administrative assistant like Gerald Jack and strength coach like LeBaron Caruthers, an equipment manager like Tank Conerly and a trainer like Bill McDonald.

Coach (Paul) Bryant once told me that if you're going to have success, you have to have a President who is interested in your program. Well I can't express how important Dr. Roger Sayers is to our program. He comes to practice after practice. I can't remember a time after a game that Dr. Sayers hasn't been in our locker room.

And it's important to have an athletic director like Hootie Ingram, and I appreciate him more than he'll ever know. I'll assure you that he's second to none in his profession.

When I talk about the players, I prefer to talk about the seniors because the younger guys will get their chance later on. *(EDITOR'S NOTE: Below are the seniors who started for the 1992 national champion team.)*

Steve Busky started in his last 21 games for us, and I really believe his best game was his last one against Miami. Steve would come by my office each week and want me to put in a reverse tight end pass. I'd tell him each week, "Let's wait 'til next week." Finally, the weeks ran out.

John Copeland. What more can be said about John. He was one half of the bookends with Eric Curry. He started 25 games in his career, and we won 24 of them. He was a consensus All-American and made 17 $\frac{1}{2}$ sacks and 36 quarterback pressures in his career. He was just a pleasure to watch.

Eric Curry. He's one of the most decorated players in Alabama history, but the thing I'm most proud of is that Eric graduated on time. He was a Prop 48 out of high school, which means you aren't supposed to make it. Well Eric did, and regardless of all those other awards he's won, I'm most proud that he got that degree.

Martin Houston played in 49 games at Alabama and rushed for more than 1,000 yards, and he's got his degree in marketing. What pleases me most is when I talk to his professors is that they all tell me what a joy he was to teach. I'll second that.

Derrick Lassic played in 48 games and rushed for more than 1,600 yards. That's 11th best in Alabama history. Last year he rushed for 905 yards, and most of them came in the big games like Tennessee and Florida and Miami. The thing that bothered me most about Derrick was that he ran so hard I was worried about him staying healthy. He ran so hard north to south with total dedication to making yards. I remember when I first came to Alabama, Derrick's girlfriend had been killed in a car accident. I'd visit with him, and he didn't want to talk. He was hurting, and I was really worried about him. He's an outstanding young man, and his contribution to Alabama football will forever be appreciated.

Antonio London came to Alabama from Tennessee, where he was one of the best high school players ever. We're glad he did. He just made so many big, big plays for us. He played in the Senior Bowl and was MVP there.

Derrick Oden. When I came to Alabama, I didn't hear many good things about

185

Derrick. Everything I heard was negative, but man, did he turn it around. He started 31 straight games and showed his leadership by becoming a captain. When he comes by my office, it's always a pleasure for me.

George Teague played in 49 games, starting 37 straight. In his career he made 14 interceptions, broke up 25 passes, and made 149 tackles. Who'll ever forget the great play he made in the Sugar Bowl. I stress to the players they must make the big play — well he made one. It has been run back and run back a jillion times on the networks, and George got plenty of airtime. If you tried to buy that much advertising time, U.S. Steel couldn't afford it. Everybody knows who George Teague is now. Brother, that play he made in the Sugar Bowl was a big-time play.

George Wilson. Not 1 in 50 million could do what George Wilson has done. I use one word to describe him: courage. Here's a young man who's involved in a hunting accident and loses half of one of his feet. I used to fuss at George about having no balance. Heck, I wouldn't either if I had a half a foot missing. Well George kept on playing, and that rascal was voted one of our captains. He's also another player who completed his degree work before finishing his football career.

Prince Wimbley played in 51 games at Alabama. I don't know if anyone has played in more. Here's a young man whose family had to survive the hurricane before the season, and then one of his favorite uncles died. Despite these tragedies, he kept leading our team, and I really appreciate him. He's a great leader, and his shoes are going to be hard to fill.

I want to thank the Alabama fans for the role they played in 1992. Wherever we went we'd see those mobile homes with the Alabama flags waving. We'd go to practices on the road, and there would be hundreds of Alabama fans there cheering us. Brother, don't tell me that doesn't make a difference.

The day before the Sugar Bowl, we were going to have a final closed practice, but when we went on the Superdome floor, there must have been 10,000 fans in the stadium. The guard asked me if he wanted me to get them out, and I told him, "No, let them stay." It's that type of love for the Alabama program that makes it special for me to coach at the University, and I'm proud to be the coach of the Alabama Crimson Tide.

"How do you bail out on a team that refused to lose?"
— Tucson sportswriter Corky Simpson

Throughout the 1992 season, Tucson, Arizona, sportswriter Corky Simpson voted the Tide No. 1 in the Associated Press poll. By mid-season, fans across the country (particularly Miami and Washington) were demanding to know which kooky media type from Alabama was donning his crimson colors. After Alabama's 37-0 win over Tulane, the culprit was exposed, and Corky got corked pretty good from some irate fans who questioned his sanity as well as his football knowledge.

Well Corky, as he put it, did his homework, and by January he was a folk hero in Alabama. University officials invited him to come to Tuscaloosa to participate in the honoring of the national champions and to be grand marshal of the championship parade. Treated to several ovations by the fans and the awarding of a Crimson No. 1 jersey by Gene Stallings, Corky basked in, as he called it, his 15 minutes of fame. Corky in turn made these statements about his No. 1 team.

CORKY SIMPSON:

Alabama should be eternally grateful to the Phoenix Cardinals whose owner, in his infinite wisdom, decided a few years ago he wanted to make a change in his head coach. In America when we don't like the music, we shoot the pianist, and in Phoenix's case, the owner got rid of the most popular sports figure in the state. That owner had such a commitment to excellence, he got rid of Gene Stallings. I think Alabama came out the winner.

During the season when it became public knowledge that I was the lone voter picking Alabama No. 1 each week, I received quite a few messages, mostly from the state of Florida. On January 2, 1993, when the final AP poll came out and Alabama was unanimously No. 1 with all 62 voters casting their ballots for the Tide, I guess I could have said, "I told you so." I did tell them so back in August, and when people asked me why I'd vote for Alabama, I'd tell them I did my homework. Here are a few of the messages I received before the Sugar Bowl.

From Maitland, Florida, I got a note saying, "I never wrote a pollster before, but your stupidity moved me to action — of throwing up." One from Miami wrote, "You say you did your homework. Well how long did it take you to read *The Weekly Reader?*"

Another said, "You say your name is Corky. Is that your name or is that a description of your gray matter?" Another wrote, "Don't let the sun set on your (bleep) in Florida, pal!"

One from Orlando commented, "Disney World needs someone to wear a new Goofy suit, and you qualify." Another irate Miamian penned, "You idiot. You have exposed yourself not only to the wrath of the Hurricane fans but showed your ignorance of college football. Corky, baby, when Alabama played Miami in the Sugar Bowl in 1990, it was like a high school team playing the Dolphins."

My favorite of them all read, "Hey, (bleep) for brains, how can you vote for someone with a cupcake schedule for No. 1? I am going to fax you a picture of my rear end, and when Miami is No. 1, then you can kiss my fax." And finally, one wrote: "Your vote should be taken away and given to someone who knows something about college football."

Alabama, you have a great thing going here, and thank you for making this one of the most memorable weekends of my life.

One of the mainstays on the 1992 squad was fullback Martin Houston.

MARTIN HOUSTON:

Perhaps the one thing that set the trend for our 1992 season was our off-season program. A lot of the guys got stronger and faster, mainly because there was a determination to do well. In the past a lot of players either gained weight and lost speed or lost weight and gained speed. Before the 1992 season, it seemed as if all the players had gained speed and gotten bigger and stronger.

I really believe not getting very much respect from the media dated back a couple of years, and it carried over into the 1992 season. Before we played Tennessee in 1990, Lee Corso said we were a high school team compared to Tennessee. Even after we beat them up there 9-6, we didn't get much respect. In 1991 we were 11-1, and everyone kept saying we weren't very good. All we kept doing was winning. We had no control over who we played, and we were determined to defeat everybody on our schedule. We would talk among ourselves before the games and say, "We've got to tighten up and get the job done. Remember all the hard work we did in the off-season, and we did it for this opportunity."

Our senior class was probably tighter than most classes because of what we had been through since our freshmen years. We had been told we were the worst freshman class in the history of Alabama, but in five years were the national champions. I would best describe our class as a group of overachievers who refused to lose. One of the most impressive things about our class was that there were no braggarts among the group, no selfish players. We let our actions speak for themselves.

All games are important, especially if you want to win the national championship, and even though no one else talked about winning it, we did as players. We talked with some of the younger players about it before the season, and you could sense that everybody on this team felt we could accomplish this goal.

There were some roadblocks we faced, and we did it like champions. Louisiana Tech was the best defense I played against in my college career. It was a tough game for us, but our defense wouldn't budge to them. David Palmer ran the punt back, and we got a couple of field goals to win it 13-0. Those are the type games where letdowns occur, and playing a team without much national recognition, but a lot of talent is sometimes your most difficult challenge.

The game that earned us respect and really started us gaining some national recognition was the 17-10 win over Tennessee in Knoxville. It showed the country that we were a pretty good football team. I think our offense began to earn its identity that day as well. The score didn't indicate how we dominated Tennessee. We just knocked them off the line of scrimmage the entire game, and Derrick Lassic had a great day running the ball. Of course the play I'd like to forget was my fumble late in the game that gave them the ball near midfield. Our defense rose to the occasion, as usual, when Mike Rogers tipped one of Heath Shuler's passes and Chris Donnelly intercepted it. I don't know if I was the first one to congratulate Chris, but I probably appreciated his play more than anyone else.

The Alabama-Auburn game was the typical emotional game it always is. It was a sad situation for Auburn with Pat Dye retiring the night before the game, and I'm certain that lifted Auburn to an even higher emotional level. We didn't feel any pity for them because we knew we had our goal of winning the national championship, and we had to win this game to keep that dream alive. Neither team did very much offensively in the first half, although we had a couple of chances to put some points on the board and failed to execute down in the scoring zone. I feel like we dominated the second half, with Antonio Langham intercepting the pass for the touchdown. Then we just played some bruising football on both offense and defense the rest of the way. Once our running game started clicking, we pretty well took command of the game.

One noticeable difference was the lack of celebrating after beating Auburn. In 1990 we had broken the string of four losses to them, and everyone was rejoicing. In 1991 we won another one that certainly got everyone fired up, but in 1992 we had the postseason game waiting for us the next week against Florida at Legion Field. Before the season Coach Stallings had talked quite a bit about being in the first-ever championship game, about the Alabama tradition and how meaningful it would be for Alabama in its Centennial season to play in that game.

The players really wanted to play Florida, too, because they had beaten us 35-0 the year before in Gainesville. It was our only loss of the year, and it came in the second game. We felt we got better and better as the 1991 season went along, but we really wanted a chance to redeem ourselves against Florida. It was important for us to win because it was for the SEC Championship and a shot at the Sugar Bowl, but there was also an avenging factor in there, too.

It was one of those games that we seemed to have under control when Derrick (Lassic) scored in the third quarter to put us 21-7. We had moved the ball effectively on them, both running it and throwing it. Jay (Barker) hit Curtis Brown for a touchdown, and Derrick had scored in the first half. With our defense may have gotten a bit complacent because Florida really came back on us with their own vengeance. When they tied it at 21 and had the ball in our territory and all the momentum on their side in the fourth quarter, I really believed our team showed its true character. We stopped them and moved the ball back up past midfield.

When we punted back to them, our defense, in particular Antonio (Langham), was determined to stop them, get us the ball back, and put us in a position to win it. Antonio made the interception and touchdown run to give us the lead for good and got us in the Sugar Bowl against Miami.

The Miami game was by far the biggest any of us had ever played in. Three years before we played them in the Sugar Bowl, but there was no comparing our attitude in 1992 and 1989. We were playing for the national championship, and no one, other than ourselves and coaches, really felt we had a chance.

Our preparation was superb, and the attitude was intense on and off the practice field. Miami was doing all the talking about how they were going to destroy us, that we were one-dimensional, and a running team didn't have a chance against their defense. We were confident we'd move the ball and we were confident they wouldn't move the ball.

Once the game started and we started running it down the Superdome, you could sense that despite their trash-talking, they knew they were in for a struggle. I'll always feel it was one of my better games. I got a few good blocks on them, and that is what a fullback is supposed to do. I know I came to Alabama as a tailback out of high school, and I really didn't know how to block. I learned how and learned I wouldn't be carrying the football very much.

I did get one crucial run there in the fourth quarter to give us a first down and keep our final scoring drive going. Miami never did stop their trash-talking. It didn't make much difference, though. We had a job to do, we did it, and 34-13 will always be a part of Alabama's legacy.

"I'd been saying all year we hadn't played our best game. Now I can say we have."
— Alabama Coach Gene Stallings after the 1993 Sugar Bowl

Jim Goostree worked in the athletic department from the days of Ears Whitworth through Gene Stallings's third year, which was capped off by Alabama's Sugar Bowl romp over Miami. Perhaps the ultimate irony for one of Paul Bryant's most trusted aide-de-camps is the fact that the Sugar Bowl win was Alabama's 323rd victory during Goostree's 37-year stint — the exact same number of wins notched by Bryant during his coaching career at Maryland, Kentucky, Texas A&M, and Alabama. Goostree remembers his final game.

JIM GOOSTREE:

We've had a lot of great wins at Alabama during my years here, and I'm lucky enough to have seven national championship rings. But the No. 1 game that sticks out is the 1993 Sugar Bowl victory over Miami. It is the No. 1 game all-time for me. Nobody expected us to win, and we not only won, but we won it in such a convincing manner against a team that had won 29 straight games and was the defending national championship team.

I believe the total commitment to excellence by the staff and the players was clearly evident from the opening kickoff to the end of the game. It is hard to have that type of intensity and effort for 60 minutes, but it was there that night in the Superdome.

The other game that I'll never forget is the 1971 win over Southern California in Los Angeles. Those Southern Cal players were big and talented, and about eight of them went on to the pros. I remember our defense holding them time and time again. I remember our offensive line knocking them backward. Our offense had a game similar to the one our defense had against Miami in the Sugar Bowl. It was the same relentlessness — and keeping them guessing. We were big underdogs that night and won it 17-10.

That game epitomized the spirit of Alabama football to me. It is something special.

Coach Stallings's secretary, Linda Knowles, talks about her boss and his impact on the University and the football program.

LINDA KNOWLES:

The love of the program is here again — even with the new members, the ones who haven't coached here before — it doesn't take long for that love to get a grip on them. What I see now at Alabama is a total family atmosphere. We spend more time at work than we do at home, and we are all pulling in the same direction.

I think Coach Stallings has a lot to do with it. He brought together old friends, and he has a talent for mixing the new people in with the old so they just complement each other.

I'll tell you a quote of Coach Stallings that touched my heart. He dictated a letter one day that said that if today he could exchange his son for a normal child, he would not. (John Mark has Down's syndrome.) He said that John Mark had taught him so many things that he would not have learned otherwise. That's the kind of love we have here today.

We all care about each other. We care about personal lives, the children — I'm talking about 45 to 55 staff members and coaches — that's a lot of people to get to pull together in one direction. I think winning the championship is certainly evidence of that.

There are many quotes about and from the Crimson Tide players during the 1992 season. Here are just a few for the historical annals.

"Our defensive guys are so mean and like hitting people so much, they'd probably slap their own mothers."
— UA running back Derrick Lassic talking about the vaunted Bama defenders

"Florida? Tennessee? Auburn? Georgia? They're all great teams, great programs. But in the grand scheme of things, none have overtaken Alabama as THE football program in the SEC."
— An article in the *Arkansas Democrat Gazette* on game day of the Alabama-Arkansas tilt

"In the pros you usually call your head coach by his first name, but when I saw Coach Stallings and the look he had in his eye, I thought it would be best to call him Coach."
— Louisiana Tech assistant coach Pat Tilley, who played 10 years in the NFL, including one under Stallings at St. Louis

"That's somebody else's problem."
— Alabama Coach Gene Stallings when asked how he would attack the Tide's defense

"My reason for voting Alabama No. 1 is quite simple: I believe they are the best team in the nation. I realize Miami and Washington are getting the most attention, but sometimes I believe that is because of what they did last season."
— Tucson sportswriter Corky Simpson, who had been voting Alabama No. 1 in the Associated Press poll since the season started, after he was exposed as the man voting for Alabama

"If we keep winning, I'll teach it to Coach Stallings, Mrs. Stallings, and little Johnny, too."
— Alabama running back Sherman Williams talking about his Sherman Shake Dance

"The two biggest plays were when (Antonio) Langham returned the interception and when (Michael) Proctor hit the field goal. A 10-0 lead is not monumental unless you have a defense like Alabama's."
— Auburn head coach Pat Dye after the 1992 game

"He must be superman. I swear if he pulled up his shirt, I think he would have a big S under it."
— Alabama linebacker Derrick Oden talking about Antonio Langham after the Florida game

"I'm looking forward to the Sugar Bowl and a chance at Miami and the national title. Everyone says we can't beat Miami, but we are not just anybody, we are Alabama."
— Alabama receiver David Palmer

"The play George Teague made in catching Thomas from behind may be the greatest individual effort in Alabama football history."
— Alabama assistant coach Bill Oliver about the 1993 Sugar Bowl game

"They're beginning to dance in Opp and Eastaboga and Montgomery and Cullman and all over the state of Alabama."
— Keith Jackson in the closing moments of the Crimson Tide win in the 1993 Sugar Bowl

"Only in America can you be fired twice, then coach a national championship team and be Coach of the Year."
— Alabama Coach Gene Stallings after the 1993 Sugar Bowl

"We shook up the whole world tonight, baby. I'm going to take the whole offensive line out to dinner. It won't be steaks. Since this is New Orleans, it'll be something like Lucky Dogs."
— Alabama running back Derrick Lassic after the Tide win in the 1993 Sugar Bowl

"In the second quarter, I saw Torretta look over at me, and he froze for a second. I saw fear."
— Alabama defensive end John Copeland after the 1993 Sugar Bowl

Stacy Harrison in action.

Bama's Martin Houston.

Victory is sweet. Alabama is No. 1 in the nation after the January, 1992, Sugar Bowl.

THE TIDE ANNOUNCERS
"Welcome to the Alabama Football Network..."

A-Day 1992 was a special time for the University of Alabama, Tide players, and fans. It marked the 100th anniversary celebration of the Tide football tradition. On hand that day, along with many decades of Tide players, alumni, and staff, were some of the legendary Alabama football announcers. Here are some of the colorful stories they shared on that festive occasion.

JOHN FORNEY:

One game I never will forget is the Alabama-LSU game of 1948. LSU is kind of like Alabama – they're as football nutty as we are! Back in 1948 they had at least three people doing LSU, so that meant at least six people looking for places to set up and broadcast the games out of Tiger Stadium. Alabama played down there, and thank the Lord it was a day game because I got put on the absolute roof of Tiger Stadium! I mean, no walls. I was sitting in a chair about like this one, I had my legs crossed, and I was sitting on my charts and my commercials to keep the wind from blowing them, and I would pull them out one by one. I never will forget broadcasting that game in 1948 from the roof of Tiger Stadium.

Another game in Tiger Stadium that I remember is back when Doug Layton and I were doing play by play, and Doug was doing the color. They took over the visiting broadcasters' booth for ABC network, and they fixed up a little lean-to with a couple of two-by-fours again on the roof right back of the LSU students and the LSU band. As God is my witness, I'm sitting at least this close to Doug – it was before we started using headphones – and I'd look over and see Doug's lips moving, but I had no idea what he was saying, and he had no idea what I was saying!

MAURY FARRELL:

In 1938 when we did the Alabama-Boston College game, the temperature outside was 28 degrees at kickoff, and 30 minutes before the start of the broadcast, one of the priests from Boston College came up to the booth where we were set up and said, "I hate to tell you this, but you've got to get out of this booth — we're going to use it for some press people." They put us on the roof of Braves Stadium with a card table — we didn't even have a lean-to. When that game was over, I called Lionel Baxter in Birmingham to see how it had sounded, and he said they'd had a lot of trouble on the line and "eeeevvvveeeerrrryyy ttthhhhiiinnnggg yyyyooouuu ssaaaiiddd ccccaaaamme oooouuuuttt..." We froze to death up there!

The players just wore leather helmets on their heads back then, and played in whatever clothes they had. I'll never forget some of those Baton Rouge games – we tried to close the windows in the booth to keep the noise out. The glass was all cut, and every one of us came out with our fingers bleeding. I'll never forget the game down in Mobile when the stands collapsed.

JOHN FORNEY:

I will never forget that game either. I was doing color, and Maury was doing play by play. It was Coach Bryant's first game, September 27, 1958. We were playing LSU, and LSU was trying an experiment that year with three teams – the Go Team, the Chinese Bandits, and the White Team. At the end of the first half of play, we were ahead 3-0. Maury, I never will forget it – we both sat there with tears in our eyes, and people were screaming because this was after 3 years of being 4-24-2, I think it was, and we had come back to lead LSU. Duff Morrison recovered a Billy Cannon fumble in midair and ran it down, and only a great play by one of their centers knocked him out of bounds at the 2. Alabama's offense that year was nonexistent except for quick kicks, so Freddie Sington had to kick a field goal, which put us ahead at the half.

We eventually lost it 13-3, but during the third or fourth quarter all of a sudden I saw what looked like a cake falling down – the bleachers in the north end zone just sank. It was really unbelievable, and I said "Maury!" And he said, "The stands are falling!" There were ambulances and sirens, and thank God nobody was killed, but there were some people hurt.

PAUL KENNEDY:

Do you remember the comeback game with Penn State in 1983 at the base of Mount Nittany? We're up there, and so was Jerry (Duncan). They wouldn't let you on the field – Joe Paterno didn't want to have any radio people on the field. So in a small booth, we had five people, including our producer Bert Bank.

Alabama was getting ready to go in with the winning touchdown. Jerry was jumping up and down, and Doug was jumping up and down, and Alabama throws to Preston Gothard. He catches the football and lands in the end zone – and they say it's NOT a touchdown! Jerry's going, "It's a touchdown! It's a touchdown!" And I said, "Let's do this deductively. Doug Layton, he caught the football." And Doug says in his baritone voice, "He caught the football." I said, "Doug, he landed in the end zone." Doug said, "Yes, he landed in the end zone." I said, "That's a touchdown." Doug said, "At Penn State, that's not a touchdown."

Another time we're playing Tennessee at Tennessee, we're on the air live with our pregame show with 90,000 people filling the stadium, and I say, "Doug, what better setting for college football — can you imagine anything nicer?" And Doug says, "No, Paul, I can't. This is magnificent. And oh — across the way, down on the field, there's Old Smokey, Old Smokey the blue-tick hound, the venerable mascot of Tennessee. If I had a gun, I'd drop him from here!"

CHARLIE ZEANAH:

Coach Thomas called me one afternoon while I was at WJRD radio station — I was working at the radio station and trying to go to school at the same time. Thomas said that Rea Scheusler, who was the former athletic publicity director, was hung up in Japan and wouldn't be able to get home, and Thomas needed somebody to handle the job until he could get there. I said, "Coach, there's no way." He said, "There is a way. I've already signed you up at the University, we'll give you $150 a month, and I'll see you at 3 o'clock tomorrow afternoon." It was that simple.

Another thing I remember about Coach Thomas was when we were going over to Biloxi. He had scheduled a game to open the season. Albert Elmore, who had played for Wallace Wade back in the thirties, was in the military and was in charge of this game. Coach Thomas got a little bit concerned since Duke had beaten us 29-26 with the Navy Preflight players, who made a much better team than Alabama at that particular time, so he called me over to the bus and asked me if I had told the "press" — we didn't say "media," we said "press" — that this was a practice game and that it wouldn't count. I said, "No, sir." He said, "Well, you'd better get ready to do so."

Well we got busy, and frankly I got so busy I forgot. We won the game, and Coach Thomas says, "Where's Zeanah?" I said, "Here I am, Coach, at the back of the bus." He said, "Did you tell the press this was a practice game?" I said, "No, I haven't had the chance." He said, "Don't!"

Anyway Alabama went to the Rose Bowl, and I went on the trip. It was one of the outstanding events of my life. We went by train, and we stopped in New Orleans, stopped in Houston, stopped in El Paso, had a workout, and picked up a jaw brace for Lowell Tew who had a broken jaw in the last game of the year. We went on to Alhambra, California, and checked into the Huntington Hotel, as Alabama teams had always done when they went to the Rose Bowl. That turned out to be one of the most magnificent teams that Alabama has ever had, and I'll try to qualify that. They scored 396 points during the regular season and allowed only 80. If you add the 34 points they scored in the Rose Bowl game, that will give you 430, and that was the highest scoring team at Alabama until 1973. Only one other team has scored more points — Bryant's 1973 team scored 477.

MAURY FARRELL:

I remember one time Bert Bank, our director-producer, had been giving us a lot of static, and we decided we were going to get even with him. So we walked down the street to McClellan's 5 & 10 — they don't have those anymore — and we bought a pair of ladies' underpants. We took them back to the hotel, and we crumpled them up, rubbed them in the carpet, and messed them up real good. While Bert was in the shower, we stuck them in the bottom of his suitcase. The next night I get a phone call from Tuscaloosa, and Bert said, "Will you please tell my wife where these ladies' pants came from!" I said, "I don't know!"

JERRY DUNCAN:

The bowl game we played in my junior year — 1965 when we squared off with Nebraska in the Orange Bowl — was played for the national championship because the two teams that were ahead of us had gotten beaten earlier that day, and we were playing the night game. When it came across the PA system that we were playing for the national championship, if I didn't already have butterflies, I certainly got some. I think that was one of Coach Bryant's and that particular staff's greatest moments because of the game plan they had put in.

We had been a very conservative football team all year, and that particular game we were outweighed 65-70 pounds a man, and our defense faced a great offensive unit that had scored more points than any Nebraska team had to that time. Our defense let them score 28 points that night, but fortunately our offense put 39 points on the board, and we came away with a national championship. That was certainly a great thrill.

You people, the fans, are the ones who make all this happen, and your support for and love of this program is something I'll cherish all my life. I just urge you to continue your support of Hootie Ingram and Coach Gene Stallings because they're class people, and I promise you, there will be another national championship.

(EDITOR'S NOTE: This was a prophetic statement made in April 1992. As we all know, that was a championship year.)

THE TEAM OF THE CENTURY
Golden Gala Acceptance Speeches

On the weekend of July 17-18, 1992, the University of Alabama's Team of the Century was officially honored with a festive get-together in Birmingham. A Black Tie Golden Gala Dinner, which was emceed by ABC-TV's Keith Jackson and featured acceptance speeches from team members who were on hand, highlighted the event. The Team of the Century represents the top 25 players, by position, that were chosen by Crimson Tide fans. Here are the words from the all-time Crimson Tiders that night.

TOMMY WILCOX:

Thank you. I'll tell you — what a way to start this thing off, with a boy from Louisiana who half of you probably won't be able to understand! This honor means so much to me and my family — I do not have the vocabulary to tell you how much it means. You work all your life to try to make your dreams a reality, and when some of those dreams come true, you've got to pinch yourself to make sure you're not sleeping and still dreaming. So these last few days, I've been doing a whole lot of pinching, wondering if this night is really for real.

It's nice to know that people have enjoyed the way you've played the game and have enjoyed you in such a way that they think you're deserving of such an honor. On behalf of my family and myself, I'd like to thank the people who voted for me — it's something that I'll always treasure.

Along with the people who voted for me, there's a lot of other people I'd like to thank. There's too many names to mention, but let me just say to the many coaches who have coached me, to the many teachers who have taught me, and to the many friends and players who fought alongside me, thank you for helping shape and mold Tommy Wilcox into what he is. I'll always be deeply indebted to you for that.

I'd especially like to thank my high school coaches and the coaches here at the University of Alabama. Since the first day I arrived at this University, they've been nothing but first class to me, and it's the same way today. I certainly appreciate it.

I'd like to thank Coach Bryant for giving me a chance. A lot of other major college coaches didn't think I could play — they didn't think I was big enough or talented enough to play. But he proved them all wrong — he took me from quarterback and moved me to safety so I was able to play! I'd like to thank my wife and two of my greatest coaches, my mom and dad. They taught me never to back down from anyone or anything no matter how great the challenge and to not be content just doing your best — they taught me to strive to be the best. And that's something I'll always cherish and hold dear, even in life today. So to Mom and Dad, thank you.

I'd like to end tonight with a question that's been asked of me many times, probably a thousand times or more since I first came to the University fourteen years ago — "Why did you choose to come to the University of Alabama?" I think I can best answer that in the words of John F. Kennedy. He said that we were going to put man on the moon, and he said we choose to do so not because it will be easy, but because we know it will be hard. And as I stand up here before you tonight, I can honestly say that I didn't come to the University of Alabama to play for Coach Bryant because I thought it would be easy. No, I came because I knew it would be hard. But I knew that if I could play here, then hell, I could play anywhere in America!

So I guess that just as NASA was successful in putting man on the moon, tonight I can say to my mom and dad that I, too, was successful at not just doing my best but as being honored as one of the best. And I'd like to thank them and all of you and to congratulate the rest of the people who are being honored tonight — it's a tribute just to be associated with them. And thanks to the many fans. Thank you for letting a little boy from Louisiana up and play for you.

JEREMIAH CASTILLE:

I'd like to thank Mr. Jackson for the introduction and all of you here this evening. I'm kind of lost for words, to be honest with you. I sat down and contemplated what could I say and what could I write down, and as Mr. Jackson shared with you, I'm an evangelist, a preacher. So I don't really know how to write things down and read from it. I like to share with people from my heart at the moment that I get that chance to let them know what's on my heart. This evening is a tremendous honor, and it's a tremendous time for me. I look back at all of the people, all of the coaches who have been influential in my life, and there are a lot of people. But most of all I just want to thank the Lord Jesus Christ for the opportunity to come to the University of Alabama. I want to thank my parents for raising me up and giving me the opportunity and having a dream of being able to accomplish some things one day.

I look at some of the players here on the podium tonight, and they played a big part for me as a young kid growing up. Seeing them play, seeing Alabama win the national championship year in and year out, and seeing great players like Joe Namath, Ken Stabler, Woodrow Lowe, and some others — they played a tremendous part in helping me have a dream and wanting to do something with my life. Growing up in a low-income housing area, football was a way out for me. I owe a lot to football — it's taken me out of low-income housing and done some tremendous things for me and my family. I'm very proud of that, and I'm very proud to be a part of this team. I feel very honored.

I just want to share with all of you — the fans, the University of Alabama, and the supporters — that if it weren't for your support and for Coach Bryant most of all, I wouldn't have been able to stand before you and be a part of this team tonight. I'd like to close with just one moment that I have vividly in my mind of the greatest coach who ever coached the game, and I believe the reason he was a great coach was because he was a great motivator and a great teacher. It was after the Liberty Bowl game, when we were on the stand and I was accepting the MVP trophy. One of the commentators asked Coach Bryant about his last game and what he thought about it and the victory. Coach Bryant very calmly put his arm around me and said, "Well, if it wasn't for little men like this being able to go out and do the things that they do, I wouldn't have been able to win the games that I won and receive the recognition that I've received."

So he always gave back what recognition was due, and that's what I want to do this evening is to thank the University of Alabama and all the supporters for giving Jeremiah Castille the opportunity to be on the Team of the Century.

DON McNEAL:

Thank you. It's so good to be here and such a great honor to be among such great football players and great fans. I'm just so elated and so excited about being here, that I have to calm down a little bit.

That play in the 1978 Sugar Bowl against Scott Fitzkee and the Nittany Lions — I was just one of 11 players at the time, 22 players to make that play possible. I was just so glad to have been there and to have made that play because you make plays like that and you don't even think about it. I attribute that to my coach Bill Oliver because when I first got to Alabama I was a green individual. I had all kinds of talent but he had to harness that talent, and he stayed on me tremendously. He said, "Don McNeal, I'm going to make you something!" I thought he hated me — he stayed on me constantly for a year. After that year, he saw that I had some potential, and then he let me go. Coach Oliver, I'd like to thank you for that. I really appreciate that because it helped me become the individual I am today. I am successful because of that, and I will be successful for a long time.

I just want to thank the Lord Jesus Christ for being the head of my life because without Him I am nothing, but with Him I am already successful. I'd like to thank my wife, Brenda, who's here tonight. I met her after I had my Achilles tendon injury in 1982. She was very instrumental in my coming back, and I want to thank her for that.

I want to thank all of my coaches here at the University of Alabama who helped me become the person and the player that I could be — Ken Donahue and again, Coach Bill Oliver. Without those guys, I wouldn't be successful today. I needed those guys up front, those guys behind the line, and of course, the secondary to help me make the play I made in the Sugar Bowl. So I'm so glad to have had the coaching staff that I had.

And of course, Coach Bear Bryant. The thing I remember about Coach Bryant was he said, "Wherever you go and whatever you do, always, always show class." That's what I've tried to do, and that rings so loud in my soul today — to always try to do the best that I can possibly do and always show class. That will ring heavily in my soul until I go to my grave.

This award means so much to me. I'll tell my little girl Jessica about this award and about this day, and I'll show her the film from tonight. I'm so glad to have been here.

There's so many people that I can name and say thank you. Last but certainly not least, I would like to thank the fans who were on our side in the stands and hollering. And especially a lady, Miss Jo Hazen who really stood in my corner when I needed someone to go to, someone to talk to, somewhere to lay my head when things weren't going so well. I'd like to thank Miss Jo Hazen for being there for me. And thank you fans for being there for me — I appreciate it.

CORNELIUS BENNETT:

Good evening. Looking at that play (his tackle against Notre Dame) again, I still say it was a fumble — because I recovered it! It's great to be here to see some of the old faces. I look back on my college career, and if it hadn't been for Jon Hand and Emanuel King and those guys pulling me aside when I first came to the University and saying, "We need you, you young buck, come on!" And Mike Dubose, who was my initial coach at the University, getting on my butt. I had never had a coach in my entire football career who did that — I guess because God had blessed me with so much talent, I had never had a coach who chewed me out. I was always a little spoiled brat on the football field. I always did things *my* way, I guess, because I could do them pretty good!

But Coach Dubose got on me so bad one day the spring of my freshman year that I went into the locker room — I was ready to go home. I called my mother and told her, "I'm coming home." She asked what was wrong, and I told her my coach had gotten on me and I had to get out of there. She said, "Why? You're a starter and you've moved out a senior." I'd moved out a senior — Steve Booker — my freshman year. I already had enough pressure on my shoulders from Coach Perkins tabbing me the way he did coming out of high school — I had my mind made up to be an All-Star tight end, but Coach Perkins saw it a little differently. But after that day with Coach Dubose, I knew — he was a special person and I was in a special place at the University of Alabama. I was just doing things my way, and my way was getting things done — but his way was the right way as far as technique, I realized that right away. I do a lot of talks at camps for kids, and I try to teach them the fundamentals because whether it's football or life, you've got to have the fundamentals to be successful in whatever you do. And I'd like to thank Coach Dubose for doing that for me — but I still hate you for getting on my . . . ! Seriously, Coach, thank you.

I saw Coach Ken Donahue, and I can still remember that ugly hat he wore all the time while he called, "Dog! Cat! Bird!" Those were the signals — if he called an animal that could fly, he was alerting us to a pass; if he called an animal that could run, he was alerting us to a run. He would scream those things out down the sidelines — "Dog! Antelope!"

Here I was going into a situation where I really didn't know what to expect. People said I must have really wanted to go to the University because Ken Donahue recruited me. And I did. I almost made the terrible mistake of going to Auburn — I committed to Auburn for about a week — because I wanted to play tight end or running back. Believe it or not, I was a pretty good running back — but that's another story.

It's great to be here to see some of these faces, like Derrick Thomas. I can remember when he first came to the University. I thought, boy, this kid's going to be great. Probably the same thing some of the guys said about me when I first came! And here we are chosen for the same team, together. Van Tiffin — I played four years with Van, and he was a quiet guy. He's still a quiet guy, doesn't say anything. Like after that kick in the Auburn game — he didn't say a word — same old Van Tiffin in the mirror combing his hair all the time! That's Van.

It's a great honor to be chosen for the Team of the Century. It's something special to be here, to see guys like Joe Namath, Kenny Stabler, Billy Neighbors, Lee Roy Jordan, and so on. It's something special that I'll always cherish. I don't have any kids yet, but one day I'll be able to show them a videotape or a photograph and say, boy, your pop was something because he's on a picture with all these great guys. And I was looking at John Hannah's Hall of Fame ring, and he told me, "Keep it up, and one day you'll be there." I don't know if that would take the place of this, though, because this is home and this is where it all started — with the great people of the University of Alabama. And I love you all for loving Cornelius Bennett. Thank you.

BARRY KRAUSS:

Thank you, Mr. Jackson. I always wanted to do this: "Hello, everybody! I'm Keith Jackson, and this is the University of Al-A-Bama." He was great — I mean, he covered me very well.

I was fortunate to grow up on the beaches of Pompano Beach, and I was telling Johnny Musso that I used to run the option against the waves. I was a big Alabama fan in those days, and I crawled up to the TV one time and saw Johnny Musso playing and a couple of other guys when I was real young (it's a joke, OK). But after I committed to the University of Alabama, Coach Bryant came to my house. My mom tried to take his houndstooth hat. It was a pleasure to have Coach Bryant in my house, but when I got to the University, I had to do a lot of growing up. My mom and dad pretty much kept me in the house most of the time, with an 11 o'clock curfew. So when I got to the University of Alabama, as the governor Jack Rutledge knows, I had a little wild streak in me, and I needed to be tamed. And Clem Gryska, who recruited and brought me up there, told me one day at practice, "Krauss, I'm going to give you a surfboard, and you're going to surf down Lake Tuscaloosa all the way back to Pompano — because we don't want you anymore!" And it was like, "Oh, no, I'm in trouble." And Coach Donahue tried running me out of here, too. Talk about Ken Donahue, it was, "Up, up, up, Barry Krauss, get out of here!" Everybody wanted me out of here, I don't know, but it worked out.

When I look around at all the great athletes — this is fantastic. I'm trying to think of all the things I could say — thank my wife, thank everybody, and thank my family.

When I came here, one of the things Coach Bryant taught us was to always call your mama. He said, "If I find out about it that you didn't call, you're in a lot of trouble." Through the years I discovered that Coach Bryant wasn't just a teacher of football — he was a teacher of life. It's an emotional thing for me because Coach Bryant really instilled winning in my life and believing that I can win. I think about all the years that I played — I think I lost probably five or six games in four years. We won a national championship and three Southeastern Conference championships. When you talk about one player and two plays, I was fortunate to even get a chance to play on the field. A lot of my friends in high school had told me that I'd never get a shot or a chance to play, and I felt that if I played for Alabama, Coach Bryant would give me a shot. Fortunately for me, he did, and in the Liberty Bowl I got to play with Bob Baumhower and Marty Lyons and all these great players. When you talk about the Goal Line Stand, that's more than just a stand — it's a representation of a team that worked hard together for four years and WON at the end. I won my last game with Alabama, and we won a national championship. It's what Coach Bryant was all about. I made a lot of good friends, which I'll carry the rest of my life.

It's a big honor for me to be chosen for this team. as you can tell, I'm fighting back some emotion. It's really an honor and a thrill. I'm in a transition — I just retired from the NFL, and you go through some ups and downs, but I know I'll always be a winner and I'll be successful because of Coach Bryant. I just want to say thanks to Coach Bryant — we miss you, and I wish you were here.

LEE ROY JORDAN:

Thank you very much. I'm delighted to be here. It's really a special, special treat to be on the podium with this group of people. When I look around, I start to tremble thinking about it because it's something that's really special.

I started thinking about the 100-year celebration that we're starting here at the University of Alabama. I went through the museum earlier today and saw all the great people who have been produced by the University of Alabama. It's awesome, and if you haven't been through the new museum, please go — we have so many things to be proud of in our state and so many people who are unbelievable representatives of our state and have done such a great job not only in athletics but also off the field. If you haven't had a chance, go through the new museum — I think you'll be really impressed with it. I was talking to Joe Namath earlier tonight and encouraging him to go because you won't believe there's anything like it in the state of Alabama.

This is home. I love Alabama, and I'm so delighted to be here. You probably know that I'm really partial to the University of Alabama. I've been away since 1962 — Bitty and I have been living in Dallas, raising three boys, playing football, and I've been trying to be a businessman these last 15 years. All the things that have happened to me have been primarily because of my relationship with the University of Alabama — the things that I learned from Coach Bryant, the staff, and all the people who were involved at the University. I love the University, and I'm so delighted to be a part of the recognition that we're giving to all the athletes that have participated over the last 100 years. We have so much to be proud of — 11 national championships — for a little state like Alabama. You know, that's unbelievable. Coming from California or Notre Dame or somewhere like that, you would say, well that's not that big a deal. But for a school located in Alabama, that's unbelievable. And for the people who we have up here on the podium tonight — the accomplishments that they've had, and so many others who are not here tonight who have accomplished so many great things representing the state of Alabama and especially the University Alabama. I'm delighted to be a part of it, I'm delighted to be here tonight, and I'm so glad everyone could be here tonight, Joe. It means a lot to us. It's really special that you all made a commitment to come back to this reunion. I want to thank the University of Alabama and all of you supporters — you're really special to all of us. Thank you so much.

DERRICK THOMAS:

Thank you. It's a tremendous honor to be here tonight. From one standpoint I'm the baby of this team — when a lot of these guys played, I wasn't even thought about! To have the opportunity to sit on the podium with them and talk with them is truly amazing, and for me it's very special.

The University of Alabama has stood for a lot for me. Each and every day in Kansas City, I try to talk with youths and try to instill in them what I learned at the University of Alabama. This past week I received an award, the White House Points of Light, from President Bush for my program "Third and Long," and a lot of that can be attributed right back to what I learned here at the University of Alabama — the lessons I learned, the speeches Cornelius Bennett spoke about. Coach Dubose didn't give me mine — Sylvester Croom did, and on many occasions he had me wanting to go home.

I didn't like Cornelius because he watched me practice — the reason he did that was because he had already paid his dues and I had to pay mine. So he enjoyed the practices where I got all the yelling that he had received two years prior to my coming. One evening after a practice when Coach Croom had gotten on me as much as he possibly could and we had made it up to the building, I was standing there, and Coach Croom said, "What's wrong with you?" I started to talk to him, and tears just started rolling out of my eyes, and I was huffing and puffing. I said, "Coach, I just can't take this any more — you're on me too hard!" And he said, "You know what — if it's the last thing I do, I'm going to make you a football player!" And before he left, he put the mark on me that made me a football player, and for that I thank him. I didn't see him in the crowd tonight, but I'd like to say a special thanks to him because he really put me on line to being the player I am today.

I'd like to thank Cornelius Bennett because before I came to the University of Alabama, I didn't even know what an outside linebacker was — we had defensive ends in my scheme at high school. They told me they were switching me to outside linebacker, and I had the opportunity to watch Cornelius work, and I tried to pattern myself after him. Once you start doing something, you start developing your own style, so I varied a little bit from Cornelius to try to develop my own style. I thank Cornelius for being a leader, for being a mentor to me, for helping me become the player I am today, and I'm going to thank him a lot more if he signs for 2.5 million or better this year! That's a different story — my contract isn't up till next year, but they may redo me this year if he signs for a lot.

I'd like to thank all the fans for the many memories we've given each other. I've made a lot of friends and had a lot of tremendous times over the course of my tenure at the University. My professors and my coaches were very instrumental in my becoming the person I am today. Not very many of the people here had coaching changes, but I endured the coaching change and the period when everybody looked down on the University. But we players kept our heads up and said that we still had to win, we still had to carry on the tradition. We won a lot of games during that period, and we also lost some. But since then, the players who remained after I left have continued the tradition, and I think the tradition is every bit as strong as it's ever been. So I'd like to say thank you, and God bless.

JON HAND:

First of all, I'd like to say it's an honor to be here. I never thought that in my lifetime my name would be included with the greatest people in this pro sport of football. I don't know where to start. Well, yes I do. It all started with my mother because she was the driving force behind everything I did. She gave me the strength to try out new things, to stay with them, and to see them through to the end. For that, I say thanks to her.

I say thanks to the coaches I had while I was here because they worked me harder than anybody ever worked me in my life. Starting with Coach Donahue — he ran me so hard that, like Cornelius and Derrick, I said that's not for me, it's too much work. He'd take us out on that track and have us run quarters in full gear long after everybody else was inside. They'd be eating dinner and getting ready to go wherever they were going, and we'd still be out there working. I'm like, "Man, this is too much work!" But it paid off, and I have to say thanks to him. Because of his work habits, there's nothing they can do to me now in the NFL that I haven't been through already.

I'd also like to say thanks to Coach Dubose. He took over my senior year, and I have to say that I and the rest of the guys were terribly afraid of him, too. We saw what he had done with Cornelius and Derrick! So he came in, and he had a veteran group of defensive ends, and he let us play. That was the best time of my life, and because of that, all three of us went into the NFL. Thank you.

The University gave me my shot in life. I didn't speak with Coach Bryant that much, but I do remember that after my freshman year, he called me into his office and said, "Jon, do you want to play?" I said, "Coach, yes, I do." And he said, "Well, you've got your chance." And I thank him, because that's all I ever wanted — a chance to play ball.

MARTY LYONS:

It's truly a pleasure to be here tonight, and the first person I'd like to thank is the Good Lord for giving me the ability to play the game of football — because without the ability to play the game, I would have been at Auburn!

I'd like to thank Jack Rutledge. Barry Krauss and I roomed together freshman year right over Coach Rutledge's bedroom. And thank God he didn't send us home! But we got close because we had a motto back then that if we had to practice hard and play hard, we were going to party hard!

I'd like to thank Dude Hennessey. He was my first coach, and besides being a good coach, he is a good friend. And now we'll get to Ken Donahue. I know everybody's been picking on you, Coach, but I'm going to do the same. I remember the day that you told me you were going to run me till I dropped. And I vowed that I'd be damned — that if I was still running in the morning, I was still running. And you stopped me and said, "You know what, you just can't be doing that. You have an opportunity to play, you have an opportunity for people to look up to you." And Coach, I appreciate that because it made me grow as a person, and it made me grow closer to my teammates.

I'd like to thank Coach Bryant not so much for what he did for me on the field but for the values he put into me as a person in the game of life. He said that you should always be proud of your family and your friends. And to come back tonight to the Team of the Century and to be recognized by the fans as part of this family, as part of this team is a great honor. I want to encourage all of the fans to continue to support the next decade because Coach Stallings and his staff and the Crimson Tide will have you up in the stands for the next 100 years saying, "Roll, Tide, Roll!" Thank you very much.

BOB BAUMHOWER:

Thank you. I'm not from Tuscaloosa. I moved to Tuscaloosa as a senior in high school, and I wasn't really caught up in this "Bear" thing or this Crimson Tide thing or this crazy "Roll, Tide" thing I heard. I didn't really know what it was all about when I moved to Tuscaloosa. But during my brief time at Tuscaloosa High School, I became a big, big fan of Alabama football — not because of the University or Coach Bryant, but just because of my love of the game. I really wanted to go play for a winner, and at the time, I saw Alabama as a winner. I wasn't very sought after as a football player — in fact, Alabama was the only scholarship I was offered. I hadn't had a whole lot of experience as a football player, but through my year at Tuscaloosa High, I was fortunate enough for Coach Bryant to take a gamble on me.

I want to tell a story that kind of sums it all up for me and what Alabama means to me. Because I wasn't from Alabama and wasn't really caught up in the aura or the tradition — I had moved from Florida to Tuscaloosa — football didn't mean a whole lot to me. I really didn't have a direction when I went to Alabama. When I went, I was just happy to be one of the guys. I was just happy to be out and be seen as one of the Alabama football players. I was just happy to be associated with the tradition.

But to make a long story short, the spring of my freshman year they moved me to the defensive line, and as the spring went on, I earned a starting position as a defensive lineman. And at the end of the spring season, I was assured by the press at that time that I would be a starter in the fall. Well, I was really feeling my oats — I thought I had made it as an Alabama football player, I was one of the guys. When fall came around, I reported back, and Coach Bryant put us through conditioning tests where they check out your conditioning through all kinds of sprints — long-distance running. Marty (Lyons) used to be a marathon runner, thanks to Coach Donahue, he used to be able to run forever! Anyway, I made it through all the tests, but I hadn't worked that hard since spring training and when I reported to practice to get my jersey, I was expecting to be on the first team. Mike Dubose was on the team at that time, and maybe he remembers this — I got an orange jersey, which I think denoted below the scrubs. I was just non-existent, and I really didn't understand what was going on. Back then, the first three days of practice were in shorts, so there wasn't a whole lot you could do to prove yourself on the field as far as going head to head with the pads and stuff. After three days, I had had enough — I was still on the scrub team. The press had been touting me as an unknown being a starter, and I was thoroughly embarrassed. I felt that Coach Bryant was wasting my time, and I had better things to do than let some guy like that waste my time. So I quit! I walked off. I threw my basket at Willie Meadows and almost hit him in the head with it, and I went to see my father. I told him what had happened, and naturally he was pretty upset about it.

But I got a phone call a few hours later from a couple of my teammates and Bud Moore. They said Coach Bryant wanted to see me, and in my infinite wisdom at that time, I knew Coach Bryant knew he'd made a huge mistake in putting me on the scrub team. I knew that this meeting would be Coach Bryant getting on his knees asking me to come back and save the team.

I went to the meeting with my dad. I think he was more nervous than I was — he was shaking in his boots. Coach Bryant's desk backed up to a big window, and if the sun was shining in, it looked like you were looking at God. You sat down on a couch where you hunkered down really low, and you were looking up at this huge man. He was a big man, and you had the big picture window behind with the sun shining through, and it looked like you had gone to heaven and the Great One was talking to you. When we got there, he welcomed my father, and then he looked at me and said, "What the hell are you doing here?" I said, "I heard you wanted to talk to me, Coach." And he said, "I don't want to talk to you — I don't need any quitters on the team!"

Basically I got one of those patented, well-known Coach Bryant attitude adjustments that have affected so many guys in their careers at the University of Alabama. And for me to be here right now and to be participating in this unbelievable honor, to be up here standing next to Joe Namath, a guy who I worshiped growing up, I have to attribute it all to the ability of Coach Bryant and the coaching staff at the University of Alabama at that time to motivate and teach you how to win. I wasn't a winner when I came to Alabama. I came from a great background — my mom and dad are two of the best people you'll ever meet in your life, but I didn't have a direction, I had no focus. But when Coach Bryant got through with me at that meeting, you could have put me in front of a freight train and I wouldn't have moved until he told me to!

I remember it just as clearly as if it were yesterday. I had quit, but at the end of the meeting, Coach Bryant said he was going to give me a second chance. He told me that if Coach Donahue didn't kill me first, then he'd see what I could do. You've heard a lot about Coach Donahue, I hated that man with a passion! Jon Hand, Marty Lyons, and I all played under this guy. Dubose knows what I'm talking about, and so does Dude Hennessey. There's nothing we can tell you that will help you imagine the pain he put us through! It was unbelievable! When I was drafted by Miami, I heard about all their tough, tough practices — Coach Shula is such a tough coach, it's going to kill you, three days down there in the heat. After my first practice in Miami was over, I said, "Is this it? Coach Donahue's warm-ups were tougher than their practices!"

It's really a great honor for me to be up here, and I have a lot of people to thank. Coach Donahue is one because I have to attribute all the things I did after the University of Alabama to him, and all the lessons I learned under Coach Bryant and all the other coaches. There's not a day that goes by that I don't draw back on the things I learned at Alabama. I'd like to thank all the fans and all the coaches at Alabama. Like Barry was saying, I wish Coach Bryant could be here because he's such a big part of my life, and Alabama's such a big part of my life. Thank you very much.

ALF VAN HOOSE FOR JOHNNY CAIN:

Legalistic minds in the audience tonight will have a problem granting credibility to hearsay testimony, but please hear this old newspaper man, Alf, who is substituting for the great John Cain, who was selected as punter for the Team of the Century at the University of Alabama. I never saw John Cain play, but I knew him as a professional friend many years after he wore the crimson and white from 1930 to 1932. I remember strongly an interview I had once with Coach Hank, who was the rock of Alabama football from 1922 through 1957. Coach Hank had a dictum that said if you had sophomores good enough to make your team, you were fixin' to get beat. The NCAA had recently legalized freshmen, and during the course of the interview, I asked Coach Hank how many freshman football players he remembered at the University of Alabama who could have helped a real good varsity team. As was his wont, he studied out and finally said he could think of three: Pooley Hubert, Walter Merrill, and John Cain.

Cain was voted onto this team as a punter. I personally voted him in my back field, first team — and I'll tell you why. Yesterday, when I was renting this suit that we don't wear every day at dinner at the Van Hoose house, I was talking to Butch Baldone, who is an Alabama nut. From the year Papa came back — 1958 — until now, he knows more about Alabama football than just about any other fan. He asked me what I was doing, and I told him I was giving the acceptance speech for John Cain.

Now this was a guy who played both ways. I asked Fred Sington about John Cain, and the first thing he said was that he was a team man. I think that if John were here tonight, he would with great dignity and proper humility accept his role as a kicker, when he could have just as well been in the other category.

He was a native of Montgomery. Legend has it that Dr. John Blue, a very famous surgeon in Montgomery, found out about John Cain as a young star football player at Memphis. Dr. Blue is remembered in medical history for performing the first open heart surgery — and this is true, no kidding. Two railyard workers had gotten in to a fuss, and one hit the other in the chest with an ax. They took him to Dr. Blue, and he stitched him up — it was the first open heart surgery in history. He was also a great Alabama man!

In my memory we have had half a dozen outstanding recruited running backs in the state of Alabama: Tommy O'Brien in the late thirties, Tommy Lorino in the fifties, Tony Nathan in the seventies, and Robert Davis last year (1991). But John Cain, I understand, was the most widely recruited player in the history of Alabama high school football. I know John would appreciate this honor, and I appreciate the honor of standing in for a great football player.

VAN TIFFIN:

When I came to Alabama, I walked on, and to be honest with you, I was just hoping to get to play a little football. I had no idea I'd ever be among such distinguished people as these around me tonight. This is the most incredible thing that's ever happened to me.

Every Saturday to me was the greatest thrill in the world. I'd wake up Saturday morning and get ready and be real intense. Then we'd get out to the stadium, and the atmosphere would be just blossoming over. And that was what it was all about — I just can't express how grateful I am for the privilege and opportunity I had to be able to participate in football at Alabama. To this very day, if I go out somewhere and people ask me where I went to school and I say Alabama, they kind of look up at me. And if later on they find out I had a part in Alabama football, they really look up to me. I feel very fortunate to have played football here at the University and to be associated with such a great tradition and fans who are so loyal to the athletic program.

It seems most everyone associates me with the last few seconds of the Alabama — Auburn game of 1985, and almost always they ask, "What were you thinking when you walked out there with the last 6 seconds on the clock?" I usually give different answers, but to be honest with you, I was thinking, "What am I going to do if I miss this? How am I going to get out of this place alive?"

I was fortunate enough that that didn't happen, and I didn't have to cross that bridge — and I'm real grateful for that. Every time I watch a rerun of it, I get sweaty palms and break out in a cold sweat and hope I don't miss it!

Probably the greatest experience of all that I had was being associated with coaches and players who had the character and class of the people at the University of Alabama. I've carried that with me, and it's helped me in the last few years. I want to thank everybody for the support of me and the University.

FRED SINGTON:

Thank you. As I look out over the audience, there are very few people here tonight who were here when I had the privilege of playing for the University. I'm very pleased about this honor.

Keith Jackson is at a tremendous disadvantage introducing me. It's like when I was inducted into the Alabama Sports Hall of Fame, they introduced me by showing pictures and film — sound pictures were just invented in 1931 — so I have that disadvantage. Some people don't remember Bull Connor. but I do. I remember him as an announcer with a megaphone on the steps of City Hall broadcasting football. Those were the days!

I played for Wallace Wade, who was a tough coach. I've heard you fellas talking about your young days and about your young coach Paul Bryant, whom I had the privilege of helping sign out in Houston, Texas. I think about the history of Alabama football. I'll say one thing about it—when the ball is kicked in September in Alabama, everybody starts breathing. This is a great football place, and the University of Alabama people are very sincere in their love for the school.

Coach Wade was a tough guy. One time when we were not performing correctly out on the field, he divided us into squads and told us to run signals. We didn't have lights in those days—that shows you how old I am—so we were running in the pitch-black dark. We couldn't pass because nobody could see the ball. Coach Wade got a long-distance telephone call, and he answered the call, took a shower, and went home. And we were still out there running! Jess Neely (assistant coach) finally went in, called him up, and said, "Coach, they're still running." He said, "Let 'em go!" I'm happy that Coach Neely called him—or I'd still be there!

Frank Howard introduced Coach Wade at the luncheon when he received the Hall of Fame award, he said, "You've wondered about the coach. You've wondered if he's gotten softer and if he really smiles. I want to tell you—he rode from Clemson to Tuscaloosa with me, and he's really mellowed—he smiled twice!"

Southern football is a great institution. I am tremendously proud to be here tonight and to be a part of this organization and this team of one hundred. I told the story the other day about a fella who walked into my store and told me he'd just been at Central Bank's new building. I said, "It's a tremendous place. Didn't you admire it?" He said, "What I really admired out there was the plaque that marks the site of the first Alabama-Auburn game, 1892." Then he asked, "Fred, were you on that team?" I said, "No, I didn't make that team!"

Anyway, I'm happy to be here with all of you young fellas. And Keith, I don't know what position you had in 1927 and 1928—there was no television, and radio had just been invented. We've come a long way, and I'm happy to have Keith Jackson back here in Alabama, in Birmingham—he's a true Alabama guy. I don't care where he says he's from, he belongs to us! Thank you so much.

VAUGHN MANCHA:

It's a real honor to be here. I don't know how lucky a person can get to get elected to this beautiful panel of great athletes for the University of Alabama. You know, as we get older we think our dreams will come true, and I think my dream came true in getting this great honor.

I want to thank the University of Alabama, Dr. Sayers, Hootie Ingram, and all the Centennial Committee for this tremendous, magnificent affair. I want to congratulate my teammates—what a thrill it is for me to be around these kind of people, to shoot the bull for a couple of days, and get to know them. And I know they feel the same way I do—we're so deeply grateful to the University of Alabama for honoring us in such a magnificent way.

We're reminiscing, and I grew up right here in this neighborhood, right here where this civic center is. In 1931 I had a hundred papers that I used to deliver right down the street. I trained at the Boys' Club here, and I went to Powell Grammar School—this is home. This means so much to me to me to come back, and what an honor it is tonight. I'm so grateful to the University for giving me the opportunity to play and represent the University.

I think about when I finished high school in 1941 and Coach Burnum and Coach Crisp came to my house and took me to lunch. You know, Coach Crisp didn't say much — he mumbled a lot. But I did make out that he said they would feed me three meals a day and they thought I would be a good football player and we'd probably get a chance to play in the Rose Bowl and I had an opportunity to get a good education. Well, we did go to the Rose Bowl, and with this honor tonight and all the other honors I've been getting lately, maybe I did get pretty good. And I was so fortunate in leaving the University with a couple of strong degrees, which has helped give me opportunities and afforded me a great career in athletics and academics. And I've had so much fun, and all of this is attributable to the University of Alabama. I was a little ol' poor kid right over here on the corner, and I'm thankful so much for this. I want to tell all the fans out here and all the beautiful people of Alabama how grateful I am to be a part of this great affair. Thanks, folks.

BILLY NEIGHBORS:

Thank you very much. It's a great pleasure and honor for me to be here and to be selected for this team, especially a team for Alabama. When I was seven years old, it was my dream to go and play football for Alabama. There's never been any doubt as to what I wanted to do. I was born one-and-a-half miles from Denny Stadium, and I started to go to games there in 1948, when I was eight years old. I never even talked with another college team — I didn't even want to! In 1957 Alabama went 2-7-1, and my brother was on that team. I went to see Auburn beat them 40-0 in Birmingham, the first Alabama-Auburn game I went to — we usually just went to the games in Tuscaloosa. But I had already made up my mind to go there — I didn't care if they went 0-11, it didn't make a damn bit of difference.

I had never heard of Paul Bryant. I knew Coach Whitworth and Coach Crisp. Coach Crisp recruited me — it didn't cost him a lot of money because I was just a mile and a half down the road! They didn't buy me anything, they didn't give me anything, they didn't offer me anything! They told me that if I wanted to come to Alabama and play, I could. And that's all I wanted.

Coach Bryant came in the winter of my first year, and somebody gave me a copy of *Sports Illustrated* — I had never read *Sports Illustrated.* It said that the way they chose the members of the team at Texas A&M was to dig a big hole about six feet deep and threw in four or five of them, and the one that came out got to play. I got a little nervous — I had had a few fights, but I had never had to fight off six or seven at one time. And I'm not very tall, and I was worried about getting out of that damn hole! Well, I talked to a few people around town, and they said they wouldn't believe *Sports Illustrated.*

So I went, and the day that I went, my brother got kicked off the team for being two pounds overweight! I heard some of these guys talking about running people, but they didn't run you then — boy, if you didn't do what you were supposed to do, you were gone! He got kicked off, and I went out there looking for him. I couldn't find Sid. I asked some of the coaches, and nobody would say a word to me. It was picture day for the freshmen, so they put a uniform on me. I weighed about 260 pounds then — that was mighty heavy for an Alabama football player in 1958 — and I didn't stay at that weight very long. I was sitting under the old shade tree on Thomas Hill — it was a hundred damn degrees! — when Coach Bryant came up to me and said, "Neighbors, get your fat tail out from under that tree and go sit in the sun. You need to lose some weight! And I don't ever want to catch you driving a car or riding in a boat!"

Well I didn't know what the hell he was talking about! I couldn't drive a car because I didn't have one, and I didn't have a driver's license to begin with! What had happened was he had caught my brother skiing behind a boat on the river, and he had a car. I guess what Coach Bryant was trying to tell me was he didn't want me to do those things. So I never went close to the river again!

There were 113 guys (freshmen) out there that day. Can you imagine having 113 football players on scholarship? They had them on every kind of scholarship in the world: golf, basketball, tennis. You know, I didn't know they had any rules, but I heard some of these guys say they were on a basketball scholarship. I think they changed the scholarship rules the next year!

They gave all 113 of us uniforms and lined us up in teams. I was on the eighth team — when I had made All-State in high school! I was a pretty good football player, I thought — and they had all these damn guys who were littler than me, and shorter than me, and fatter than me in front of me! So I figured he was going to check me out, and he did. Out of those 113 people, they chose 11 of us — guys like Jack Rutledge, John O'Linger, Brother Oliver, Mal Moore, Pat Trammell — hell, you can remember when you only have 11 left! And Jimmy Wilson, Jimmy Sharpe, and Charlie Pell. Tommy Brooker from Demopolis, Alabama — Coach Bryant took that little bunch, and we went on and won 11 games. We had only 25 points scored against us — that's unbelievable! Alabama had only won 3 games in four years, and four years later, we went on to win the national championship and gave up only 25 points.

You know, that's a dream come true right there! Nothing else ever has to happen to you. I see us 11 guys today, and what a close bunch of people — even after 30 years. Coach Bryant took us kids and molded us into a team. We never had any Heisman Trophy winners — isn't it great to have 11 national championships and no Heisman Trophy winners? I think that's what's so wonderful about Alabama football — you've got great fans and great players, and we've always had good coaches — except on occasion.

It's wonderful to go back to the University and see familiar faces, people who you know. You see, I know Brother Oliver, Mal Moore, and Coach Stallings. Coach Stallings used to coach me — he was 22 years old, and he could holler and scream and grab and shake, but he never cussed us out. But he was one of the few that didn't! Coach Stallings came here from Texas — Coach Bryant brought a bunch of little babies with him. I guess the oldest coach was 25 years old, and Coach Bryant worked them just as hard as he worked us.

It was so much fun — well, it wasn't fun to start with, but it got fun at last. I guess you have to work your tail off to get to the point where you feel comfortable. Our last year here, we probably didn't do anything — we just played the games. And I'm so proud to be part of that football team and part of the Alabama tradition. I know it will continue. God bless you.

JOHN HANNAH:

I want to thank everybody for letting me be here also. I had four other family members who played at Alabama, and one of the things that Coach Bryant used to stress to us was that there are no stars, there was no one man — there was a team. So even though we're up here, those four guys in my family and all the other guys who played deserve to be up here just as much as we do. And my hat's off to you for putting up with those four years that all of us endured. And I applaud you.

As an offensive lineman at Alabama, you're an unwanted stepchild. If you weren't good enough to play defense, Coach Bryant put you on the offensive line — and that's the honest-to-God truth! If we could get 10 points ahead, he'd sit on the ball for the rest of the day, so we didn't get to show a whole lot while we were at Alabama.

One thing I remember is walking down the halls of the coliseum and seeing the walls covered with the pictures of the people I wanted to be like — I wanted to earn the credentials they had earned. I was honored by being in the same building and walking the same grounds that those gentlemen walked.

To be honest with you, I chose to be an offensive lineman at an early age. I was around football all my life — my dad was a high school coach, and I got a chance as a young man to look at football and decide what position I wanted to play. I looked at all those guys who got all the glory for carrying the football and noticed that everybody was trying to hit them and hurt them — and I didn't want to do that. Then I looked across the way at the defensive linemen who were always running and trying to hit the guys carrying the ball, but I noticed that they were always getting hit — and I didn't want to do that either. I finally found this one group of guys who looked like they were really well fed, they usually walked to the line of scrimmage, and everybody on the field was trying to get *around* them so they could get to the guy with the ball — I said, "That's for me!"

I've got a few stories about Coach Bryant. When I was a sophomore (Scott Hunter will appreciate hearing this), I gave up about 15 sacks one night. They were sending every blitz in the book at us, and Coach Jimmy Sharpe — contrary to what he might tell you — didn't really teach me what to do against those blitzes. They were coming from the left and right, and I didn't know what was going on. It was third quarter, and I was heading toward the sideline — my head was in the ditches. The ABC camera shot down, right along the sideline, and got a closeup picture of Coach Bryant as he kicked me right in the butt and knocked me to the ground. Well I was embarrassed and ashamed — all my friends saw Coach Bryant kick me. So I thought I'd call my mom and get a little sympathy. I called her, and I'll never forget what she said that Sunday afternoon. She said, "Son, what did you do to make Coach Bryant mad at you?"

Coach Bryant always had a way of making you think you hadn't arrived — of always keeping you humble, always wanting to strive a little further. you never were quite good enough. I remember that right before the last bowl game I was in, I had heard inklings that I might get drafted into the NFL. So I was feeling pretty good about myself, and I went to Coach Bryant and said, "Coach, I may get drafted into the NFL, and I wondered if you could help me find a good attorney to represent me when I go to do my contract negotiations." Coach Bryant looked at me and said, "John, you ain't good enough to need no damn lawyer!"

The most compassionate thing I remember about Coach Bryant happened at a game we played in Birmingham against the University of Tennessee. It was about 120 degrees on the Astroturf that day — it was awful. We had one more series going, and I wasn't feeling real well. I looked over at Jim Goostree, who is one of the kindest, most compassionate people I've ever known, and he said, "John, just do one more series. You just gotta do one more series." And I said, "All right, Coach, I'll go one more series."

So I wobbled out there, and it was awful. I remember coming in to the sideline, and Coach Bryant knelt down, and we said a little prayer. I looked up at my old buddy Jim Crawford, and I said, "Jim, I don't feel real good." And that's the last thing I remember — I passed out. When I came to, I looked up and saw Coach Bryant looking at me, and I could tell from his eyes that he was worried, he was concerned, he was really fearful. I'll always remember that. Despite all the punishment and things he did to me, I know from that time I woke up from a pretty deep sleep that he cared about me as an individual and that everything he did for me and to me was for my own good. I appreciate the man, I appreciate Alabama, the University of Alabama football program, and the coaches today. Thank you.

JOHNNY MUSSO:

I really wasn't expecting an opportunity to stand before this group and express the way I feel. I thought they'd show a clip, and I'd wave and say thank you. But after a couple of people stood up here with all that calm and poise and starting talking, I started making a list. I started writing down things. But I'm not real good verbally expressing my emotions. In fact, I wish I could hire someone like Mr. Van Hoose to stand up and tell exactly how I feel. Perhaps he could do it a lot better than I could — and I might even become a better runner and blocker in the process! *(EDITOR'S NOTE: referring to Alf Van Hoose's acceptance speech in behalf of Johnny Cain.)*

I don't know what they did with the highlight film. They showed Bobby Marlow and Humphrey making all these long, beautiful runs down the sideline. I don't know — they must have lost some of them or something — I'd like to think that, anyway.

It would be hard for me to tell you how God has richly blessed me in so many ways. High on that list of things I am grateful for is my association with the University of Alabama. The fan support I felt here is just really unique. And living out of the state for a period of time, I guess I've come to appreciate how truly unique that is.

I'd like to thank each one for the vote that they've given me in this honor that I'm receiving tonight. Of course, the biggest fan I'd like to thank is my sister. I think she was personally responsible for about 50% of the 400,000 votes. I told her, "Really, Mary Jo, if I win this, I'd like to do it on my own." She said, "Well, I only voted once." But she handed out the ballots, and even though she didn't tell anyone how to vote, she patiently waited while they did vote.

I think Alabama is truly blessed with the support it's received through the years from the fans. I feel blessed just by the players who are on this platform. There are many here who had a big impact on the way my life evolved and the focus I had as a young person. I didn't live far from here... and I used to go to Alabama games — I sneaked in when I was 10 or 11 years old. I vividly remember Joe Namath's first varsity game at Legion Field. I remember Kenny Stabler running down the sideline in the rain and the mud against Auburn. I remember Lee Roy — just the descriptions on the radio, not that there wasn't TV back then (that came out wrong!) — but I remember them describing him running down the running back and intimidating without even hitting. Just hearing the descriptions of that, the legend of Alabama grew in my mind. It really shaped what I wanted to do with my life.

I really appreciate the people who have preceded me on this platform and the legacy and tradition that have been passed down. And also the people who have followed me — the Goal Line Stand and Van Tiffin's kick and all those memories of people who have carried on that tradition. I really appreciate that, and I feel really blessed to have the opportunity to watch other people hold that love and tradition of Alabama football constant through these years.

I've received more credit than I ever deserved. I played with people, particularly the senior class that I came up with, who really didn't get the credit they deserved. I remember our first meeting with Coach Bryant as freshmen. He told us to look around the room, and if we were a typical class, there would be one out of four of us there in four years. And we were very typical_ out of the 44 there that day, 9 of us graduated four years later and two were redshirted and came later. So I would like to openly thank and recognize my teammates, particularly those who were signed and came through those four years with me. There's one teammate I'd like to thank particularly, though, who had more to do with me being here than anyone else, and when I say his name, you'll understand. Of course, it's John Hannah. I can't even imagine John Hannah contemplating playing any other position.

I'd also like to thank Coach Bryant for the quality of coaches he allowed me to be associated with. First of all, Coach Gryska, who kept my head from being turned and going to Auburn. He told me that one day I would look back and see that going to Alabama was the right decision. And Coach, I think I've come to that day.

Thank you for the opportunity to work with folks like Jimmy Sharpe and Richard Williamson and Mal Moore and two other people who have really had a particular impact on my life. One is Steve Sloan — what a wonderful opportunity it was to day-in and day-out rub shoulders with him — and John David Crow, who was just a hero in my eyes. He was the backfield coach at Alabama, and he had just retired from the Cardinals after a long career. I had the unique opportunity of playing under him, and I thought that was a great honor.

Most people think of that game (the 1971 game against USC) as just a real turnaround in Alabama football — the upset, the wishbone being shown for the first time. It brings back two horrifying memories for me — I died twice in the game before the first quarter was over, and it had to do with the two people I admired the most, John David Crow and Coach Bryant. Early in the first quarter I broke my little finger, and everytime I bent it, it would just flop back. It was very painful — I could put up with that, but it was hard to hold the ball. I tried running a couple of plays, and then I thought I'd better get it taped up. I took myself out of the game and went over to Coach Goostree, who of course was very sympathetic. He immediately started to wrap up my finger. And if there were just two things that I could erase from my memory of my career at Alabama, they would be these two things, which happened within 30 seconds of each other. One is when Coach Crow came over and asked Coach Goostree, "What's wrong? Is he all right?" Coach Goostree said, "Well, he hurt his little finger." John David Crow is a tough-looking guy, and I wish I could erase the memory of his face as he looked at me in stunned silence. Not two seconds later, Coach Bryant pushed into the huddle and said, "What's wrong?" Before Coach Goostree could say anything, Coach Crow said, "Johnny hurt his little finger." Everything I had tried to establish in three years was completely out the window!

I would like to say a personal thanks to Coach Bryant — to his family that is represented here tonight. Many people have analyzed why Coach Bryant was such a great coach. He was a wonderful motivator, he was a great judge of people — he knew what was in people's hearts and somehow he could bring out the best in them. There is one thing, it's my own opinion, I think Coach Bryant succeeded at the University for one reason above all others — he really loved the University. He certainly had a lot of competitiveness and he certainly had a lot of ability, but I think the thing that drove him most was that he died a little bit every time Alabama came off the field with a loss. And he just wouldn't allow anybody to go on the field if he didn't think they had the pride and the class and the determination to carry out and wear that jersey with a lot of special feeling. And I think Alabama football is going to continue to be held in high regard and that tradition and legacy will endure simply because he passed that feeling on to a lot of people. He passed that love of the University on to his players, to the people he coached with, and to hundreds of thousands of fans across the state who I don't think will allow Alabama football to do anything but increase that legacy. Thank you for this honor.

JOE NAMATH:

Thank you. Our family exists on love — love is the pulse and the heartbeat of our family. Alabama football is a family affair — it has been for many years. And the pulse and heartbeat of Alabama football is you, the fans. You keep us players going. You demand the best, and you get the best effort from us. I've had some success as a football player, and it's been because of you Alabama fans. It's certainly been because of Coach Bryant, Lee Roy Jordan, Brother Oliver, Billy Neighbors, Mal Moore, Billy Battle. These guys demanded the best that we could offer as underclassmen. Because these guys tried harder, we tried harder, and we tried to live up to the expectations of the Alabama fans. And we're so glad to be a part of the Alabama football family. The family keeps growing. That pulse and heartbeat keep beating strong and the tradition of the Alabama family is just wonderful.

We are here because of memories — memories of our friends who aren't necessarily here with us. A lot of fans remember "the Snake" and Joe and the other guys up here, but not one of us here would say we did it on our own, by a long shot. We're here because football is a team game, just like life is a team game. All of us up here realize that. We're here because of memories and the people we share those memories with, and man, it's wonderful. God bless you, and thank you.

KENNY STABLER:

Thank you. When I received word of being chosen as a member of the Team of the Century, a million names crossed my mind, an awful lot of people, people who are the reason that I get to stand up here. The first people who came to mind were three high school coaches and guys I played with in high school who helped give me the opportunity to come here to the University of Alabama, to walk in the footsteps of Joe Namath and Pat Trammell and Steve Sloan and try to carry on the tradition that had been established at Alabama. It was a tremendous responsibility and one that I welcomed. Baseball was a choice, but not really when you get the opportunity to come up here and play for Paul Bryant, and the type of players I was blessed with playing with.

It's a team game, and there are so many people to thank. I look at the guys I played with, and what a great receiving pair I had: Dennis Homan on one side and Ray Perkins on the other side. We had an offensive line that took great care of us, with Tom Somerville, Jerry Duncan, Bruce Stephens, Terry Killgore, Cecil Dowdy, Wayne Cook — a great tight end, David Chatwood, Les Kelley. They were all great football players.

And of course, the opportunity to play for Coach Bryant. Looking back on my career, I have him to thank for so many things. I had an opportunity, and I might have thrown it all away if it had not been for Coach Bryant's discipline, which I needed dearly — and he gave it to me. He picked me up by the back of the neck and kicked me in the pants and made me realize that I was throwing away a tremendous opportunity by not conforming to his rules. He did know what was best for me, and through his discipline I was able to be with those players I just named, I was able to experience national championships, SEC championships, Orange Bowls, Sugar Bowls, Cotton Bowls. It's just a wonderful, wonderful feeling to be the family of the University of Alabama and to be associated with all of these players, and I want to publicly thank every one of my teammates for everything they did for me. I want to publicly thank Coach Bryant for what he established. I try to take the lessons he taught us — self-sacrifice and discipline and all those things — and apply them to my two little girls. Those lessons are coming in might handy.

This is a wonderful occasion. The University has a lot to be proud of. I'm very honored to be up here with this cast of characters, this wonderful football team. I'd like to take this group and knock some years off and go again. Thank you very much.

MARC TYSON FOR PAUL BRYANT:

(EDITOR'S NOTE: Marc Tyson is Paul Bryant's grandson.)
This has just been great, being up here with all of my childhood heroes and getting to visit with them and getting to look at Johnny Musso, who used to wear 22 — that would always be my jersey in all the sports I played. It still makes me a little sad when I think about how much Papa would have enjoyed being here tonight. It's such a great event, and he would have enjoyed sharing stories. He would have probably stayed up until 4 in the

morning just going over things with people like John Forney and Jerry Duncan and all these fellas up here.

Tonight and all my life I've heard people say how much Papa meant to them — players, coaches, fans, friends. I'd like to take this opportunity to tell you how much you meant to him as well as to our family. A day never passed without him telling one of us a story about y'all and what y'all meant to him. You may not realize it, but each of you touched his life in a very special way. You gave his life much happiness and much cheer, and we thank you for that.

It seems like just yesterday that he was here laughing and telling stories. I kept watching the tapes and everything, and I think all of us thought he'd walk up here tonight, and that's the way it should end.

This award would mean a lot to him, but as you all know, he would not have won this award without y'all. Our family thanks you for it from deep in our hearts. Thank you.

THE NEXT HUNDRED YEARS
by Steve Townsend

Certainly only a few of the many heroes whose exploits at Alabama contributed to the 100-year legacy of excellence can be chronicled in any literary work, and no doubt there be literally thousands of additional pages added to this or any of the many other books that have been penned on Crimson Tide football.

Alabama football is as much a part of the heartbeat of its legion of followers as the sun is to daytime. "When the football is kicked off in September in Alabama, everybody starts breathing again," remarked legendary football star Fred Sington, and perhaps that embodies the importance of the sport to a state and its people.

Will the love of the program sustain itself in its second 100 years? Well, back in 1922 thousands of Alabamians welcomed home the conquering team that rode the rails to Pennsylvania and stunned the college football world with an improbable 9-7 win over Penn, and a few years later thousands lined the railways from New Orleans to Tuscaloosa to dole out gifts to the Rose Bowl winners en route home from stunning victories on the West Coast. Nearly three-quarters of a century later, the streets of Tuscaloosa sparkled in crimson when the 1992 national champions were honored in January 1993.

Frankly it seems a safe bet that as enthralled as Americans are with sports, there will be little diminishing of the love affair between the Alabama fans and their football program. Perhaps the central figure of Alabama's first 100 years, Paul Bryant, put it best. "I don't know if I'd ever get tired of football. If I ever get that notion, I think back to one day I was out on the practice field wondering whether I'd get tired of the sport. Then I heard the Million Dollar Band playing over there on the parade grounds. When they started playing 'Yea, Alabama,' I got goose bumps all over me. I looked out there at those young rascals in crimson jerseys, and I just wanted to thank God for giving me the opportunity to coach at my alma mater and be part of the Alabama tradition."

Steve Townsend

July 1993

"No one can help but be aware of the rich tradition that is associated with this team and with this university. Tradition is a burden in many ways. To have a tradition like ours means that you can't lose your cool; to have tradition like ours means that you always have to show class, even when you are not quite up to it; to have tradition like ours means that you have to do some things that you don't want to do and some you even think you can't do, simply because tradition demands it of you. On the other hand, tradition is the thing that sustains us. Tradition is that which allows us to prevail in ways that we could not otherwise."

— University President David Mathews talking to an Alabama team in the early 1970s

ORDER FORM

JOHN FORNEY & STEVE TOWNSEND

Share the tradition. Together, for the first time, in one unprecedented book — over 100 behind-the scenes interviews with Tide players and coaches from 1920-1993. A great gift for every Tide fan!

Only $24.95 plus $3 shipping & handling
Ala. residents add 7% sales tax

Use this form to order by mail.

— —

Please send me _____ books.

Ship to:

Name _____

Address _____

City _____ State _____ Zip _____

Phone (_____) _____

*Please note we cannot ship to PO boxes, so include street address if necessary. If no street address is available, please add $2 to your shipping and handling charge to ensure parcel post delivery.

Method of payment:

❑ Check enclosed   ❑ Money order   ❑ VISA   ❑ MasterCard

Card Number _____

Expiration Date _____ Signature _____

Make checks payable to and mail to: CRANE HILL PUBLISHERS
2923 Crescent Avenue / Birmingham, AL 35209
(800) 841-2682 / Fax (205) 871-7337